SOCIAL PROBLEMS

SOCIAL PROBLEMS

An Introduction
to Critical Constructionism

FOURTH EDITION

ROBERT HEINER

Plymouth State University

New York   Oxford
OXFORD UNIVERSITY PRESS

Oxford University Press is a department of the University of Oxford. It furthers the University's
objective of excellence in research, scholarship, and education by publishing worldwide.

Oxford   New York
Auckland   Cape Town   Dar es Salaam   Hong Kong   Karachi
Kuala Lumpur   Madrid   Melbourne   Mexico City   Nairobi
New Delhi   Shanghai   Taipei   Toronto

With offices in
Argentina   Austria   Brazil   Chile   Czech Republic   France   Greece
Guatemala   Hungary   Italy   Japan   Poland   Portugal   Singapore
South Korea   Switzerland   Thailand   Turkey   Ukraine   Vietnam

Published by Oxford University Press.
198 Madison Avenue, New York, NY 10016
www.oup.com

ISBN 978–0–19–985907–8

Printing number: 9 8 7 6 5 4 3 2 1

Printed in the United States of America
on acid-free paper

for Laurel

CONTENTS

PREFACE

All around us are social phenomena that could possibly be seen as problematic; yet, only a few of these capture the public's attention for a brief period of time and these are replaced by another few in a subsequent period. The problems that capture our attention are not necessarily the worst ones and they are not replaced because they have gotten better. There must, therefore, be forces other than the seriousness of these problems that explain their procession through the public imagination. This book applies a synthesis of conflict theory and social constructionism (herein called "critical constructionism") to the examination of the forces that influence the public's understanding of social problems.

Special thanks go to Jeffrey Hadden, who has passed away since the publication of the first edition of this book. I started out as his teaching assistant at the University of Virginia, and his definition of a social problem lent much to the paradigm used throughout this book. It was an honor working with Jeff and I miss our communications.

My editor at Oxford University Press, Sherith Pankratz, has worked with me over the past two editions of this book as well as two other projects. It's always been a pleasure working with her and I appreciate her encouragement, her knowledge, and especially her responsiveness to my concerns. I also want to thank Cari Heicklen, and all the others at OUP who worked on this book. Their efficiency and professionalism were never less than impressive and they made the completion of this book as painless as possible.

To the reviewers who provided detailed comments, I extend my appreciation for their careful reading and insight:

Cara Bergstrom-Lynch, Eastern Connecticut State University

Walter F. Carroll, Bridgewater State University

Jennifer L. Dunn, Southern Illinois University, Carbondale

Stevan R. Jackson, Radford University

Karen Kendrick, Albertus Magnus College

Joseph W. Ruane, University of the Sciences

Ira Silver, Framingham State University

An incomplete list of others I want to thank for their assistance, expertise, and moral support includes Julie Bernier, Joyce Bruce, Peng-Khuan Chong,

John Krueckeberg, Kathy Melanson, Bryon Middlekauff, Nikki Nunes, Christian Roberson, and Cynthia Vascak.

Lastly, I want to thank my wife, friend, and colleague, Sheryl Shirley. Her training in political science and international relations complements mine in sociology and her compassion for the disenfranchised has always been an inspiration.

NEW TO THE FOURTH EDITION

- A new chapter on inequality of life chances in the United States. This chapter includes updated material on race as well as a new discussion of gender inequality. In this chapter, you will also find updated material on health care and a new section on education and inequality.
- Chapter 4 on family has a new section on same-sex marriage.
- Chapter 5 on crime and deviance has a new section introducing the sociological concept of social control as it relates to the medicalization of deviance.
- Chapter 6 on the environment extends the discussion on environmental injustice from previous editions, using Hurricane Katrina as an example of environmental racism.
- This new edition also includes discussions of the "Great Recession," the Occupy Wall Street movement, and the U.S. Supreme Court decision in *Citizens United v. Federal Election Commission*.

While holding to my original goal of producing a brief and affordable social problems textbook, all of these changes along with other smaller ones will make this text more relevant to today's sociology students. But, as always, this is as much an exposition on recent history as it is on current events and no one knows as this book goes to press what will happen afterward.

An Introduction to the Sociology of Social Problems

To begin our study in the sociology of social problems, we should note that "social problems" is a subdiscipline of sociology. Sociology is a very broad field, encompassing such subdisciplines as the sociology of the family, of crime and delinquency, of race relations, of the environment, of education, of law, of medicine, of science, of knowledge, and yes, even of sociology itself. Sociology is so broad that most sociologists specialize in just one or two subdisciplines. The point is that the sociology of social problems is a subdiscipline; it is *not* simply a current events course. The sociologist who specializes in social problems is not a news journalist or simply a social commentator; he or she brings to the analysis of current events the perspectives, tools, and theories specific to his or her sociological training.

THE SOCIOLOGICAL PERSPECTIVE

Sociology is a social science, and as a science, it attempts to approach its subject matter objectively. The social sciences include such disciplines as sociology, psychology, and anthropology. The natural sciences include such disciplines as biology, chemistry, and physics. The social sciences are often called "soft" sciences, referring to the fact that they are less scientific or less objective than the natural, or "hard," sciences. Indeed, there is truth to these charges. Value judgments do come into play more often in the social sciences than in the natural sciences. The social sciences are more subjective because humans are conducting the research and humans are the subject of the research. One cannot study oneself objectively. However, the natural sciences are not totally objective either. Implicit judgments underlie the conduct of research in the natural sciences, such as, What is important to know? What is the best way to study it? What constitutes sufficient evidence? *Important, best, sufficient*—these are all value judgments.

We can, then, conclude that the social sciences are less scientific than the natural sciences because they are less objective. However, we cannot conclude that the social sciences are not truly sciences on the basis of their lack of objectivity (as the term *soft* implies) because if we use objectivity as our primary criterion, then the natural sciences are not sciences either; in fact,

1

there would be no such thing as science. What the natural sciences and the social sciences have in common is that they systematically strive for objective understanding.

This is an important point in the sociological study of social problems because most people assume that "social problems" are bad and need to be eliminated. Indeed, the very use of the word *problem* promotes such connotations. However, if we approach the study of social problems assuming that they are bad, we are not being objective and we will not achieve a sociological understanding.

Let us take crime, for example. Most students of social problems and of criminology begin their study of crime presuming that it is bad and needs to be eliminated. *Bad* is a value judgment, and it impedes our objective understanding of the phenomenon of crime. One who presumes crime is bad is likely to overlook many of the "good" aspects of crime. For example, crime provides us with nearly 3 million jobs in the local, state, and federal criminal justice systems as well as in private security.[1] Perhaps it could be argued that without crime these people could find other jobs. However, many people who work in these areas like their jobs, so for them crime is good. As will be discussed later in this book, Emile Durkheim[2] and Kai Erikson[3] both argue that crime plays an essential role in uniting a society against common enemies and in establishing the moral boundaries of a community. To the extent that crime performs these functions, it is good. Further, sociologists have pointed out the role organized crime has played in American history in terms of providing ethnic minorities with a ladder to the middle class.[4] Through organized crime, minority members have acquired wealth, and with that wealth they have established legitimate businesses, hiring others of their own kind who were previously excluded from the workplace. This process began with the Irish in the late nineteenth century, then the Jews at the turn of the century, then the Italians, and now Hispanics and African Americans. If you are of Jewish, Irish, or Italian descent, perhaps you or someone you know can afford to be in college because your or his or her great grandfather was hawking drugs in the 1920s (i.e., alcohol during Prohibition). Likewise, 10 or 20 years from now, more Hispanic and African American kids may be able to afford to go to college because their grandparent was hawking crack in the 1980s. Consequently, crime has been good for millions of immigrants and minorities in American history. Only a small proportion of them participated in organized crime, but countless more were helped into legitimate business by the participation of a few.

To suggest that crime has its positive aspects is not to argue that the United States' relatively high crime rates are reason to rejoice, nor is it to suggest that crime should be encouraged; but it does suggest that the layperson's assumption that crime is bad and needs to be eliminated is a limited and limiting view. One who takes this perspective will not likely be open to a more complex understanding of the phenomenon. The same can be said of all social problems. Thus, as social scientists, it is important that we suspend some of our moral beliefs and value judgments as we pursue a fuller, more objective understanding of social problems. Unfortunately, *problem* is a value-laden term; to the layperson, it connotes an element of undesirability. The sociologist striving for some degree of objectivity, therefore, defines the phrase *social problem* very carefully. Sociologically, *a social problem is a phenomenon regarded as bad or undesirable by a significant number of people or a number of significant people who mobilize to remedy it.* To understand the scientific advantages of this definition, it is important to understand the concept of *social structure.*

In a society, there are individuals, groups, and institutions. These individuals, groups, and institutions are all related to one another. These relationships may be very strong or very weak, very direct or very indirect. The totality of these individuals, groups, and institutions and the relationships between them make up the social structure. It is presumed that there are rules governing these relationships. Sociology is the study of these rules, and a sociological theory is an attempt to describe such a rule.

Now, let us get a little abstract and graphically depict a social structure (Figure 1.1). The social structure is arbitrarily represented as a grid (A), a set of intersecting rules and relationships.

Contained within this social structure is a phenomenon (B) that is a *potential* social problem. According to our sociological definition, this phenomenon does not become an actual social problem until it is defined as such by a group (C). To repeat our definition, a social problem is a phenomenon regarded as bad or undesirable (B in the diagram) by a significant number of people or a number of significant people (C in the diagram) who mobilize to remedy it. The group (C), which is either significant in size or significant in composition, is often called a *social movement organization.* So important is this group that in their classic formulation Malcolm Spector and John Kitsuse define a social problem solely in terms of its activities: "Thus we define social

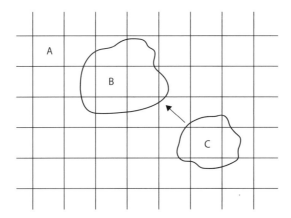

Figure 1.1

problems as the activities of individuals or groups making assertions of grievances and claims with respect to some putative conditions."[5]

To understand why this group forms, one must understand the social structure (A). The point of this conceptualization is that a phenomenon (B) does not become a social problem because of its inherent badness; it becomes a social problem because of factors *external* to the problem itself—namely, the social structure (A) and the social movement organization (C). Here is the scientific advantage of this conceptualization: the sociologist cannot objectively say that phenomenon B is bad, but he or she can objectively say that group C says phenomenon B is bad. Hence, the sociologist is able to establish a degree of objectivity over the otherwise value-laden phrase *social problem*. We will call this conceptualization the *social problems perspective*.

To illustrate the social problems perspective, let us take the example of child abuse. Children have been physically abused for hundreds or thousands of years. There were brief periods in history when a group would organize on behalf of abused children; but for the most part, what we call "child abuse" was overlooked or tolerated by most of Western civilization throughout most of its history.[6] That is, it did not meet our definition of a social problem. One might be inclined to argue that child abuse was a social problem, even though it was not recognized as such, because countless children were being hurt, even killed, at the hands of their parents, and that is bad. However, *bad* is a value judgment. How badly do the children have to have been hurt and how many have to have been hurt for child abuse to constitute a social problem? We cannot objectively say. Where do we draw the line in terms of injury or numbers of injuries before we can call something a social problem? This is a matter of opinion, and science cannot answer this question.

It was not until the early 1960s that physicians began to organize, opposing the previous medical practice of overlooking evidence of child abuse. According to Steven Pfohl,[7] there were a number of features of the medical profession that help to explain this timing. First, in the late 1950s, pediatric radiology had advanced to the point where long bone fractures could be identified. Long bone fractures travel up and down the bone and are almost certainly the result of periodic trauma occurring over a long period of time, fitting the pattern of child abuse. Before this advance in pediatric radiology, emergency room doctors encountering injuries resulting from abuse could be pretty certain that abuse was the cause; but they generally refrained from reporting their suspicions to the authorities. They were inclined to overlook child abuse because, at the time, what went on between family members was considered a family matter; parents had almost absolute property rights over their children. Furthermore, norms of doctor-patient confidentiality made the reporting of child abuse a difficult ethical decision. At the time, it was not clear exactly who the patient was: the child or the parents, who "owned" the child and were paying for the doctor. On the other hand, pediatric radiologists acted largely as consultants, having little or no direct contact with either the child or the parents. They also received little or no respect within the medical profession because they were "merely" consultants, they did not perform surgery, and their connection to life-or-death decisions was indirect. They, therefore, had something to gain by their "discovery" of child abuse. So they became the "experts," and they were often called into court to testify about life-and-death decisions involving children. They stood to gain more prestige within the profession as a result of the discovery of child abuse. Soon, psychiatrists joined in the mobilization against child abuse. They, too, had previously enjoyed little prestige in the medical profession and could only stand to elevate themselves by aligning themselves with what was becoming a popular cause. Then, with the help of the media, the police, and various political leaders, child abuse became a full-blown social problem.

Note that we just explained how child abuse became a social problem without stating or implying that it is bad, without making a subjective evaluation of the harm that it causes. Instead, we explained how the phenomenon (B in Figure 1.1) became a social problem because a group (C), made up of pediatric radiologists and psychiatrists, mobilized against it. This group came about because of features and changes in the social structure (A). Remember that the social structure is made up of individuals, groups, institutions, and the relationships between them. That is what we described: the relationships between parents and their children, between doctors and parents, between doctors and children, between pediatric radiologists and the rest of the medical profession. Child abuse became a social problem not because of the harm done by the phenomenon but because of features external to the phenomenon.

A Few Drawbacks

While sociology is a social science and while we strive to control our subjectivity, it must be noted that objectivity is an impossible goal. All of us are products of our society, and as such, we cannot study society objectively. We are subject to the same rules of society that we are trying to study. The social problems perspective should be recognized as merely a device, a flawed device, that enables us to achieve some degree of objectivity. Now let us take a look at the flaws in this device.

Our definition of a social problem is a good deal less than purely objective. According to this definition, a social problem is a phenomenon regarded as bad or undesirable by a significant number of people or a number of significant people who mobilize to eliminate it. The problem with this definition is, of course, the word *significant*. Significance is a value judgment. How many people make up a significant number? Also, how significant do the people involved have to be? Having this word in the definition allows the researcher to identify virtually any phenomenon he or she wants and to justify this identification by calling the group opposed to it "significant."

Let us take a look at the diagram again. It has been redrawn in Figure 1.2. Another flaw in the social problems perspective is that the sociologist lives, breathes, and conducts her or his research in that social structure. (The sociologist is now represented by the little speck [D] marked on the diagram.) In other words, the sociologist is not looking at the social structure from above, as you are looking at the diagram on this page. The sociologist is part of the social structure that she or he is studying, subject to the same norms, values, and beliefs that characterize that social structure. Consequently, his or her objectivity is compromised.

A Few Advantages

These flaws notwithstanding, there are certain advantages to this perspective for the sociologist interested in social problems. The social problems perspective emphasizes that it is not the objective harm done by a phenomenon that makes it a social problem; instead, the activities of parties external to the phenomenon give it the status of a social problem, and those activities must be understood in terms of their social structural context. Therefore, this perspective allows us to ask two very important questions: (1) Why does a seemingly harmful phenomenon that has been around for a long time suddenly achieve the status of a social problem (e.g., child abuse); (2) Why are some seemingly harmful phenomena considered social problems while other seemingly harmful phenomena are not? (For example, why is street crime so often defined as a social problem, while corporate crime is not?) These two questions ("why all of a sudden?" and "why this and not that?") are of fundamental concern from the sociological perspective referred to in this book as *critical constructionism*. From the social problems perspective and from the critical constructionist perspective, the answers to these questions do not have to do with the relative harm done by the phenomenon.

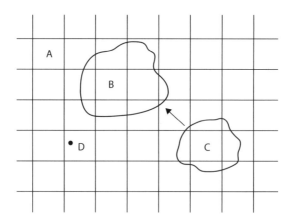

Figure 1.2

CRITICAL CONSTRUCTIONISM

Critical constructionism is largely a synthesis of two very influential theories in sociology—namely, *conflict theory* and *symbolic interactionism*. It will be useful to review these theories before turning to our discussion of critical constructionism.

Conflict Theory

Conflict theory is derived largely from the works of Karl Marx. Writing at the time of the Industrial Revolution, Marx was concerned with the struggle between the bourgeoisie and the proletariat. The *bourgeoisie* owned the factories and the *proletariat* worked in them. The relationship between the two classes, according to Marx, was one of exploitation. With the state representing the interests of the bourgeoisie, the social structure itself favored the interests of the bourgeoisie; the proletariat were unable to do anything but work for them. All terms of employment favored the employers, and they worked their advantage to the hilt, underpaying their workers and treating them like replaceable parts. Modern conflict theory is concerned not only with the struggle between employers and employees but also with the struggle between all interest groups: rich and poor, white and black, men and women, etc.

Conflict theorists are concerned mostly with inequality. Those interested in social problems usually attribute them to inequality and to the use and abuse of power. *Power is the ability to influence the social structure.* Those with power—the elite—influence the social structure in ways that will enhance their power. Generally, the elite tend to use their power to prevent change and maintain the status quo. It is, after all, contemporary social arrangements—the present social structure, the status quo—that allow them their power. Those with relatively little power tend to accept the status quo, not necessarily because they are forced to, but more often because they believe in it. Our norms, values, and beliefs are products of the social structure. Therefore, the ability to influence the social structure is the ability to influence the way people think. People are socialized by society's basic institutions—government, education, religion, and the media—to think that those in power should be in power.

Like their predecessor, Marx, modern conflict theorists tend to be very critical of capitalism. Contrary to what most people think, the people in power, referred to above, are not the nation's political or military leaders. The real power in the United States, they argue, is in the hands of the capitalists, specifically the nation's corporate leaders and major shareholders. Controlling as much money and resources as they do, they are able to influence legislation and policy for their own interests. The free market economy of the United States, with its relative lack of regulations, benefits American corporations often at the expense of the American people. According to the neo-Marxists, the American people, on the other hand, often tend to believe that anything that is good for corporate America is good for them, not because this is true, but because that is what they have been socialized to believe.

It is not surprising, then, that conflict theory often comes across as a very terse critique of capitalism. Americans tend to be far less receptive to such ideas than their European counterparts. During the 30-plus years of the Cold War, everything Marxist was considered bad and most things capitalist were considered good. Besides being ideologically unpopular, conflict theory also suffers in that it is easily interpreted to suggest that the elite make up a united, all-powerful conspiracy. This, however, is not the intention of the conflict theorist. First of all, the elite are not all-powerful. Their ability to influence the social structure is not boundless. There is a certain give-and-take. All legislation and policy does not favor their interests; but their influence is such that the totality of legislation and policy favors their interests. Second, few conflict theorists would suggest that the elite conspire to subjugate the rest of society. Instead, the elite have a *unity of interests* that makes it seem *as if* they conspire. That is, most powerful people, for example, have more interests in common with other powerful people than they do with poor people; therefore, the same policies that would benefit one powerful person will also benefit most powerful people; when each pursues his or her individual self-interest, it produces the same effect as a conspiracy.

Another feature of conflict theory that may or may not be problematic is the primacy it gives to the value of equality. There is an inherent value judgment implicit to most conflict theory. The pain and suffering that are the result of inequality are viewed negatively. Objectivity is often willingly suspended in the name of equality. In fact, many conflict theorists often take an activist role, feeling it is their moral duty to promote social and political change. Even though its objectivity may be compromised, conflict theory is generally highly regarded among sociologists. Many would argue that the human rights that conflict theorists study and promote are universal or inherent rights and, therefore, do not constitute subjective values. Whether this is true or not is a philosophical matter, but their perspective remains sociological because their emphasis is on the social structure and the inequality built into the relationships between individuals, groups, and institutions. Conflict theory's emphasis on social justice has added the elements of liberalism and humanitarianism for which sociology is renowned and for which it is sometimes reviled.

Symbolic Interactionism

Unlike conflict theory, which focuses on the broader social structure, symbolic interactionism focuses on the day-to-day interactions between people. Symbolic interactionism is considered a branch of social psychology because it focuses on the ways people think and give meaning to the world. Virtually all human interaction involves the act of interpretation. George Herbert Mead argued that human beings are different from other animals because their communication is based on language. The communication of other animals is genetically programmed; therefore, their utterances have inherent meaning. Human communication, on the other hand, is based on language; language is based on words; and words are symbols. A *symbol*, by definition, is something that signifies something else. Symbols, then, have no inherent meaning and, therefore, require interpretation.[8]

The act of interpretation is critical to all of our social experiences, not just the processing of language. Between us and our environment is our interpretation of the environment. People do not respond directly to the environment; instead they respond to their interpretation of the environment. The way we interpret the environment depends upon our past experiences. Since no two people have the same history of experiences, no two people interpret the same event or object exactly the same way. Hence, the word *college,* for example, has at least a slightly different meaning for everyone who uses it. Likewise, any given social problem will mean something different to all who conceive of it. Based on their different histories of experience, people will interpret and prioritize social problems differently.

Though no two people's experiences can be the same, members of different groups within the social structure will have experiences more similar to each other than they will to members of other groups. Their interpretations of the environment, therefore, will be more similar to each other's than to those of members of other groups. For example, members of the upper class have more experiences in common with one another than they do with members of the lower class. Therefore, if not for the power used by the elite to influence the way people think, upper-class and lower-class individuals would be likely to label or define social problems differently.

We have already been introduced to the logic of symbolic interactionism in our discussion of the social problems perspective, illustrated in Figure 1.1. In this diagram, the potential social problem (B) does not become an actual social problem until it is defined, or *labeled*, as such by a significant number of people or a number of significant people (C). Like a symbol, the potential social problem (B) has no inherent meaning. Before it can become a social problem, it has to be interpreted as such by a significant group (C). Symbolic interactionism, then, directs our attention not to the social problem itself but to meanings that are assigned to it. This leads us directly to a discussion of critical constructionism.

Critical Constructionism

Some seemingly harmful phenomena meet our definition of a social problem, while other seemingly more harmful phenomena do not meet this definition. Put another way, some phenomena come to be interpreted by a significant number of people or a number of significant people as social problems that need to be addressed and some do not, irrespective of the amount of harm done by these phenomena. *Social constructionism* is concerned with how the meanings of social problems are constructed. Problem construction involves the identification of a phenomenon as problematic, the providing of explanations for the causes of that phenomenon, and the persuasion of the public that the phenomenon is problematic and needs to be addressed. The social constructionist examines these processes. *Critical constructionism* is different from social constructionism only in that it emphasizes the role of elite interests in the process of problem construction. Borrowing from conflict theory, the critical constructionist argues that the way social problems are constructed, conceived, and presented to the public, more often than not, reflects the interests of society's elite more than those of the mainstream and often at the expense of those with the least power.

It was suggested above that the social problems perspective allows us to ask the question, Why are some seemingly harmful phenomena considered social problems and not other seemingly harmful phenomena? The example of street crime versus corporate crime was given. Most Americans would consider it common sense that street crime is more "dangerous" than corporate crime. The critical constructionist might argue that street crime is considered more of a social problem than corporate crime because the groups that have the power to frame social problems have an interest in diverting public attention away from crimes committed by the upper class and directing it to crimes committed by the lower class. Thus, the way the crime problem is constructed reflects the interests of the elite (whose crimes do more harm), to the detriment of the poor (who are punished more severely for their crimes).

Symbolic interactionists argue that all interpretations of reality are influenced by our experiences. To put it more strongly, all knowledge is socially constructed. All constructions of social problems are, therefore, worthy of constructionist analysis. Without denying this position, however, the critical constructionist is most concerned with those constructions of social problems that are in the popular domain—namely, those that receive a great deal of media attention—and how those constructions are influenced by elite interests. Popular constructions of social problems are those that sway social policy, and elite interests are most in need of critical scrutiny because they are so often obscured or confused with societal interests. Consistent with conflict theory from which it is derived, critical constructionism strives to give voice to the less powerful groups in society, a voice that is typically overwhelmed in public debate by the resources of those groups with more power.

Though the term *critical constructionism* may be unfamiliar, this type of analysis is not new to sociology. Many of its components were described by Marx and later developed further by Antonio Gramsci. Gramsci, a socialist, was incarcerated by the Fascist government in Italy in the 1920s, in the words of the prosecutor, "to stop that brain from working for twenty years."[9] Gramsci wrote many of his ideas down in what have come to be known as "the prison notebooks." Gramsci addressed what many have argued is a critical flaw in the work of Marx, the question of "inevitability." Marx argued that it was inevitable that the workers would rise up in revolution and overthrow their capitalist oppressors. Such a revolution did not take place in a great many countries, including the United States. In these countries, Gramsci argued, the capitalist elite have been able to thwart a revolution through their influence on institutions associated with the production of knowledge and culture. Gramsci called this influence *hegemony*, and through their hegemony, the elite are able to shape what the public considers "common sense."[10] For example, in the United States, it is considered common sense that the country is both the "the land of the free" and "the land of opportunity" despite, as we shall see, evidence to the contrary. However, as long as Americans believe these to be matters of common sense, they feel no need to change the status quo, let alone revolt against the capitalists. Thus, Gramsci and the critical constructionists are in agreement that, through their influence on the production of cultural knowledge, the elite are able to influence the public's perceptions of social problems to their own advantage.

Critical constructionists do not argue that the social problems that are successfully constructed are inconsequential and harmless. Instead, they argue that our view of the problems that exist in society has been distorted by the power relations involved in their construction. In this regard, critical constructionism is not very useful in terms of providing solutions to problems; but it is useful in terms of providing a perspective that allows us to discern alternative ways of constructing and framing social problems and to prioritize them on a basis that is concerned with the societal welfare and that does not weigh more heavily in favor of society's elite.

NONSOCIOLOGICAL PHILOSOPHIES

Very often, nonsociological philosophies dominate the public debate about social problems. The most popular of these is the notion of free will. Sociology, as well as the other social sciences, is based on the principle of *determinism*, arguing that human behavior and the choices we make are largely determined by forces that can be empirically studied. The principle of *free will*, on the other hand, asserts that our choices are voluntary and not determined by such forces. Philosophers have been debating these two points for millennia, but perhaps we should see the issue as being a matter of degree. The question is, How free or how determined are the choices we make?

Americans tend to favor a free will explanation for social problems. American religious life is dominated by the Judeo-Christian ethic; the United States is among the most capitalist societies in the world; Americans place a high value on individualism. Free will is the ideology that ties all these features of being "American" together. Whether a person goes to heaven or hell is a matter of the free choices that the individual makes (the Judeo-Christian ethic); whether one becomes rich or poor is a matter of the free choices that one makes (capitalism); we, as individuals, have a right to make our choices freely and to be rewarded accordingly (individualism). On the determinism–free will continuum, debates in the United States concerning social problems tend strongly to favor free will, and sociological explanations often face a good deal of resistance.

Here are some examples of the types of argument put forth by free will advocates: if we cut welfare recipients from the welfare rolls, poverty will decline because people will make the rational choice and go to work; if we toughen sentencing, crime will decline because people will make the rational choice and not commit crime. Compelling as it may be in U.S. culture, the free will explanation for social problems does have a serious drawback. One problem with free will is that it fails to explain some of the *patterns* that characterize these problems. For example, why are African Americans more likely to be poor in this country than white Americans? To say that African Americans are more likely to be poor because they are less likely to make the decisions necessary to move out of poverty amounts to a nonexplanation. It leaves out why African Americans are less likely to make those decisions. Obviously, there are forces that influence (or "determine") the choices we have to make, that influence the choices we have available, and that influence the way we derive our decisions.

Another nonsociological philosophy that enjoys considerable popularity in relation to social problems is the *human nature* argument. Like sociology, it is a form of determinism; but it is quite the opposite of sociology. Human nature proponents argue that we are the way we are because that is what nature (or God) has ordained. Sociology, on the other hand, holds that we are the way we are because of our culture and our experiences within the social structure. Human nature is a form of biological determinism; sociology employs a form of social or cultural determinism. Again, philosophers have been debating these two points for thousands of years; the debate is often referred to as "nature versus nurture." Human nature, thus, has its legitimacy; however, with regard to social problems, it shares a serious flaw with the free will argument. Both philosophies often fall short when it comes to explaining crime, poverty, and other social problems by failing to account for patterned and cross-cultural variations.

THE CROSS-CULTURAL AND GLOBAL PERSPECTIVES

One of the first things that sociologists and anthropologists learn from their studies of other cultures is that statements about human nature are usually *ethnocentric*, or culturally biased. That is, we think that it is human nature to be the way our culture has made us. Virtually from the time we are born, we are exposed to the norms, values, and beliefs of our culture. They are omnipresent, and we learn to take them for granted. We do not question them, we live by them; we have no basis for questioning them. We come to think of them as "natural." This is ethnocentrism. People all over the world are ethnocentric, believing their culture to be superior to the "strange" ways of other cultures.

The problem with ethnocentrism is that it is limiting. It does not just limit our ability to understand other countries, their people, and their practices; it also limits our ability to understand our own country, our policies, and ourselves. Understanding requires perspective; the kind of perspective we seek in this book is a "cross-cultural" (or a "comparative") one. Comparisons are an essential element of the scientific process. Paleontologists may compare fossils over time. Medical researchers may compare the relative effects of different drugs. Behaviorists may compare the ability of mice who have been exposed to different stimuli to get through a maze. Likewise, an essential tool of the sociologist is cross-cultural comparison. Through comparisons, we can gain new insight into social problems in the United States. For example, if another country has considerably less violent crime than we have in the United States, an explanation for its lower rates will help us to understand our high rates of violent crime. If another country is able to avoid the problem of poverty, then an understanding of its culture and practices may provide us with insight into our own problem of poverty. And so it goes with other social problems.

We must be wary, however, when we engage in comparative sociology. Cultures are very complex and not easily compared. For example, just because another country executes its robbers and has a lower robbery rate than the United States does not mean that it has a lower robbery rate because it executes its robbers. There are many more factors that may affect robbery rates that need to be considered, such as religion, family structure, media, distribution of wealth, unemployment, urbanization, the availability of guns, and so on.

Though we may be tempted to look to other countries for solutions to our social problems, the complexity of cultures makes this problematic. One country's solutions may not be applicable in another country. This should not, however, deter us from comparative inquiry. While an examination of other countries may not provide us with all of the answers to all of our problems, we can acquire insight from these other countries; and it would be the height of ethnocentrism to believe that we have nothing to learn from them.

A cross-cultural perspective allows us to see the variety of possible ways of looking at and solving different social problems, while a global perspective allows us to look at the interrelations between countries and their social problems. For better or worse, the world is becoming increasingly globalized. Current economic trends and telecommunications are making the world smaller and smaller. Countries throughout the world are becoming more and more interdependent. Geopolitical boundaries are becoming less relevant. One country's social problems may well impact problems in other countries. One country's refugees flood into another country, threatening its political stability. Another country's population is exploding, which may cause mass starvation or may motivate its leaders to expand its borders beyond their present position. Another country expends far more resources per capita than most other countries, causing it to look to other countries to exploit their resources and contributing to a disproportionate depletion of the earth's natural resources. There is no question that more and more social problems will be global in their scope, and a global perspective will be necessary to confront them. It is time we shed some of our provincialism and look at social problems and social solutions throughout the world.

CORPORATE AMERICA

As we examine our neighbors, it becomes apparent that the United States is unique among the modern nations of the world. The United States has a short history, and that makes it somewhat easier to characterize it in a few words. American culture is highly individualistic and places a great deal of emphasis on freedom. This notion of "freedom," however, is quite elusive. Freedom of religion was suppressed by our ancestors, who persecuted the pagan Native Americans. Freedom of speech was suppressed by the Espionage Act of 1917, later during the McCarthy era, and at various other points in our history. The freedom of homosexuals to marry continues to be suppressed in most parts of the country today. The degree to which we enjoy such freedoms as those of the press, speech, religion, and sexuality does not distinguish us from many other countries in the world. What does distinguish the United States, however, is the degree of emphasis that we place on freedom of the market. Though not absolute, the one freedom that we have historically enjoyed more than any other country is freedom of the market. Market freedom is the linchpin of capitalist ideology, and this explains why the United States is often characterized as one of the most capitalist societies in the world.

Consistent with critical constructionism, it is the opinion of this author that many of the social problems we experience in the United States stem from our capitalist extremes, that many of our social problems would be amenable to improvement were we not so individualistic in our personal affairs and in the economic affairs of our country. Community and compassion are often sacrificed in the name of individualism and the free market. It is not that the values of individualism and the free market are inherently bad; in fact, they are often good. It is the extreme to which these values are expressed in the United States that results in a good many of our social problems.

What is worse is that these extreme values are rapidly spreading throughout the world. In the past, deregulation has benefitted American corporations so much that other countries have been forced to deregulate their markets in order to compete. The result has been the momentous and incredibly rapid restructuring and deregulation of the world market through programs and treaties such as GATT (General Agreement on Tariffs and Trade), NAFTA (North America Free Trade Agreement), CAFTA (Central America Free Trade Agreement), the WTO (World Trade Organization), and the EU (European Union). The American style of capitalism spreading across the globe glorifies efficiency and profit at any cost. Large corporations stand to gain considerably from the freedom of the world market. That would not be bad if their profits did indeed "trickle down" to the workers and improve the general standard of living in the societies involved. This, as we shall see, has not been and is not likely to be the case. Instead, millions of American workers are being—or face the threat of being—"downsized." Because corporations seek to trim the fat, American workers and workers all over the world are facing cuts in their benefits. Environments throughout the world are being devastated as *transnational* corporations (TNCs) set up shop wherever the labor is cheap and environmental regulations will not interfere with their quest for profit. As the world economy is being restructured and as corporations throughout the world are racing to cut any "excess" labor costs, we need to consider seriously whether corporate interests and societal interests are one and the same.

THE MEDIA

The critical constructionist is very sensitive to the role of the news media in defining social problems. In what amounts to a constructionist claim about the media, Brent Cunningham writes in the *Columbia Journalism Review,* "The press has the power to shape how people think about what's important, in effect to shape reality."[11] The chances that a problem will receive much attention—or have societal resources mobilized against it—are almost nil without media coverage. Politicians often manipulate and/or criticize the media to highlight social problems that fit their own political agenda. The media have their own agenda as well. In recent decades, the media have merged into huge conglomerates. In the early days of television, providing the news was largely considered a public service; profits were to be made from other programming, and news bureaus were less concerned with "the bottom line."[12] Today's network and cable news programs are evaluated in terms of their profitability. The network executives are responsible to their shareholders, and their principal concern is profit. The way to make a profit is to sell commercial advertising; the way to sell commercial advertising is to attract a large audience; the way to attract a large audience is to entertain. While a democracy depends upon an informed citizenry, the goal of today's media is to entertain, not to inform.[13] Unfortunately, we depend upon the media for much of our information about contemporary social problems, and the media have found that certain problems sell advertising better than others.

Most of the television networks and major newspapers and magazines now belong to some of the largest corporations in the world. These corporations make most of their profits from sources other than their news agencies. Large corporations are large investors in other large corporations. They share the unity of interests discussed earlier in this chapter. As owners of other subsidiaries and investors in other corporations, they have an incentive *not* to provide information through their news agencies that might cast a negative light on these subsidiaries or corporations. For example, if a corporation is invested in the timber industry, their news agency will face a conflict of interests in deciding whether or not to report the devastation of our forests caused by clear-cutting. General Electric is engaged in the production of military weaponry. Along with Comcast, GE is also co-owner of the NBC television network. Thus, a company that profits from war was also providing us with news and information leading up to the war in Iraq. The conflict of interests here is both transparent and Orwellian and the potential for good investigative journalism from NBC News was seriously compromised.

The corporate media face similar conflicts of interests in deciding whether or not to report transgressions committed by the TNCs with whom they have multimillion-dollar advertising accounts. This is not to say that the news agencies will never make such reports. Their biases would become too transparent if they only reported stories favorable to their financial interests. But there is substantial incentive to avoid certain kinds of reportage. In other words, news agencies cannot objectively report the effects of corporatization because they themselves are corporations, invested in other corporations, and profiting from still other corporations by broadcasting or publishing their commercial advertising. They have an interest in portraying the country's social problems in some ways and not in others.

As this book goes to press, tens of thousands of people have been organizing in cities in the United States, Europe, Hong Kong, and elsewhere, protesting the influence the corporate elite have over government policies, calling themselves the Occupy Wall Street movement. The American media must walk a delicate balance in covering the issue. On the one hand, there are enough people on hand in enough places that they must cover the protests; otherwise, their image of being "fair and balanced" will be compromised. On the other hand, if they give the protests too much coverage, the audience may want to know more about the issues that concern the protesters, their cause may receive more legitimacy, and the media's corporate interests will be threatened. As of now, the mainstream American media cover the protests by selectively focusing on the marginal people in the crowds—the "hippie," weird, and scary types—the people with whom the mainstream audience is less likely to sympathize. ("Whenever I write about Occupy Wall Street," writes *New York Times* columnist Nicholas Kristof, "some readers ask me if the protesters really are half-naked Communists aiming to bring down the American economic system when they're not doing drugs or having sex in public."[14]) Another tactic employed by the media in this and all other large protests that threaten the status quo is to focus on confrontations between the police and a very small proportion of the protestors, projecting an image of the protesters as radical troublemakers and ignoring or, by implication, downplaying the fact that the vast majority of protesters are reasonable and peaceful.

That television and print media depend on corporate advertising for nearly all of their operating expenses and profits cannot help but influence their programming. The Public Broadcast Service (PBS) once received the bulk of its operating expenses from the government and was noted for its "liberal," sometimes anticorporate bias. But when Congress slashed its budget in the 1980s and PBS came to depend increasingly on corporate sponsors, it became far more centrist in its news reporting. It began broadcasting more financial affairs (procorporate) programming and presenting conservative viewpoints as a matter of course. It is quite likely they changed their programming and point of view because they did not want to offend their corporate sponsors. In 2010, Congress again slashed their budgets and they are becoming increasingly dependent upon corporate revenues.

Defenders of the media argue that the competition among a diverse array of corporate owners with a diversity of interests ensures that the public will be exposed to a healthy diversity of viewpoints. However, the array of corporate owners is not quite so diverse; they have a unity of interests and very often cooperate rather than compete with one another. Consider the facts as presented in Box 1.1.

Box 1.1 enumerates only a small proportion of the interconnections between media conglomerates. Competition, which is the linchpin of capitalism and is supposed to ensure diversity in the media, is rapidly diminishing as media conglomerates spread their reach. It is no wonder that the news media spend so little time covering monopolistic enterprises. If they were to do so, they would have to cover themselves. Expecting a real debate about capitalism and corporate power in the U.S. media, argues media critic Ben Bagdikian, is the equivalent to expecting the former Soviet media to provide a comprehensive debate on the value of communism.[15]

There are more reasons to suspect the media's coverage of critical economic issues. Corporations have been paying a smaller and smaller percentage of the overall tax revenues in the United States. This issue could easily generate important political debates, but the media have a financial interest in deemphasizing (or not covering) the issue. Proper coverage could well result in the enforcement or passage of tax laws that could increase the taxes of their parent and subsidiary corporations. Furthermore, the media generally have an interest in painting a rosier picture of the U.S. economy than the situation might deserve. Coverage of a bleak economy could reduce investor confidence and lower the value of the parent company's stock and of the stocks in which the parent company is invested. Media critic Arthur Rowse reports that the president of NBC once received a phone call from the chief executive officer (CEO) of General Electric, its parent company. The

---

BOX 1.1. GEAOLDISNEYFOXATTMICRIVIACOM, INC.

[T]hrough joint ownership of cable channel MSNBC, Microsoft and General Electric are partners. And so are Microsoft, AT&T and AOL Time Warner through Microsoft's ownership stake in AT&T, which will own part of Time Warner through cable system MediaOne, which AT&T is buying. AT&T also has a share in Excite At Home, a high-speed Internet access competitor of Road Runner, which is jointly owned by Time Warner, Microsoft, and MediaOne. AOL Time Warner also shares ownership of AOL Europe with the large German media conglomerate, Bertelsmann, which is buying a share of Time Warner's Book-of-the-Month Club.

By sharing ownership of MSNBC with Microsoft, GE/NBC also is an indirect partner with AT&T and AOL/TW, which is allied with Viacom/CBS through their joint ownership of Comedy Central cable channel and with ABC/Disney and Hearts through their joint owner-ship of Arts and Entertainment (A&E) and The History cable chan-nels. GE/NBC also shares fortunes with Rupert Murdoch's News Corporation and its Fox News Network through joint ownership of the National Geographic cable channel.

Source: Arthur E. Rowse, *Drive-By Journalism: The Assault on Your Need to Know.* Monroe, ME: Common Courage Press, 2000, 18.

CEO "was fuming about NBC news reports about the calamitous dive of the stock market the day before. . . . He reportedly insisted that reporters stop using such phrases as 'Black Monday' and 'precipitous drop' because they were depressing the price of General Electric shares."[16] (For further critique of the media, see Chapter 6.)

Americans have a choice: to have society run by "big government" or by "big business." Big government is run by people who are elected by the citi-zenry, who are serving specific terms of office, and who, to be reelected, must at least present the image of concern for the society's welfare. Big business is run by CEOs not elected by the citizenry, whose goal is to increase profits and who are under little or no pressure to attend to society's welfare. Big government means regulation. Big business means deregulation.

In the mid-1990s, ABC's prime-time newscast featured a segment, usu-ally several times every week, called "Your Money," showing how the gov-ernment squandered your tax dollars. This segment clearly was designed to foster a distrust of "big government," and this clearly served the interests of "big business." ABC could just as easily have presented a nightly seg-ment on the abuses and negative effects of American corporate capitalism, but this clearly would not have been in its corporate interest. This is just one example of the media's procorporate bias. What is remarkable about it, though, is that this segment was broadcast almost every night for about a year, yet few people seemed to recognize it as antigovernment or procapitalist propaganda. "By discrediting government," writes sociologist Charles Derber, "such diversion undermines the most important check on corporate power."[17]

Segments such as ABC's "Your Money," financial affairs programming on all the major networks (including "public" television), and the hundreds of thousands of television commercials that most people have seen by the time they graduate high school—all of these represent instances of probusiness propaganda that are rarely, if ever, recognized as such. Instead, they have become so much a part of the media landscape that they are taken for granted and never questioned.

It would be difficult to overemphasize the importance of these and other media reporting biases. A democracy depends upon an informed citizenry, and the media is our primary source of information about the world. This is why freedom of the press is expressly guaranteed by the Bill of Rights of the U.S. Constitution. If the information we get from the media is tainted by corporate interests, then so too are our voting behaviors and our government policies. In his book *Rich Media, Poor Democracy*, Robert McChesney writes,

> A media system set up to serve the needs of Wall Street and Madison Avenue cannot and does not serve the needs of the preponderance of the population.... [T]he U.S. media system is an integral part of the capitalist political economy...and this relationship has important and troubling implications for democracy.[18]

THE HOMOGENIZATION OF CULTURE

While some question whether the United States will remain ascendant in the world economy, there is no question of its ascendancy during the latter half of the twentieth century when the foundations of the global economy were being established. As American corporate capitalism spread around the globe, so did American products: its tennis shoes, its cars, its music, its films, its television programming, its tastes, its language, and its values— especially its consumerist values. The American value of consumption used to be distinctively American. In the recent past, and still today, people, government representatives, and pundits from around the world are complaining that the citizens of their countries are becoming too wrapped up in American culture; they are abandoning their own culture, striving to be like Americans, and striving to consume what Americans consume. If you have done some traveling outside the United States, you have probably observed different aspects of this trend.

Cultures throughout the world are being homogenized to the American model. This can be seen in both a positive and a negative light. On the one hand, it is good for American exports, and that has been good for American workers. It also has its advantages for American travelers. It is sometimes comforting to find a McDonald's or to hear your favorite music in foreign lands. On the other hand, this trend makes some of these other countries susceptible to the same social problems we face in America. That is why people, government representatives, and pundits around the world are complaining; they realize that they will soon face the same problems that we face because of our glorification of free markets and individualism.

A related problem that arises when other countries adopt American values lies in the fact that the *American Dream* is not a realistic goal for most of their citizens—just as it is not for many American citizens, given the nature of inequality in our society—and intense frustration will be the result. Further, the "homogenization of culture" threatens to end millennia of cultural diversity. People throughout the world are concerned that their traditional cultures are giving way to modern American culture. Some people strive to be "modern" like Americans; others are virtually forced to be. For example, when rainforests are cut down, their inhabitants are forced out so that the wood can be provided to the Americans or the Japanese. Once in the cities, these former forest dwellers are exposed to the same American values as their urban neighbors. Whether voluntary or forced, much of the cultural richness of the globe is being absorbed into one extended American culture. Though this may somewhat exaggerate the situation—cultures generally change slowly—it still concerns many; certainly foreign travel is becoming less and less exotic. Ethan Watters writes,

> To travel internationally is to become increasingly unnerved by the way American culture pervades the world. We cringe at the new indoor Mlimani shopping mall in Dar es Salaam, Tanzania. We shake our heads at the McDonald's on Tiananmen Square or a Nike factory in Malaysia. The visual landscape of the world has become increasingly familiar. For Americans the old joke has become bizarrely true: wherever we go, there we are.[19]

SUMMARY

Sociology is a social science, and the sociology of social problems is a sub-discipline within that science, not simply a study of current events. One important goal of social scientists is to minimize the influence of values in their research endeavors. While the layperson is inclined to view social problems as inherently bad, this is a value judgment; and the sociologist tries to avoid making such an assumption. The sociologist, instead, seeks to understand the complexity of the social problem and its interrelatedness to the social structure. Consequently, it is not the inherent badness of a phenomenon that makes it a social problem but the fact that it has been identified as such by a particular group, a social movement organization. Features and changes in the social structure explain the emergence of that social movement organization.

Throughout this book, social problems will be addressed from the perspective of critical constructionism, which is largely a synthesis of two classical sociological perspectives: conflict theory and symbolic interactionism. Conflict theorists are concerned primarily with inequality and the use and abuse of power. Those in power have the ability to influence the social structure, and they do so to promote their own interests. It is not that the elite conspire to maintain their power and subjugate the rest of society, but a unity of interests makes it seem as if they conspire. This is the more liberal branch of sociology; conflict theorists often implicitly or explicitly advocate change, with the goal of reducing inequality. Symbolic interactionists are concerned with the process of interpretation that goes on in human interaction. Accordingly, people do not respond to their environment but to their interpretation of that environment. The same can be said of social problems: people do not respond to the problem itself but to the meaning the phenomenon has for them.

Critical constructionists examine how the meanings of various social problems are constructed and how these constructions often favor the interests of the elite at the expense of the middle and lower classes. The critical constructionist does not argue that all social problems are merely fabrications of the elite but that the attention accorded to a given problem often does not correspond to the objective conditions associated with that problem vis-à-vis other potential problems. Critical constructionism attempts to provide a perspective that facilitates the prioritization of social problems that does not favor the upper class to the detriment of the other classes.

Competing with sociological theories in the public arena are the philosophies of free will and human nature (or biological determinism). Free will, especially, plays an important role in the American psyche because of American religious, capitalist, and individualist traditions. Both philosophies are antisociological in that they downplay or ignore the role of the environment in determining human behavior. They also suffer in their inability to explain the patterned characteristics of various social problems within a country as well as between countries.

A cross-cultural analysis calls into question the validity of free will and human nature as explanations for social problems. Cross-cultural analyses are necessary to overcome our ethnocentric views of social problems and their solutions. In addition to a cross-cultural perspective, a global perspective is important because the world is becoming increasingly interdependent and problems in one country often impact other countries.

One pronounced global trend has been the restructuring and deregulation of the world market. Though certainly not limited to American corporations, this represents an extension of American corporate capitalism to the rest of the world market. Individualism and the quest for profit in an unregulated world market work to the advantage of the large TNCs but not necessarily for

American citizens or their counterparts throughout the world. The TNCs are becoming exceedingly powerful, but their interests are in profit and not in the welfare of the people in the countries in which they operate. An informed world public could slow down or shape this process into something more beneficial. That is, the most recent crisis in the global economy might have been averted, but the media that are responsible for informing the public are part of the deregulation engine that was responsible for the crisis.

THE PLAN OF THIS BOOK

Unlike many social problems texts that deal with a dozen or more social problems, this short text will deal with only a few of the problems commonly addressed in most texts. We will analyze how these problems have been constructed and why they have been constructed the way they have; alternative theories (whether sociological or not) will often be presented; cross-cultural data will be provided. In the "Application" section of each subsequent chapter, specific alternative constructions will be supplied. The goal of this book is to impart to the reader a different, more sociological, cross-cultural, and global manner of conceiving social problems compared to what he or she had before approaching the sociology of social problems.

Author's Note

A major emphasis in this book is a global analysis of contemporary social problems. Such an analysis has to make a distinction between "rich" countries and "poor" countries. Past editions of this book have, with some trepidation, referred to the former as "First-World" countries and the latter as "Third-World" countries. This is terminology that dates back to the Cold War when the United States and its allies were referred to as the "First World," the Soviet Union and its allies were referred to as the "Second World," and all other countries were referred to as the "Third World." Though these terms still continue to be used in some corners, with the end of the Cold War, this terminology became *passé*; and some find it objectionable because it implies a moral kind of ranking of countries.

Another possible alternative is to simply refer to "rich" countries and "poor" countries. The problem with this distinction is that it implies some kind of monetary cutoff between the two (which there is not) and it obscures the critical fact that there are poor people in rich countries and rich people in poor countries.

One of the most frequently heard distinctions is that between the "developing" world and the "developed" world. The problem with referring to poor countries as "developing" is that it implies these countries are on the right track and well on their way out of poverty. As we shall see, this is obviously not the case. Further, opponents of the developed/developing distinction are concerned that "developing" means developing with Western assistance (particularly Western corporate assistance) along the same path taken by Western development, with all of its negative consequences (exploitation of workers, an overemphasis on consumption, and environmental destruction).

Another terminological distinction being used in the current literature is that between the North and the South. Most of the affluent countries in the world today are in the northern hemisphere and most impoverished countries are in the southern hemisphere. There are, of course, notable exceptions and gradations of affluence and poverty. Most notably, Australia and New Zealand are in the southern hemisphere, while Haiti, North Korea, and Albania are in the northern hemisphere. And when talking about issues like exporting labor to "the South," China and India have certainly been big players on the receiving end of outsourced jobs, but they are in the northern hemisphere. Nonetheless, despite its imprecision, the North-South dichotomy will be the language adopted in the chapters that follow. Recognizing that all such distinctions have their deficiencies, the reader is asked to bear with this terminology.

Discussion Questions

1. Look through a newspaper or watch the evening news and identify a social problem. Provide an individualist explanation and a sociological explanation for the problem. Which do you find more compelling? Why?

2. Watch the evening news on one of the broadcast networks tonight and take note of the kinds of corporations sponsoring the advertisements. In what way(s) might the advertising revenues from these corporations skew the content of the news broadcast? (Keep in mind that the broadcast news is a major source of information about what is happening in the world, especially for older Americans, the people most likely to vote. So the question is not how do the commercials influence the viewers, but how do the commercials influence the content of the news which influences the viewers?)

Inequality and Capitalism

AN INTRODUCTION TO CRITICAL ECONOMICS

As this book goes to press, the world economy is being wracked by an economic crisis which many fear could have dire consequences. Millions more Americans than "normal" are out of work and their near-term prospects for reemployment are not good. Economists say the recession technically lasted from December 2007 to June 2009; but the median household income dropped *more* in the two years following the recession (6.7 percent) than it did during the recession (3.2 percent)[1] and for the millions of people who have been out of work for an extended period, it feels like a depression. To try and capture the feelings of despair of these people and the apprehension being experienced by most others, this book will be referring to this economic period in history as the "Great Recession."

Most economists are coming to believe this crisis resulted from the failure to implement commonsense regulations on the financial industry. This failure reflected the extreme form of capitalism that prevailed in the United States prior to the onset of the crisis and continues unabated. A major part of President Reagan's platform was to "get the government off our backs" and deregulation began to escalate in the 1980s. By the 1990s, the effect of deregulation on the American class system was becoming increasingly pronounced. To understand how we got where we are, it will be useful to critically examine some of the economic trends taking place over the past several decades.

Just as "problems" in society are socially constructed, so too is the "health" of a society. In the late 1990s, Americans were being bombarded with news of a healthy, booming economy. This "boom" provides a good illustration of critical constructionism because it demonstrates how the economy is balanced in favor of the elite while at the same time it is widely believed to serve the interests of the middle and lower classes as well. A truism that was popular then and now is "A rising tide lifts all boats." If this were true and if the economic prospects of the lower, working, and middle classes were ever to improve, then they should have improved during the boom. The late 1990s proved this to be untrue, however. During the "boom," a great preponderance of the resulting wealth poured into the coffers of the upper class, economic inequality grew, the incomes of the working and middle classes remained virtually stagnant despite the fact that people were working harder, and the poor continued to suffer as they always had, some even more so than before. Before we examine these phenomena in detail, a basic primer in critical economics will help us to understand how they came about.

On a national scale, *economics* refers to a system employed by a nation to produce and distribute goods and services. There are two basic types of economic systems: *capitalism* and *socialism*. In a capitalist economy, the means of producing and distributing goods and services are privately owned; in a socialist economy, they are publicly owned. However, there are no purely capitalist societies and no purely socialist societies in the world. Generally speaking, the United States is considered among the most capitalist societies in the world and North Korea, among the most socialist. The United States is not purely capitalist because certain services are publicly owned (e.g., public schools, police and fire departments) and there are restraints on what private owners can do with their property, their businesses, or their employees (e.g., antitrust laws, minimum-wage laws, rent control). North Korea is not purely socialist because people can conduct certain business transactions free from public regulation. Thus, we might conceive of different nations as falling on a continuum, somewhere between pure capitalism and pure socialism, as depicted in Figure 2.1.

Now, let us put these terms in present-day vernacular. Note that socialism is on the left, as it is associated with the political left (or liberalism), and capitalism is on the right, as it is associated with the political right (or conservatism). In a socialist society, the government is much more involved in running the economy; hence, socialism in the American vernacular is associated with "big government." From the critical perspective, the fewer restraints on businesses in a capitalist society, the more the economy will be run by large corporations; so maintaining the same vernacular, we will say "big corporations." Governments have a tendency to regulate; corporations tend to despise regulations.

Keep in mind that "socialism" and "capitalism" are economic and not political terms. This is an important distinction because Americans are socialized into associating socialism with totalitarianism, as seen in the former Soviet Union and in North Korea. Totalitarianism, however, is a political system and not an economic system. Socialism, at least in its moderate forms, does not have to be enforced by a totalitarian government. This is apparent in most of the Western European countries. They have an economic system that can be located toward the center of the continuum, known as *democratic socialism*. In these economies, the state frequently owns strategic

Socialism ⟵――――――――――――――――――――――――――⟶ Capitalism

Figure 2.1

industries and services, such as mining, steel, banking, airlines, television stations, and education and health-care systems. Further, these economies provide extensive welfare services paid for by public taxes, often including higher education, retirement pensions, family leave, and health care. Note that these are democratic societies; the governments that enact these policies are freely and popularly elected in democratic political systems. A more detailed diagram is seen in Figure 2.2. As we will see throughout this book, contrary to popular constructions of "big government" in the United States, both American political and economic policies—from tax laws to labor laws to environmental laws—strongly favor "big corporations" and their wealthy investors. While the United States does not have a purely capitalist economy, as we have mentioned, it is located toward the extreme end of the continuum. It is not surprising, then, that its extreme form of capitalism is supported by very powerful ideological systems that influence social problem construction. The mainstream media, for example, while often accused of being "liberal," are components of very large transnational corporations and, therefore, have an interest in deregulation. Since the media belong to such corporations, it should be expected that, more often than not, they will represent the interests of these corporations. We must, therefore, develop a degree of circumspection when reading or viewing their coverage of various social problems.

If an American is asked why he or she is proud to be an American, the word most likely contained in the answer is "freedom." Yet, when it comes to the most important of freedoms, political freedom, the United States' record is less than remarkable. While we have been socialized to equate "democracy" with "freedom," Americans only have the freedom to choose between two political parties, both of which are capitalist. There are only two political parties in the American democratic system that can raise enough money to run viable campaigns: the Democrats and the Republicans. While the Democrats are considered liberals in the American political system, in the world scheme of things, economically, they fall considerably to the right of center. Bill Clinton, for example, a Democratic president, championed the North American Free Trade Agreement (NAFTA) and other free trade agreements that have reduced government regulation of business and opened up the free flow of capital across international boundaries. Clinton's trade agenda was unabashedly procapitalist. Barack Obama, another Democratic president, signed a free trade agreement with South Korea in 2011. Economically, both

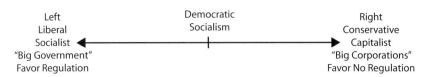

Figure 2.2

parties are procapitalist and would lie on the right side of our continuum, as is roughly shown in Figure 2.3.

Americans have been socialized to believe that there are enormous differences between the Democrats and the Republicans; but given their closeness on issues of trade and some other economic issues, many critical theorists argue that the United States has, essentially, a one-party system, a capitalist party system. Meanwhile, countries in Western Europe and elsewhere have multiple parties ranging across the continuum (e.g., Communist Party, Socialist Party, Green Party, Labor Party, Conservative Party, etc.). When most Europeans go to the polls, they have far more choice (freedom) than Americans. Sometimes they elect leaders from the left and sometimes from the right, and sometimes candidates from multiple parties win enough votes that they have to form coalition governments—a freedom not possible in the American winner-take-all system.

The United States is famous, at least among Americans, as a bastion of freedom, yet it has historically had very little tolerance for left-wing ideology and its proponents. In the past (some would argue even today), proponents of the left have been the targets of intense government scrutiny, discrimination, and smear campaigns. Eugene Debs, the last notable leader of the Socialist Party, ran for president of the United States five times. The last time, in 1920, he received nearly a million votes, a sizeable number given that the electorate was much smaller back then. This was an exceptional campaign not just because he was the last prominent socialist in the United States but because he ran his campaign as an inmate from a federal prison. Deprived of his freedom of speech, he had been imprisoned for speaking out against U.S. participation in World War I, claiming that it was a war fought in the interests of wealthy capitalists. Later, in the 1950s, left-wing writers and entertainers had their careers destroyed by inquests conducted by the U.S. Congress under the leadership of Senator Joseph McCarthy. And in the 1960s and 1970s, the FBI was illegally investigating and disrupting the activities of prominent leftists.

Thus, political freedom has been rather limited in the United States in that it does not seem to encompass left-wing economic ideologies that are considered mainstream in much of the rest of the world. The fact that the image of the United States as being a bastion of political freedom does not correspond to the reality of a two- (or, according to some, a one-) party system or with the reality of its history of political persecutions suggests that the image of American freedom is itself a social construction and not a fact.

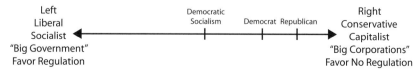

Figure 2.3

In short, when the very idea of capitalism is seriously questioned, the government steps in to defend it. Further, the way the two-party system has evolved, Americans do not have the freedom to elect any presidential candidate other than one who is procapitalist. Moreover, we cannot expect the media to challenge this system.

While it seems that we may have digressed from the topic of inequality, the relatively extreme form of capitalism that is found in the United States explains a great deal of its inequality. Much of the wealth generated by the boom of the 1990s was indeed generated by capitalism; and the failure of that wealth to "trickle down" to the middle, working, and lower classes is also explained by the U.S. position on the socialism/capitalism continuum.

THE GAP BETWEEN THE RICH AND THE REST

Despite the booming U.S. economy of the late 1990s, the gap between the rich and the poor was growing, while the incomes of working-class and middle-class families remained more or less stagnant. There is no doubt that there had been a substantial expansion in the U.S. economy during the decade of the 1990s, but the vast majority of the profits from that expansion were reaped by the upper class. Writing at that time, British economist John Gray noted, "The United States is the only advanced society in which productivity has been steadily rising over the past two decades while the incomes of the majority—eight out of ten—have stagnated or fallen."[2] In the face of numerous recessions, median family income had been declining since the 1970s; the 1990s were remarkable in that the expanding economy had virtually no impact on the poor or on working-class and middle-class incomes.

The Gini Index is a measure of inequality reported annually by the U.S. Census Bureau. If everyone received the same income, there would be absolute equality and the Gini Index would equal 0; on the other hand, a 1 on the Gini Index would indicate total inequality. As Figure 2.4 illustrates, the index has been rising steadily since the 1970s.

In fact, the Gini Index of .469 in 2010 was far higher than the index scores of most countries in northern Europe but quite similar to those of Russia and China and many countries in the South. Table 2.1 indicates the kind of company the United States keeps with regard to inequality. Further, the gap between rich and poor is larger in the United States than in any other industrialized country.[3]

The conservative agenda of President Reagan's administration was guided by a policy known as "trickle-down economics." The reasoning behind this policy held that if the government made it easy for the rich to get richer (through fewer regulations and lower taxes on profits), they would spend their money and it would trickle down to the poor. History demonstrates that this did not happen. Instead, the rich invested their newfound gains and/or sent them overseas. During the 1980s, the income of the top 1 percent

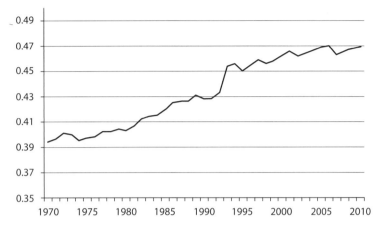

Figure 2.4 Gini Coefficients (Income Disparity): U.S. 1967–2009
Source: "Selected Measures of Household Income Dispersion," U.S. Census Bureau.

of U.S. families soared 78 percent,[4] median family income remained stagnant, and the income for the bottom 20 percent of workers fell 10 percent.[5] While Reagan was easily identified as a conservative—friend to the rich and nemesis of the poor—the same trends continued under the following administrations, including the "liberal" Clinton administration. The tax cuts spearheaded by the next administration of George W. Bush benefitted the rich far more than the rest. Between 2001 and 2006 corporate profits grew at an annual rate of more than 14 percent;[6] but, again, as we observed earlier, those profits did not trickle down to the average worker. Overall, the Congressional Budget Office reports that between 1979 and 2007, after-tax

Table 2.1 Inequality (Selected Countries)

		Gini Index*	
in the 20s	in the 30s	in the 40s	in the 50s
Austria	Australia	Argentina	Bolivia
Belgium	Canada	China	Brazil
Denmark	South Korea	Dominican Repub.	Colombia
Finland	Italy	Jamaica	Thailand
France	Japan	Russia	Guatemala
Germany	Spain	Philippines	Mexico
Sweden	United Kingdom	*United States*	Zimbabwe

* Data were not all collected the same year, but pertain to different countries between 2005 and 2009.

Source: Central Intelligence Agency, *The World Factbook,* https://www.cia.gov/library/publications/the-world-factbook/rankorder/2172rank.html. Retrieved October 6, 2011.

income of the bottom 20 percent of families went up by 18 percent, those in the middle three quintiles (i.e., the 21st through 80th percentiles) saw their incomes rise by 40 percent, the 81st through 99th percentile of households' income rose by 65 percent, and the top 1% of households' income shot up a dramatic 275 percent.[7]

Figure 2.5, compiled and released by the nonpartisan Congressional Budget Office in 2011, shows that the bottom 80 percent of households reaped smaller shares of overall income between 1979 and 2007, while only the top tier was able to increase its share. Figure 2.6, below is somewhat unusual in that it is derived from data collected by the Internal Revenue Service (rather than the U.S. Census Bureau) and it breaks out the growth in income of the top 5 percent up to the top .01 percent—that's one-hundredth of 1 percent—of U.S. taxpayers. Here we find that over the past 25 years the rate of income growth accelerates with each step up the economic hierarchy, with the top .01 percent increasing its share of the economic pie at rates exponentially higher than the other groups (let alone those below the 95th percentile).

That .01 percent of taxpayers represents about 13,000 taxpayers; it is represented largely by corporate executive officers (CEOs) and people receiving the greatest share of their income from investments. While incomes for the vast majority of workers have stagnated or fallen, CEOs have done quite well indeed. In 1982 the average CEO compensation was 42 times the salary of the average worker. By 2004, CEOs were making 431 times the average

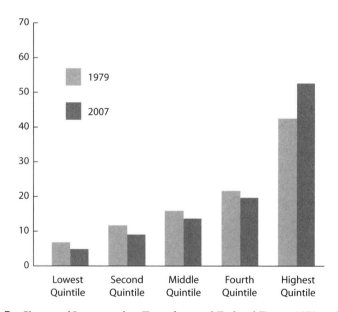

Figure 2.5   Shares of Income after Transfers and Federal Taxes, 1979 and 2007
Source: Trends in the Distribution of Household Income between 1979 and 2007, The Congress of the United States, Congressional Budget Office, October 2011.

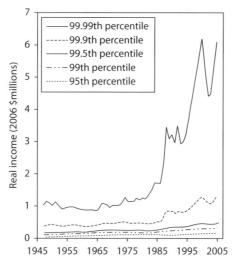

Figure 2.6 Top Incomes by Income Percentile, 1947–2005

Source: Bartels, Larry M., *Unequal Democracy.* © 2008 by Russell Sage Foundation. Published by Princeton University Press. Reprinted by permission of Princeton University Press. Data obtained from Thomas Piketty and Emmanuel Saez, "Income Inequality in the United States, 1913–1998," *Quarterly Journal of Economics* 118: 1–39, 2003. Updated with data from Saez's website, http://elsa.berkeley.edu/~saez.

worker. In Germany the ratio is 11 to 1 and in Japan CEOs only make about 10 times the average worker.[8]

Today, with high unemployment rates so often in the news, proponents of trickle-down economics talk in terms of job creation rather than income. They argue that if we free the rich to make more money, they will create more jobs. But if there were truth to this assertion, then given the enormous rate of income growth among the elite that has taken place in recent years, today's unemployment rates should be much lower than normal instead of the unusually high rates that have been dominating the news.

While many of those in power fervently seem to believe in trickle-down economics and while corporations and their investors have profited handsomely from its application, the problem is that there is little to no evidence indicating that it works. Tax rates on the highest income earners have fallen dramatically from the mid-twentieth century onward. Figure 2.7 shows the top marginal tax rates since 1920. These are the highest rates that could be imposed on the highest incomes. As we see in this figure, during the 1950s, 1960s, and early 1970s incomes of the wealthy were taxed far more heavily than today, trickle-down theory was not driving the economy, and the American economy boomed.

Taxing the rich did not stifle economic growth and prosperity was shared across the income spectrum (as seen in Figure 2.6). Between 1947 and 1973

Figure 2.7 Top Marginal Tax Rates 1920–2010

Source: Data obtained from Tax Policy Center, "Historical Highest Marginal Tax Income Rates," Urban Institute and Brookings Institute. http://www.taxpolicycenter.org/taxfacts/displayafact.cfm?Docid=213 Retrieved November 4, 2011.

real family income went up 104 percent; during the next 32 years, it only increased 23 percent.[9] And the gap between the rich and the rest started its precipitous expansion. Figure 2.8 reveals the pace of this expansion in the past few years, showing that between 1948 and 1979 the top 10 percent of families reaped 33 percent of all income growth, whereas between 2000 and 2007 the top 10 percent of families reaped *all* of the growth in income.

"[T]he United States," writes sociologist William Julius Wilson, "has had the most rapid growth of wage inequality in the Western world."[10] The Luxembourg Income Studies, comparing the United States with many other industrialized nations, found that the rich in the United States had more disposable income (between one-quarter and one-half more) than the rich in any of the other nations studied and the poor in the United States had the least disposable income, suggesting that the rich in the United States are better off than the rich in most other industrialized nations and the "poor are among the poorest in the industrial world."[11] "Levels of inequality in the United States," writes Gray, "resemble those of Latin American countries more than those of any European society."[12]

Income disparity is only one way of measuring inequality; an equally important measure is disparity in wealth. If one has wealth (or assets), then income becomes less important. Most Americans have little or no wealth because they cannot afford to invest much of their earnings.[13] While the majority of Americans are living in debt and are only a few paychecks away from financial catastrophe, wealthy individuals either do not have to work or can easily survive an interruption in income. Wealth also has a convenient

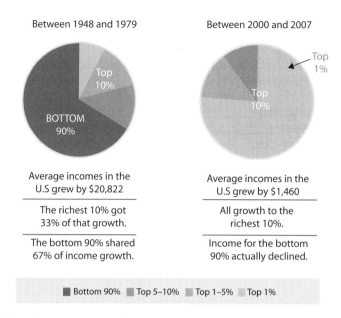

Figure 2.8 When Income Grows, Who Gains

Source: "Income Inequality: It Hasn't Been This Way," Economic Snapshot, Economic Policy Institute (using data from this table: http://www.econ.berkeley.edu/~saez/ TabFig2008.xls on Emmanuel Saez's website at the University of California, Berkeley), February 9, 2011, http://www.epi.org/publication/income_inequality_it_wasnt_always_ this_way/. Retrieved October 6, 2011.

way of generating more wealth through investments, interest, and dividends. Wealth, notes New York University economist Edward Wolff, is a "better indicator of long-run economic security.... Without wealth, a family lives from hand to mouth, no matter how high its income."[14]

Wealth inequality in the United States is greater than income inequality; just as the income gap between the rich and the rest has been expanding, so too has the wealth gap. In 1976, the top 1 percent of families in the United States held 19 percent of all wealth; by 2000, this figure had increased to roughly 40 percent of all wealth.[15] Remarkably, during the "Reagan revolution" of the 1980s, two-thirds of all gains in financial wealth were reaped by the top 1 percent of Americans.[16] The same trends continued under the following presidential administrations, both Democratic and Republican. According to Wolff's estimates, between 1983 and 1997, the top 1 percent of Americans reaped 86 percent of all stock market gains.[17] Wolff writes, "Equalizing trends during the 1930s through the 1970s reversed sharply in the 1980s. The gap between the haves and have-nots is now greater—at the start of the twenty-first century—than at any time since 1929."[18] Since most of the average American's wealth is derived from his or her home and since the Great Recession hit home values as hard as it did, the average American's wealth plummeted in recent years, thereby contributing to an expansion of

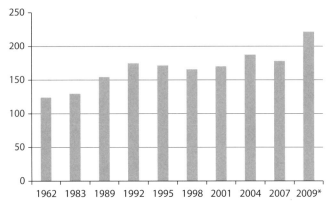

*Figure for 2009 estimated using Federal Reserve Flow of Funds data.

Figure 2.9 Ratio of Wealthiest 1 Percent of Households to Median Household Wealth

Source: "State of Working America Preview: The Rich Get Richer," Economic Policy Institute Analysis of Survey Consumer Finances and Flow of Funds Data, Economic Snapshot, December 22, 2010, http://www.epi.org/publication/the_rich_get_richer/. Retrieved October 6, 2011.

the already large gap between the wealth of the rich and the wealth of everybody else. Figure 2.9 shows the ratio of the wealthiest 1 percent of households to the median household wealth. We see that the ratio has been very high for decades, but note the jump between 2007 (before the Great Recession) and 2009 (during the Great Recession) when the wealth of the richest 1 percent of families jumped from 181 times greater to 225 times greater than the median family wealth—by far the biggest increment on the chart in just two years.

High concentrations of wealth at the top are an indicator of how well entrenched the social classes are in a society because these concentrations are almost always passed on from generation to generation. For most of the twentieth century, the wealth gap was generally greater in European societies than in the United States, leading to the assertion that the class system was more entrenched in Europe and that there was greater opportunity to advance in the United States. "By the early 1990s, however," writes Wolff, "the situation appeared to have completely reversed, with much higher concentration of wealth in the United States than in Europe. Europe now appears to be the land of equality."[19] Wealth in the United States, notes Gary Wills, is "concentrated in fewer hands than at any time in our past—and in fewer hands than any other modern democracy tolerates."[20]

Many Americans, it seems, tolerate such concentrations of wealth because they would like to see themselves among those who possess great wealth. Such dreams are part of one of the most powerful constructions in American society, frequently referred to as the "American Dream." The American Dream will be discussed in more detail later in this chapter, but for now we should note that one of its most important components is the belief in "America as the land of opportunity." This belief is easily identified as a social construction in that the power with which it is held does not correspond to the degree with which it can be supported by facts. Certainly, there is the opportunity to improve one's class position in the United States, but that opportunity does not distinguish the United States from many other countries in the world.

Summarizing the research on class mobility, sociologist Harold Kerbo writes, "The United States has the reputation of being the land of opportunity among many people in the world. [The data], however, indicate that the United States is only about average with respect to its rate of circulation mobility, or the equality of opportunity in general."[21] In another summary of the data, Doug Henwood writes, "In fact, the U.S. is a lot less mobile than people think; most people don't move far from their station of their birth, and the U.S. is no more fluid than other countries." Although conservative economists argue the great advantage of capitalism is that it allows for increased economic mobility, research comparing the United States to the even more socialized countries of Scandinavia shows that children of poor fathers in the United States are more likely to stay poor than those in Norway, Sweden, Denmark, and Finland.[22] While the media abound with rags-to-riches stories, "statistics on class mobility show these leaps to be extremely rare."[23] Research indicates that the majority of wealthy individuals featured in the *Forbes* 400, writes Holly Sklar, "inherited their way to the roster, inherited already substantial and profitable companies, or received start-up capital from a family member."[24] Noting the enormous gap between rich and poor in the United States and the slow rate of wage growth during the past several decades, Jeremy Rivkin wrote before the Great Recession, "Today, the U.S. can no longer claim to be the model of upward mobility for the world. That does not mean that there isn't opportunity for both native-born and newcomers. But the kind of unfettered upward mobility that made America the envy of the world no longer exists."[25]

Just as the image of America as the land of freedom is socially constructed, so too is the image of America as the land of opportunity. The proof that there is not equal opportunity in the United States is simple and irrefutable: if one is born poor, it is far more difficult to become rich than it is for one who is born rich to stay rich. Most people remain in the social class into which they were born, and the United States is not exceptional in the proportion of individuals who move up or down the class hierarchy.

The Middle Class: Working Harder to Stay in Place

Economist Jeff Faux writes, "For the quarter of a century following World War II, Americans got richer faster and *together,* reinforcing the notion that our common citizenship contained claims on the American dream."[26] From the mid-1940s until 1973, average household earnings rose continuously and considerably in the United States, increasing 104 percent from 1947 to 1973 in constant dollars. Thus, it is quite possible that during the period in which your parents and grandparents grew up, there was considerable economic optimism and that optimism had a basis in reality. Until recently, most middle-class parents took it for granted that their children would advance beyond them in their economic well-being. However, as we have seen above, since 1973, the rate of income growth dropped precipitously.

Women continue to earn less than men for comparable work, but there has been some improvement in women's earnings relative to men's earnings. Much of that improvement has been largely due to a decline in men's earnings. Consequently, even though at the beginning of this century more families are dual-income families than in the 1970s, there has been only a modest change in the median household income since then, up a mere 4 percent since 1973.[27] In other words, today it takes two breadwinners to earn the approximate standard of living that it used to take only one breadwinner to earn earlier.

The remarkable thing about the stagnating wages during the most recent boom and declining wages today is that the average worker then and now is better educated than the average worker of 1973 and puts in more hours at work.[28] In 2005 the Organization for Economic Cooperation and Development (OECD) reported that Americans worked more hours than most of their European counterparts. Employers are getting better-educated workers, who work longer hours at more or less the same labor rates they were getting in the 1970s.

In 1985, average hourly compensation (wages plus benefits) in the United States was higher than elsewhere in the industrialized world. In 2009, at an average of $33.53 per hour, the average production worker received less than his or her counterparts in at least 13 other countries.[29] This is good news for American corporations, which are getting by with lower labor costs; it is bad news for the workers and their families.

Much of this can be explained by the fact that corporations have been able to wring more work and productivity out of their workers without commensurate compensation. The resulting profits inflated the price of stocks in the late 1990s and were passed along to shareholders. While improved worker productivity has improved the fortunes of the rich, workers themselves have seen little in the way of improvement. In the recent past, we expected workers to benefit more from the fruits of their labor and a booming economy. The productivity of the American worker made much of the boom of the late 1990s possible, yet the worker shared few of the fruits of his or her labor. Indeed, the 1990s may have signaled a turning point in modern American labor relations, with increased worker productivity no longer translating into higher wages, a trend that continues today. During the boom, Richard Freeman noted that "Americans work considerably more hours and take less vacations than Europeans.... [W]e even work more than the Japanese. The experience of prolonged earnings declines and rising inequality in the

"WE'RE NUMBER ONE! WE'RE NUMBER ONE!! U-S-A! U-S-A! U-S-A! GO! AMERICA!
BE COM-HEY!! WHERE'S YOUR COMPETITIVE SPIRIT?!?"
Source: © Matson, St. Louis Post-Dispatch, by RJ Matson, politicalcartoons.com.

context of job growth and economic expansion is unprecedented in U.S. economic history."[30]

THE PLIGHT OF THE AMERICAN WORKER

In the nineteenth century, Karl Marx devoted his lifework to writing about
the effects of capitalism and industrialization on the working class. Factory
workers of that time had virtually no protections. Working long hours in
often dangerous conditions for wages that kept them in poverty, they could
be fired on a whim. Undoubtedly, conditions have improved for Americans
and workers in other countries in the North; but many of the strides that
have been taken to establish a modicum of job security and to improve working conditions, wages, and benefits are steadily being eroded. While it is difficult to imagine we will ever see a return to nineteenth-century working
conditions, work for most people in today's economy is far more precarious
than it has been since the Great Depression.

Popular constructions hold that in order to compete in the global
economy, U.S. businesses and industries must be able to change and adapt at
a moment's notice and that the success of the U.S. economy in the twentieth
century had been due to its "flexibility." The first and most precious casualty
of such flexibility has been job security. The three decades following the end
of World War II were marked by a period of enormous economic growth and

by an unwritten "social contract" between corporations and their employees. It was implicitly assumed that if the employee dedicated his or her life's work to the corporation, the corporation was duty-bound to maintain that employment until retirement. The economy would prosper and the middle and working classes, especially, would prosper as well. Writing in the *Wall Street Journal,* Hal Lancaster declares, "the social contract between employers and employees…is dead, dead, dead."[31] Today, job security is a thing of the past. The concept often seems foreign to college students and younger workers, and they likely have only a faint appreciation of its meaning and importance for their grandparents' and perhaps their parents' generations. However, for these generations, job security enabled workers to plan a family and then to plan for the future of their children. Job security lent predictability and stability to family life, and it had everything to do with peace of mind.

The greater the flexibility of a business or industry, the greater its ability to do whatever it takes to increase profits. Replacing assembly-line workers with robots, mid-level managers with computers, full-time workers with part-time workers, the labor of American workers with the labor of workers in poor countries, reducing health insurance and other employee benefits are some examples of "flexibility" in business economics. Indeed, such flexible practices have made American businesses more competitive in the global economy; but, as we have seen above, the rewards of increased competitiveness have largely gone to the elite and, as we will see below, the costs of increased competitiveness have largely been paid for by the middle and working classes in terms of their job security and their financial and psychological well-being.

Downsizing

According to U.S. Labor Department figures, from the beginning of 1995 to the end of 1997, 8 million—one out of every 15—workers were laid off.[32] These layoffs occurred during the "boom" and signaled a new and unsettling trend. In the past, mass firings were associated with corporate failures, often accompanying a downswing in the economy; during the boom, they were associated with corporate successes and an upswing in the economy. Ever focused on the "bottom line" and anxious to cut labor costs, corporations were and are laying off employees, sometimes by the tens of thousands. Frequently, when they announce a massive layoff, the price of their stock shares rises and their CEOs are awarded bonuses worth millions of dollars.

The beginning of the end of the social contract between employers and employees is frequently acknowledged to be the mid-1970s, when manufacturing jobs became very vulnerable to the export of labor to poor countries. More and more companies were *outsourcing* labor, having their products assembled in poor countries where labor is much cheaper, and importing parts assembled in these countries. With the money saved in labor, corporations could either lower their prices and compete more effectively or pass the savings on to shareholders or both. During the 1970s and 1980s, blue-collar layoffs ran high. Corporations and their owners profited handsomely by the export of labor. Blue-collar workers often suffered abysmally.

Corporations did not actually have to outsource their labor overseas to benefit from this trend; merely being able to threaten setting up shop overseas gave them considerable leverage over employees and their unions. Much of the prosperity of the working classes during the postwar period came from the hard-won gains of the labor unions. Labor unions and corporate management have always had conflicting interests. Now, the unions are having to cut back on their demands and accept reductions in wages and benefits because management can always threaten to move their operations to another country.

In the 1970s and 1980s, blue-collar workers suffered the most from downsizing. In addition to the outsourcing, they were frequently displaced by new technologies and automation. New production techniques often required fewer workers. Robots replaced hundreds of thousands of assembly-line workers. Corporate managers have been known to replace workers with new forms of automation, which are actually more costly than human labor, for the purpose of increasing their leverage over remaining workers, reminding them of their dispensability.[33] In the long run, such automation may save costs by undercutting the power of workers and their unions.

Today, new technologies are making white-collar workers increasingly vulnerable to downsizing as well. New computerized technologies are making business and industry all the more flexible, enabling the displacement

of telephone-answering secretaries by voice-mail interactive recordings; of letter-writing secretaries by word processing, faxboards, and e-mail; of filing secretaries by electronic memories; of clerical and administrative supervisors with nobody left to supervise; of junior administrators by automated processing; and of middle managers no longer needed to supervise dismissed clerical and administrative employees.[34]

Jobs in corporate management were once among those most sought after, in part because they were among the most secure. Today, however, corporate managers are no less vulnerable to downsizing. A survey of large firms conducted by the American Management Association found that 32 percent of layoffs were suffered by managers and supervisors.[35]

New satellite technologies have improved international communications to the point where it has become cost-effective to export white-collar labor overseas, where such labor is cheaper. Katherine Newman notes, "Data-entry, airline reservations, and other clerical jobs are being exported to the English speaking Caribbean, to Ireland, and even to the People's Republic of China, where wages are one-fourth to one-fifteenth of those earned by

American counterparts."[36] Even many of the more elite, "high-tech" workers in the United States are being displaced by technology and the export of labor. Computerized simulation programs, for example, have allowed Boeing to lay off many of its better-paid aircraft design engineers. More and more of the code for computer software targeting markets in the North is being written by software designers in the South, who are being paid a fraction of what American software designers earn. The computer technicians and other service representatives that you speak to over the telephone when you call for customer service are often carrying out their end of the conversation from India or elsewhere in the South. The *Washington Post* reports,

> [W]hite-collar work is expanding beyond the customer-service call centers that many U.S. companies have moved to developing countries. In India, for example, radiologists now interpret CT scans for hospitals in the United States, and accountants assess risks on loan applications for homes halfway around the globe. U.S. architectural work is being farmed out to the Philippines, Poland and India, as well as China. Microsoft Corp. operates a sophisticated computer research center in Beijing. By 2015, according to a report by Forrester Research Inc., more than 3 million white-collar jobs and nearly $140 billion in wages will have shifted from the United States to other nations.[37]

With the ever-increasing pace of technological change, few, if any, jobs are safe. Meanwhile, CEOs with reputations for implementing mass layoffs are frequently the best paid and most sought after of those in the corporate world.

The "Downsized"

Until the most recent economic crisis, popular constructions held that mass layoffs are frequently needed if corporations are to maintain their competitive edge and, further, that those who are "downsized" could easily find another job. While the mainstream news media frequently portray rags-to-riches stories and prefer to show how individual workers who have been displaced find better jobs or start their own successful businesses, research on the subject suggests that workers are not being done such a great favor by being laid off. Many of those who are laid off take weeks, months, or years to find another job (if they do ever find another full-time job). In 2010, over 40 percent of the unemployed were out of work for over six months.[38] Even for the fortunate few who take only a few weeks to find a job, the experience can have traumatic effects on the displaced worker's family, given the fact that most Americans have very little in the way of savings and given the uncertainty of future employment. Desperation leads many of those who find a job in just a matter of weeks to settle for one that pays considerably less than their former job. Many of those who job hunt for months or years still cannot find work that pays as much as their former job. Higher-paid workers who are laid off often take longer to find a new job or circumstances may force them to take a new job with lower wages and/or fewer benefits.[39]

Jeff Faux of the Economic Policy Institute reports that in 2004 the average laid-off employee was out of work for 5 months and when he or she did find a job, it was likely to be at a salary 20 percent less than the previous salary.[40] What's worse is that the cut in pay is likely to have permanent effects, substantially reducing his or her lifetime earnings. A 2011 study by the Brookings Institution found that of those who lost their jobs during periods of high unemployment and then found another job, 75 percent were earning less than they were three years or more after losing their job. The average reduction in lifetime earnings, they estimate, was $112,000—nearly a 20 percent reduction.[41] The average displaced worker is also likely to suffer a decline in health-care benefits with the new job. Again, managerial workers are no less vulnerable to these trends. Managers laid off in their late fifties are likely to have even greater difficulties finding new employment, and when they do, they suffer an average 35 percent decline in salary.[42]

Many of those being laid off find themselves having to accept contingency work. Writes Beth Rubin,

> The contingent labor force includes both part-time and temporary workers— some voluntarily contingent, and some involuntarily so. Contingent workers receive lower pay, no fringe benefits, and little occupational protection. Their work is contingent on labor demand, and their security is up for grabs. Most would rather work full-time if they could. Research shows that since 1970 involuntary part-time work has grown 121%....The involuntary, part-time workforce is growing more rapidly than the full-time workforce and is becoming a permanent part of the modern workplace.[43]

While Rubin notes a 121 percent increase in contingency work since 1970, she notes an even more rapid increase of 250 percent since 1982. Conveniently, and unfortunately, when incumbent U.S. presidents boast about the number of new jobs created under their administration, they fail to distinguish between new jobs that are permanent and those that are temporary. Contingency workers often work for "temp agencies," such as Manpower, Inc. Temp workers average only 60 percent of the hourly wages of their full-time counterparts, and they get few, if any, benefits.[44] "[L]ess than half of the employees of temporary-help firms," states a *Boston Globe* article, "are covered by health insurance from any source."[45] Even during the '90's boom, the *New York Times* reported that more than a quarter of Microsoft's domestic employees were temporary workers, "who often call themselves permatemps because they work anywhere from six months to three years at the company."[46]

Contingency workers, of course, represent a cost savings to employers, and they greatly enhance the "flexibility" of the workforce in that they are employed on an as-needed basis. Until recently, most contingency workers were found in blue-collar and clerical positions, but employers, anxious to cut labor costs, enhance their flexibility, and maintain their competitive edge, are hiring contingency workers throughout the occupational spectrum. Rubin notes, "Lawyers, doctors, college professors, and even top managers increasingly find themselves working on a part-time or temporary basis."[47] A striking indicator of the trend to replace full-time workers with part-time workers is the fact that many firms are laying off their full-time employees and then rehiring them as contingency workers. A survey of 720 downsized companies found that 30 percent had reemployed former full-time employees on a contingency basis without their former benefits.[48]

Missing from our discussion thus far is any mention of the psychosocial impact of job displacement, involuntary contingency work, and the downward mobility that so frequently accompanies them. Anthropologist Katherine Newman studied the subject extensively for her book *Falling from Grace: Downward Mobility in the Age of Affluence.*

> The experience of downward mobility is quite different. They once "had it made" in American society, filling slots from affluent blue-collar jobs to professional and managerial occupations. They have job skills, education, and decades of steady work experience. Many are, or were, homeowners. Their marriages were (at least initially) intact. As a group, they savored the American dream. They found a place higher up the ladder in this society, and then, inexplicably, found their grip loosening and their status sliding.
>
> Some downwardly mobile middle-class families end up in poverty, but many do not. Usually they come to rest at a standard of living above the poverty level, but far below the affluence they once enjoyed in the past. They must therefore contend not only with financial hardship but with the psychological, social, and practical consequences of "falling from grace," of losing their "proper place" in the world.[49]

When people who has been employed all of their adult lives are suddenly laid off, their lives are turned upside down and they are likely to experience some degree of *anomie*. The taken-for-granted predictability to their daily life is suddenly washed away and their normal reference points no longer have any meaning. This can cause a kind of stress above and beyond the stress brought about by their financial situation. Sociologist James Russell writes,

> It is thus not poverty produced by unemployment as such that is anomic. A person who has been poor for a long time lives within a relatively predictable situation. It is when poverty comes on suddenly that it is experienced as anomic, for then the person is thrust into a new, unfamiliar situation.[50]

Making the situation of the displaced and downwardly mobile all the more difficult is the fact that most Americans believe in the American economic system and many blame the laid-off worker for his or her fall from grace. Those who are downsized also frequently believe in the system and, therefore, blame themselves. Writing before the Great Recession, Newman noted, "We are far more likely to 'blame the victim' than to assume that systemic economic conditions beyond the influence of any individual are responsible. This tendency is so pervasive that at times even the victims blame the victims."[51] The American emphasis on financial success, the media's predilection for rags-to-riches stories, the constant refrain about the United States being the land of opportunity provided little framework for the displaced worker to understand what had happened to him or her.

Those who are laid off are not the only ones traumatized by downsizing; those who made the cut and managed to keep their jobs are also psychologically impacted. Having seen their co-workers "axed" and suspecting future cuts, they find themselves in a very stressful work environment. Working units are expected to be as productive after downsizing as they were before; consequently, workers remaining on the job frequently have to work harder and put in longer hours, with the proverbial axe hanging over their heads. The respected British medical journal *The Lancet* reports a study examining the health effects of downsizing on remaining employees. The study found that "the biggest 'losers' were professional workers.... Unsurprisingly, poor general health and tense family relationships are the result for many, with 'the sheer quantity of work' being perceived as the main contributor." The article goes on to report, "but the study coordinators also discovered that lack of colleagues is pushing many professionals to the brink: half of the interviewees described their current staffing levels as either inadequate or very inadequate."[52]

The ease with which companies downsize gives rise to fear among employees, and this fear translates into increased power for the corporate executives. Though they may be working harder and longer, pulling the weight of their missing (i.e., laid-off) co-workers, the remaining employees are not likely to be asking for raises or complaining when their benefits are cut as they fear they could lose out in the next round of job cuts.

Workers in the manufacturing industries are rapidly coming to realize that their jobs are *passé*, that they cannot compete with the price of labor in the South, and that the new job openings in the United States are primarily in the service sector. "Not to worry," write Donald Barlett and James Steele,

> As Washington and Wall Street were quick to point out, new jobs were created throughout the economy to replace the old. Why, employment at Wal-Mart alone has increased by 2,890 percent in less than two decades.... Wal-Mart has roared ahead of GM, Ford and Chrysler as a major American employer.
>
> There are to be sure, several significant differences. First, 30 percent of Wal-Mart's workers are part-time; the Big Three autoworkers are full-time. As for pay, a GM assembler earns $18.81 an hour; a tool and die maker $21.99 an hour. Most Wal-Mart employees earn a dollar or two above minimum wage.... Then there's the matter of benefits. The autoworkers have a guaranteed annual pension. The Wal-Mart employees do not. The autoworkers receive fully paid health care. Wal-Mart part-time workers receive no company benefits and full-time workers must pay part of the cost of health insurance.[53]

Wal-Mart employees are not unionized and the corporation discourages them from unionizing. For most of the twentieth century labor unions served to stave off the "Wal-Martization" of the American workforce. But the corporate elite have been able to exploit the anxieties brought on by the Great Recession to undercut labor unions, forcing concessions by threatening to move their operations overseas. Public employee unions were, until recently, perhaps the most immune from Wal-Martization; but facing severe budget cuts, hundreds of thousands of public employees have been laid off and the positions of those who remain employed are far less secure. Conservative politicians and representatives of the corporate elite have rejoiced in the weakening of public employee unions, but the end result is that more have been forced to join the ranks of the unemployed and competition for jobs has become even more fierce.

With marketplace and technological changes taking place so rapidly and with millions of workers facing impending "restructuring," layoffs, and/or Wal-Mart-type employment, economists and social commentators frequently console and advise workers that they need to keep abreast of changes and learn new skills that are more appropriate in the modern labor market. They simply need to "retool" themselves. This is often more easily said than done. Also, accelerating marketplace and technological changes suggest that if the future worker is to remain steadily employed, he or she will have to spend ever-increasing amounts of time learning new skills. Today's workers are already spending increasing amounts of time at work and decreasing amounts of time with family; from where will they find the additional time to learn new job skills?

Unemployment has never loomed on the horizon of so many workers, over such a large spectrum of occupations, as it does today—not since the Great Depression. Earlier in this chapter, we mentioned working conditions in the early days of the Industrial Revolution, stating that these conditions have certainly improved. However, with regard to job security, the clock has been turned back decades, if not centuries. Gray writes,

> [I]n their ever-greater dependency on increasingly uncertain jobs, the American middle classes resemble the classic proletariat of nineteenth-century Europe. They are experiencing economic difficulties similar to those which confronted workers who have lost protective support of welfare provisions and labor unions.[54]

In short, true to critical constructionism, popular constructions of the health of the American economy are skewed toward the interests of corporate executives and corporation shareholders. As this edition goes to press, few, if any, are arguing that the American economy is healthy. But for most of the 1990s and much of the early 2000s, economists, politicians, and pundits were lauding the booming economy and the only thing that boomed were corporate profits and the accounts of large investors. Further, those booms were brought in on the backs of the working and middle classes; they were made possible by exacting more productivity from these workers—partly through newer technologies but mostly through more work hours—without compensating them with higher wages.[55]

The newest economic data suggest that the 1990s were not an aberration but signaled a reversal in the social contract that accounted for the success of both corporations *and* their employees in the post–World War II era. Corporate executives and conservative politicians have used the banner of global competition to hold back wage increases and to turn back advances made by American workers in the decades following World War II. The balance of power between employers and employees—once mediated by labor unions and progressive government policies—is now shifting rapidly in favor of the employers, where it had been from the Industrial Revolution through the Great Depression.

The United States versus Other Industrialized Countries

Before unemployment rates skyrocketed with the Great Recession, defenders of the American economic system often pointed to the fact that unemployment rates in European countries were usually considerably higher than in the United States, but cross-cultural comparisons of unemployment rates can be deceptive. Different countries calculate unemployment rates differently. For example, many European countries include "underemployed" contingent workers in their unemployment figures, whereas "Americans working a mere hour a week do not get counted as unemployed."[56] Further, most countries require a person to be actively seeking employment to be included in the unemployment rate. In some European countries, a recent look through the job ads in a newspaper counts as an active search, whereas in the United States, a person actually has to contact potential employers to be counted as actively searching for employment.[57] The extraordinarily high incarceration rates in the United States (discussed in more detail in Chapter 5) also confound comparisons of unemployment figures. Most of the people in prison today were poor and unemployed before they got there. Prison inmates are not counted in the unemployment rates, but if they were, U.S. rates would rise far more substantially than European rates. If prisoners were included in U.S. unemployment rates, the national rate for unemployed males could rise by as much as 25 percent and considerably more than that in some states.[58]

More important than these confounding factors, we cannot compare U.S. and European unemployment rates to draw inferences about levels of suffering. Whether or not U.S. unemployment rates are normally lower than European rates, the unemployed in the United States likely suffer more than those in most European countries. Most of the countries in Europe are much more generous with their unemployment compensation benefits. "The United States," writes Newman, "is conservative—some would say mean—in this regard. We provide 35 to 40 percent of an individual's prior wages for a period of twenty-six to thirty-nine weeks. Most European countries (and Japan) offer support equivalent to 60 to 80 percent of previous earnings for nearly one year."[59] Most European countries are also less stringent in determining eligibility requirements for unemployment compensation. In the United States, one must have been at his or her previous job for a certain period of time to qualify for benefits, and part-time workers are not qualified. Thus, only about one-third of workers who are out of work are qualified to receive unemployment benefits compared with 89 percent of unemployed workers in Germany and 98 percent in France.[60]

As we will see later in this chapter, European societies also have a more generous welfare system that kicks in when unemployment compensation runs out. Thanks to welfare reform in 1995, welfare benefits are up to the individual states and the states vary considerably in determining eligibility, benefits, and time limits; but most states limit welfare benefits to a fixed number of years. Thus, it is possible for an unemployed American to be without any source of cash assistance—a situation that is not possible for citizens in any Western European country.

Defenders of the stringent and relatively stingy unemployment compensation policies in the United States argue that they encourage laid-off workers to find new employment quickly. This may be true, but these policies also explain why displaced workers so often end up with jobs that pay less than their former employment. They do not have the comfort zone that their European counterparts have to take their time to look for more suitable employment; instead, financial exigencies frequently force them to settle for lower-paying jobs. The relatively rapid progression of diminished public support creates the dire threat of real hardship for unemployed Americans, but works to the advantage of corporations that can reemploy them for lower wages.

Aside from unemployment compensation, many European countries do far more to protect their workers. In most Western European countries, it is much more difficult to fire employees than it is in the United States. For example, "In Germany," Gray writes, "the slash-and-burn, hire-and-fire culture which permitted the American downsizings...is unheard of—or rejected."[61] In a bold move to reduce its unemployment rate, France recently phased in a 35-hour workweek. The rationale was that "if people work less, it will take more people to do the work. That means more jobs." Though the following conservative administration abolished the 35-hour workweek almost as soon as it was established, many companies have retained it.[62] In Japan, during times of economic recession and with the help of special government subsidies, corporations "do everything possible to keep valuable workers by making cuts elsewhere when profits are down."[63]

Many of the contrasts between European and American societies described above apply more to the Europe of the recent past and may apply less to the Europe of the near future because European societies are steadily changing in the direction of the American model. The European elite savor the dismantling of regulations, the lowering of taxes and cutbacks in social programs and they attribute the cause to the irresistible influence of globalization. Critical constructionists have a somewhat different interpretation and attribute the cause to the rapidly increasing influence of transnational corporations in a globalized economy.

Capitalism

European restrictions on downsizing, France's tenuous government-mandated 35-hour workweek, and Japan's government subsidies to reduce the need for layoffs—all of these are anathema to American corporate capitalism. The reason the United States is considered among the most capitalist societies in the world is that the government does so little to intervene in the economy. Occasionally, when the government does intervene, the proceeds go directly to corporations, as in the recent bailout of major financial institutions. Consequently, the U.S. government does far less than most European governments and those of many other countries throughout the world to protect workers from the vagaries of global competition. Such government policies, it is said, limit the flexibility of business and industry and, thereby, inhibit their competitiveness and, consequently, their profits. Few economists, American or European, dispute this claim. However, the United States is distinguished from its industrialized counterparts in the emphasis that its citizens, politicians, and economists place on the market. As we shall see throughout this text, American social and economic policies are guided by the preeminence of the market. Other countries have different priorities, and they frequently hold to the opinion that unbridled capitalism can have destructive effects on societies and communities. These governments, more than that of the United States, have policies intended to moderate, or harness, the effects of the market on the common good. "Why," asks former conservative British economist John Gray, "should a civilized and successful social institution [a government-moderated economy] be traded off for the endemic insecurity, social divisions, and multiplying ghettos of the American free market?"[64] As a spokesperson for the French employment minister states, "We say OK to the market *economy*. . . . But what we don't want is the market *society*."[65]

A government-moderated market smacks of "socialism" to most Americans, and indeed, government intervention in the economy is the critical variable distinguishing left from right on the socialism/capitalism continuum (see Figure 2.1). However, we need to remember that "socialism" and "totalitarianism" are not equivalent and that the European and Japanese governments, referred to above, are democratically elected. Their people have freely gone to the polls and chosen government leaders who would step in to moderate the harmful effects of their markets. Though perhaps some of these countries have fewer individuals who go from rags to riches, they do not have the radical inequalities in income and wealth that exist in the United States. Their workers are less threatened by the possibility of massive layoffs, and if they are laid off, workers and their families do not face the same degree of financial upheaval as their American counterparts. As we shall see later in this chapter, these nations also do not have as much poverty as the United States.

The key to capitalism's success, some say, is a process known as *creative destruction*. According to this principle, policies, practices, businesses, or industries that are not competitive will ultimately be destroyed by, or give way to, ones that are more competitive.

The modern-day version of capitalism is in many ways a new form of capitalism made possible by new technologies and increasingly permeable international boundaries. Improved telecommunications have made it possible to shift vast sums of money around the globe with a mere keystroke. Telecommunications have also made it far easier for executives in the United States, for example, to manage and direct operations in the South (i.e., to "export labor"). Further, until very recently, shipping costs were steadily declining (especially for new technologies such as computer chips, which are often light and take up little space). At the same time, it has been fashionable in the U.S. Congress to deregulate business and industry and to lower trade barriers. All of these factors add up to what Luttwak calls "turbo-charged capitalism," which has contributed to the ever-increasing pace of creative destruction. In this environment of turbo-charged capitalism, large corporations have no loyalty to local communities, or to nations, for that matter. They develop sophisticated accounting methods, shifting their profits from one overseas tax haven to the next, and when production costs rise (usually that is when living standards start to improve), they simply move operations elsewhere.

Businesses and industries that compete successfully in this environment have reaped enormous profits for their shareholders, but faced with the threat of creative destruction, they frequently have left significant casualties in their wake in the form of massive layoffs, unemployment, financially disrupted families, and communities disrupted by uncertainty and crime. Creative destruction is not new; it is the speed at which creative destruction occurs in today's economy that is new and that makes the majority of Americans vulnerable. "[A]ny production anywhere and the related employment can be displaced at any time by cheaper production from somewhere else in the world. Life in the global economy," writes Luttwak, "is full of exciting surprises and catastrophic downfalls."[66] It is the rapid pace of change, according to many commentators, that makes the U.S. government's policy of nonintervention so outdated.[67] For the past three decades, an interesting and destabilizing cycle was in effect: while the accelerated pace of change had increased the need for the government to moderate its destructive effects, the U.S. government was becoming increasingly noninterventionist in its economic policies, which, in turn, further increased the pace of change and the need for government moderation of its destructive effects. Conservative renegade and oft-times presidential candidate Pat Buchanan states, "When go-go global capitalism is uprooting entire communities and families, I ask conservatives what it is we are trying to conserve."[68]

Unfortunately, in many ways, the European democratic socialist model is competing with the American corporate capitalist model and may itself be in danger of creative destruction. The American model, with all of the flexibility described above, was a very strong competitor. In response to this challenge, many European countries have combined their economies with a common currency. Beyond this, most European countries are demonstrating a great deal of ambivalence about how they are going to compete effectively in the global economy. There is talk in the European press about how, if they are to compete, there will have to be downsizing and governments will have to cut back on some of their welfare provisions and worker protections. Indeed, on the one hand, various European countries have cut back on their welfare provisions. On the other hand, some countries, like France, as described above, have tried new worker protection initiatives. Countries like Germany have managed to maintain very strong worker protection policies, while simultaneously exporting a good deal of their labor. Ambivalence is further reflected in that people in many European countries seem to alternate between electing conservative, procapitalist candidates and liberal, prosocialist candidates. As the American corporate capitalist model spreads across the globe, countries around the world are facing the same question as these European countries: Can they effectively compete in the global economy without abandoning their government-moderated economic models that have, thus far, helped them to maintain a civil society? The recent global economic crisis which emanated from the United States has many Europeans regretting shifts they have made in the direction of the American economic model.

Private Affluence/Public Squalor

In another critique of American-style capitalism, it has been noted that the system provokes a stark contrast between private affluence and public squalor. Put simply, Americans prefer to horde their money for themselves and loathe to spend it for the common good in the form of taxes. As a result, in a great many communities, we can find hundreds of beautiful private swimming pools but no municipal pools. We have millions of private automobiles but often terrible roads and one of the worst public transportation systems in the entire world. We have thousands of excellent private schools and many more thousands of substandard public schools. More and more who can afford them have excellent private security forces protecting them, while public security forces (the police) are straining to meet the public need.

In the world's wealthiest country, the state infrastructure is in abysmal condition. The massive blackout that afflicted many of the eastern states in August 2003 was a demonstration of the U.S. failure to invest in its infrastructure. In August 2005, floodwaters produced by Hurricane Katrina breached New Orleans' levees and caused enormous devastation. In October 2005, only a weakened 173-year-old wooden dam stood between downtown

Taunton, Massachusetts, and eight feet of floodwaters. In August 2007 a bridge crossing the Mississippi in Minneapolis collapsed during rush hour, killing five and injuring more than a 100 people.

The U.S. House Committee on Transportation and Infrastructure estimates that "32 percent of our major roads are in poor or mediocre condition and 28 percent of our bridges are structurally deficient or functionally obsolete." Further, it estimates that "[n]early one-third of all fatal crashes are caused by substandard road conditions and roadside hazards."[69] In many areas, pipes carrying drinking water, storm water, and wastewater have been in the ground for more than a 100 years. Said the chair of the Highways, Transit, and Pipelines Subcommittee, "We have two choices: pay a little now to provide a significant investment in our infrastructure, or pay much more later in lost lives, lost efficiency, and the greater costs that will be needed to repair a more deteriorated transportation system."[70] Since the turn of the new millennium, at least 21 dams have failed and the American Society of Civil Engineers (ASCE) estimates that over 2,600 dams in the country are unsafe. The average public school in the United States is over 40 years old[71] and, according to the ASCE, "Due to either aging, outdated facilities, severe overcrowding, or new mandated class sizes, 75 percent of our nation's school buildings remain inadequate to meet the needs of school children."[72] Sociologist Charles Derber describes a few of the worst cases of dilapidating schools: "New York schools with exposed asbestos, rotting roof beams, and broken plumbing; Montana schools where water leaks have led to collapsed ceilings; and a New Orleans school where termites have eaten books on library shelves and then the shelves themselves."[73]

In 2009, the ASCE gave the nation's overall infrastructure a grade of D, and it estimated the necessary investment over a 5-year period to be about $2.2 trillion. A breakdown of their "grade report" can be found in Box 2.1.

In 1969, noted economist John Kenneth Galbraith addressed the endemic contrast between private affluence and public squalor.

> The final problem of the productive society is what it produces. This manifests itself in an implacable tendency to provide an opulent supply of some things and a [miserly] yield of others. This disparity carries to the point where it is a cause of social discomfort and social unhealth. The line which divides our area of wealth from our area of poverty is roughly that which divides privately produced and marketed goods and services from publicly rendered services. Our wealth in the first is not only in startling contrast with the meagerness of the latter, but our wealth in privately produced goods is, to a marked degree, the cause of the crisis in the supply of public services. For we have failed to see the importance, indeed the urgent need, of maintaining a balance between the two.[74]

While Americans may think that it is human nature to prefer to spend one's money on oneself rather than for the public good, citizens of many other countries would likely disagree. In addition to spending more money (relative

```
┌─────────────────────────────────────────────────────────────────────┐
│                                                                       │
│      BOX 2.1.  PROGRESS REPORT AMERICA'S INFRASTRUCTURE               │
│      ─────────────────────────────────────────────────────────       │
│                                                                       │
│              Aviation                            D                    │
│              Bridges                             C                    │
│              Dams                                D                    │
│              Drinking Water                      D–                   │
│              Energy                              D+                   │
│              Hazardous Waste                     D                    │
│              Inland Waterways                    D–                   │
│              Levees                              D–                   │
│              Roads                               D–                   │
│              Schools                             D                    │
│              Solid Waste                         C+                   │
│              Transit                             D                    │
│              Wastewater                          D–                   │
│              Overall GPA                         D                    │
│                                                                       │
│      Source: American Society of Civil Engineers, "2009 Report Card   │
│      for America's Infrastructure." Available at http://www.asce.org/ │
│      reportcard/. Retrieved April 30, 2012.                           │
│                                                                       │
└─────────────────────────────────────────────────────────────────────┘
```

to their gross domestic product) to support social welfare programs, many countries spend more than the United States on the upkeep of their infrastructures. Remember, many of these countries are no less democratic than the United States, and citizens of these countries repeatedly elect "socialist" leaders who they know will use higher taxes to support the common good. In 1998, for example, the German people voted the government out of office because it was trying to lower taxes and cut government spending.[75]

POVERTY

The Numbers

The nation's largest network of food banks, Feeding America, reports that their agencies serve over 37 million people each year. The organization reports that 5.7 million people receive food assistance from them each week, representing a 27 percent increase over the numbers in 2006. Thirty-six percent of those who seek their help are from working families.[76] In 2010 the U.S. Conference of Mayors reported increases in the numbers of people seeking emergency food assistance in all of the cities they surveyed; the average increase was 24 percent.[77] The United States, recognized as the wealthiest and most powerful country in the world, also has higher rates of poverty than other industrialized nations. The data in Table 2.2 reveal what sociologists

Table 2.2 Percent of Population Living in Poverty (With Incomes Less than 50% of Median Income) in the 1990s (during the "boom" years)

United States	19.1%
United Kingdom	14.6
Canada	11.7
Netherlands	6.7
France	7.5
Germany	7.5
Italy	6.5
Sweden	6.6

Source: Harold Kerbo, *Social Stratification and Inequality,* 8th ed. New York: McGraw-Hill, 2012.

refer to as *relative poverty,* the condition of not being able to afford what is considered normal in a given society. In Table 2.2, people are considered poor if their income is less than half of their country's median income. Another, more serious type of poverty, is *absolute poverty,* which is defined as the inability to afford the basic necessities of living. Using this definition, the United States ranks even worse than it does for relative poverty. In the early 1990s, other industrialized countries had an average of between 2 and 5 percent of their populations living in absolute poverty, while the United States had between 13 and 14 percent.[78] A study by the U.S. Department of Agriculture reports that in 2008, more than 17 million households in the United States experienced "food insecurity;" of these, 6.7 million experienced "very low food security."[79]

Beyond these figures, we are more used to hearing about the numbers and percentages of Americans living below the official "poverty line" or the *poverty threshold.* The poverty line was first calculated by the U.S. government in the 1960s, using data from 1955, by estimating the cost of a bare minimum diet (known as the *economy food plan*) and then trebling that figure to take into account other necessities such as clothing and shelter. That total—originally based on the cost of food—has been updated every year according to the rate of inflation as shown in the Consumer Price Index. In 2010, the poverty threshold stood at just over $22,000 for a family of four. In that year, 15.1 percent of the population lived below this threshold; this figure translated to 46 million people.[80]

Many social scientists, however, are critical of the official poverty threshold, arguing that it underestimates the true number of people living in poverty. One problem is that the official poverty threshold—other than deriving separate figures for Alaska and Hawaii—makes no allowances for the fact that the cost of living (food, rent, utilities, etc.) is higher in some areas than in others. In fact, frequently lacking transportation, the poor often have to purchase their groceries from the only grocery store in their neighborhood, which quite likely charges exorbitant prices because there is no competition in the area and its customers are "captive." The U.S. Department of Agriculture recently reported that there are 2.3 million households in the United States that are located more than a mile from a supermarket and do not have access to a vehicle.[81] Areas with high concentrations of such households, usually in the inner cities, are frequently called "food deserts" and, not only do their residents pay higher prices for food, but the stores in which they buy their food usually stock more high fat foods with little nutritional value and few, if any, fruits and vegetables.

A more fundamental problem deals with the fact that the poverty threshold is calculated by multiplying the cost of a minimal diet by a factor of 3 because the typical family in 1955 spent about one-third of its budget on food; today, however, it spends about one-sixth of its budget on food.[82] Today, the costs of housing, transportation, and utilities take up a far larger proportion of the family budget than they did in 1955.[83] Thus, if we were to follow the logic behind the original development of the formula, we would multiply the costs of food by 6 instead of 3. This would double the threshold and far more families would be living below it. Furthermore, depending on where they live, if parents are to go to work to earn their living, they quite likely need a car and must pay all the expenses necessary to keep it running—another cost not included in the formula. They often must incur child-care costs as well. In 1955, the calculation assumed a two-parent family with working father and stay-at-home mother; therefore, it made no provision for the costs of child care.

Government officials have long resisted any efforts to reform the calculation of the poverty threshold because to do so would dramatically increase the number of people considered to be living in poverty. No presidential administration wants to be associated with the year in which the number of people living in poverty increased more than 100 percent.

Even so, such reforms in the calculation of the poverty threshold take into account only needs associated with absolute poverty. Conceivably, they could also take into account needs associated with relative poverty, such as the costs of entertainment, a vacation, and perhaps an occasional sundae for the kids. Sociologist Kathryn Edin notes that the poor often feel compelled to make purchases that, at first glance, others might regard as frivolous, "such as the occasional trip to the Dairy Queen, or a pair of stylish sneakers for the son who might otherwise sell drugs to get them, or the cable subscription for the kids home alone and you are afraid they will be out on the street if they are not watching TV."[84]

Whether one accepts the official poverty threshold or not, one of the most disturbing economic trends in the United States has been the rise in the number of people who live in "deep poverty." Since 1975, the percentage of the poor with incomes below 50 percent of the poverty line has been increasing, from 30 percent in 1975 to 43 percent in 2010, the highest on record. (There was a 26 percent increase between 2000 and 2005 despite considerable economic expansion during most of this period.) More than 20 million people lived in deep poverty in the United States in 2010.[85]

The Homeless

Among the hardest to count when calculating the extent of poverty in the United States are the homeless. It is very difficult to estimate the extent of homelessness because those in this situation have no address and are frequently on the move. Until the 1980s, public discussions of homelessness almost always focused on homeless men, who were often stereotyped as tramps, hobos, or skid-row alcoholics. During the 1980s, the Reagan administration had begun cutting back on welfare programs and federal housing programs. When the issue of homelessness came up, the focus was still on individuals, and administration officials typically characterized the homeless as either mentally ill or drug-addicted. "This view, of course," writes Joseph Dillon Davey, "exonerate[d] the Reagan administration for housing cuts and [made] no distinction between the 'new homeless' and the 'old homeless' and the skid-row alcoholics who made up the old homeless."[86] The "new homeless," to whom Davey refers, is increasingly made up of families with children. According to the U.S. Conference of Mayors, each year since 1973 has seen an increase in the proportion of the homeless that is made up of families. According to the 2010 report of the U.S. Conference of Mayors, 58 percent of the cities surveyed reported an increase in homelessness in the previous year.[87] And the 2011 report of the National Alliance to End Homelessness reports that the subpopulation with the largest percentage increase over the previous year was family households.[88] In an article published in *Political Science Quarterly* Ralph Nunez and Cybelle Fox write, "Many Americans refuse to believe, however, that entire families are homeless in the richest country of the world." This, they argue, explains why there has been no effective policy response to the problem of homelessness in the United States.[89]

Why?

The widespread poverty in the United States, relative to other industrialized countries, begs for an explanation. Basically, most of the characteristics of the U.S. economy discussed above go a long way toward an explanation. The extreme form of capitalism that exists in the United States means that there is little in the way of government assistance to the poor. Yet, popular constructions of poverty and welfare in the United States suggest that the country is far too generous in its welfare provisions to the poor; but relative to other industrialized countries, welfare provisions for the poor are quite meager in the United States. Kerbo writes,

> From the political rhetoric...one gets the idea that the United States has had the most extensive and costly welfare system in the world....Nothing could be farther from the truth. To begin with, of the sixty-three most industrialized nations in the world, *only one nation* does not have some form of guaranteed income program for all families in need. That one exception is the United States.[90]

Another popular construction related to poverty in the United States is that there is plenty of opportunity for the poor to improve their economic standing. This is, in fact, the basis of what is so often referred to as the "American Dream," the belief in "America as the land of opportunity." However, like other patriotic rallying cries throughout history, it is, at best, an exaggeration. Perhaps the American Dream had its greatest element of truth in the early decades of the 1900s. It was during this period that the United States became the biggest industrial giant in the world. Factory jobs became plentiful and the American Dream became accessible to millions of Americans, even the poor. Factory jobs were good jobs because they paid relatively well and required little in the way of skilled experience. One did not even have to speak English to perform well at most of these jobs. Poor, uneducated, illiterate, non-English-speaking people from all over the world flocked to American cities for these factory jobs. In the 1920s, for example, an assembly-line worker at Ford Motor Company could earn $5 per day. That was a considerable sum of money for a poor person in those days, enough to support a family and to set some aside as savings. In this way, millions of people were able to move from poverty into the middle class. In the 1970s, however, a process known as "deindustrialization" was well under way. For the reasons discussed above (namely, automation and the export of labor), manufacturing jobs grew scarce, leaving mostly low-paying service sector jobs available for the poor. Today, it is far more difficult for someone making close to minimum wage flipping burgers or greeting people in Wal-Mart to make enough money to support a family *and* to set some aside as savings. Deindustrialization made the route from poverty to the middle class a far more difficult prospect, and the American Dream became far less viable for millions of Americans.

The American Dream, however, is such a powerful construction and is so much a part of the American ethos that it is virtually sacrosanct. To many Americans, questioning it, as critical constructionism is apt to do, is almost a form of heresy. To challenge the validity of the American Dream is to challenge both our collective and individual identities. The very presence of the poor in the United States represents such a challenge, and the response to the poor in the United States—more so than in almost all other countries—is often one of contempt. Contempt for the poor could be considered a form of American patriotism in that it is a reaffirmation of the belief in America as the land of opportunity.

Contempt for the poor explains why Americans are so frequently attuned to alleged character flaws in poor people. As a professor who talks about poverty in my classes, I frequently hear students complaining about the "welfare system," citing cases of poor people driving luxury automobiles or the time they were behind a poor person in the grocery checkout who was paying for luxury items with food stamps. These cases are likely to have been selected out of contempt because these students seem to have failed to notice the hundreds of other times when they have seen poor people driving old, beat-up automobiles or taking the bus or walking because they cannot afford an automobile or its upkeep. They have also failed to notice the scores of other times they have been behind someone in the grocery checkout purchasing cheap, subsistence foodstuffs with their food stamps. That they instead notice the "abuses" committed by poor people suggests that they want to see such abuses because these reaffirm their belief in the American Dream. Such contempt for the poor makes it all the more difficult to be poor in the United States. In terms of absolute physical necessities, it is more difficult to be poor in most countries of the South, but emotionally, it is more difficult to be poor in the United States because of all of the blame and self-blame that accompany the conditions of poverty here.

Conservative politicians can gain a good deal of political capital by tapping into and nurturing this contempt. Ronald Reagan, for example, on a number of occasions, held up the help-wanted sections of major newspapers while indicating that the problem of poverty had nothing to do with the lack of job opportunities in the United States. "[I]n the Washington daily paper on Sunday," he once said at a Republican campaign rally, "you pick it up and see 70 full pages of those tiny help-wanted ads, employers looking for people to come work."[91] The message he was imparting was simple: poor people prefer poverty and welfare to work, and the problem of poverty is a problem of motivation on the part of the poor. However, when holding up these want ads, what Reagan failed to note was that (1) most of those jobs required experience, education, or skill levels that disqualified most poor applicants; (2) of the jobs for which poor people were qualified, there were frequently several to dozens of applicants; and (3) most of the jobs for which there were ads were eventually filled, and filling them did nothing to lower the poverty rates. Sociologists John Pease and Lee Martin systematically examined the want ads in one edition of the *Washington Post*. Of the 696 ads in that edition, most required experience, education, or skill levels that disqualified most poor applicants. "Only 13% of all vacancies," they write, "and only 8% of all full-time vacancies offered work for the unemployed poor. Although these menial jobs," they continue, "paid low wages and rarely offered fringe benefits, they received an average of 21 applications and were quickly filled."[92]

Indeed, until the Great Recession, the fastest-growing category of those living in poverty was the "working poor." More of the jobs being created in the "new economy" are in the lower-paying areas of the service sector, such as fast food and retail. These jobs are often part-time and frequently pay little more than minimum wage, with few or no benefits. Even a full-time job or several part-time jobs amounting to 40 hours per week at minimum wage would put a single parent and his or her—most likely *her*—two children below the poverty line. This, in part, explains why the U.S. Conference of Mayors found that 39 percent of adults seeking emergency food aid in 2003 were employed.[93]

In the United States, the poor receive relatively meager financial assistance plus a great deal of blame. In other industrialized countries, the poor receive generous financial assistance and relatively little blame. The latter combination seems to be more effective in moving people out of poverty. Perhaps most confounding to the notion of the American Dream is the relative ease with which the poor in other industrialized countries are able to "escape" poverty. In the Netherlands and Sweden, about 40 percent of those living in poverty are able to escape in a year or less. The Netherlands has an escape rate of 45 percent; France, Germany, and Ireland have rates between 25 and 28 percent; and in the United States, only about 14 percent of those living in poverty are able to escape in a year or less.[94]

The likelihood of successfully addressing the problem of poverty in the United States is hindered not only by an ideologically based contempt for the poor but also by the class bias of the news media. From the end of World War II until the 1960s, the poor in America were largely ignored by the media. Then, in 1962, sociologist Michael Harrington published his book *The Other America*, which was instrumental in bringing poverty to the attention of the American public. Harrington wrote in a phrase that is apropos today, "That the poor are invisible is one of the most important things about them. They are not simply neglected and forgotten as in the old rhetoric of reform; what is much worse, they are not seen."[95] For several years, following the publication of Harrington's book, issues involving poverty received a good deal of media attention, culminating in Lyndon Johnson's War on Poverty. Partially in response to this coverage (and to coverage of race issues), conservative politicians began to accuse the media of having a liberal bias. This accusation continues today and is refuted in this text but, nevertheless, has had a profound effect on news reportage, causing the media to retreat from its coverage of such issues.

This is a persistent issue: until the most recent economic crisis, poverty was rarely covered in the news, especially television news. When the poor did show up in the news, it was usually in a far from sympathetic light, often in connection to the crimes they committed, the drugs they used, the babies they had, or the welfare system that they cheated. While coverage of the poor is lacking, the reporting of issues that would be of concern mainly to elite interests abounds in the nightly news, including daily reports of stock market activities, fashion reporting, and regular reports of skiing conditions from some news stations. "Besides being of practical value to the wealthy," writes Gregory Mantsios, "such coverage has considerable ideological value. Its message: the concerns of the wealthy are the concerns of us all."[96] Coverage of "wealthy issues" and not of "poor issues" leads the public to believe that prosperity runs throughout the American class system and that poverty is a nonissue. A survey by the Catholic Campaign for Human Development found that most respondents "maintained that poverty affects some one million people in this country,"[97] while the actual figure is between 35 and 40 million people—the latter estimate, writes Mantsios, "equals the entire population of Maine, Vermont, New Hampshire, Connecticut, Rhode Island, New Jersey, and New York combined."[98] With the most recent economic crisis, however, sensitivity to the plight of the poor might heighten as more people fear they may soon be counted amongst them.

Welfare versus Wealthfare

Given the contempt that so many Americans have for the poor, it is not surprising that welfare programs for the poor are popularly held in disdain. It is interesting to note, however, the contrast between opposition to financial assistance available to the poor and the toleration of financial assistance available to corporations and the nonpoor in the United States. Both money given out by the government and money not collected by the government in the form of taxes represent "tax expenditures." They both negatively impact the amount of money in the treasury. Both welfare given to the poor and tax breaks available to corporations and the nonpoor represent tax expenditures. Tax deductions could then be regarded as a form of "welfare" given to corporations and to the nonpoor. They are sometimes referred to as "corporate welfare" and/or "wealthfare." The amount of money "given out" in welfare to the poor pales in comparison to the amount given out in wealthfare; but, until the Great Recession, wealthfare has not been as controversial. While many Americans complain bitterly about the size of their tax bill, sometimes blaming welfare going to the poor, cutbacks in welfare to the rich could have a far more substantial impact in reducing their tax bills. Barlett and Steele have written extensively about the subject.

> It is possible to structure a tax system that imposes taxes in such a way that people at the top are left with sufficient money to buy several houses, and everyone in the middle can buy one house. Or it is possible to structure it in such a way that people at the top are left with sufficient income to buy many houses, and a large number of people in the middle cannot buy one. In the 1950s, the United States had the former tax system. [Today] it has the latter. Why? Because Congress effectively jettisoned the progressive income tax— which held that tax rates should rise along with income [as it does in most European countries]—and replaced it with comparatively low rates plus a generous mix of preferences, and exceptions, and deductions that are designed to benefit the more affluent individuals and families.[99]

Over the past three decades, Congress has cut the tax rate for the wealthiest taxpayers by more than half.[100] With the deductions and exceptions available to them, it is not the least bit uncommon for rich people to pay similar or even lower rates of tax than people in the lower and middle income ranges.

Corporations have enjoyed similar tax privileges. The proportion of all federal taxes paid by corporations has fallen from 30 percent in the mid-1950s to less than 7 percent in 2009. Much is made in the corporate media about the 35 percent corporate tax rate in the United States, one of the highest rates in the industrialized world. Much less is said about how, thanks to various deductions and loopholes, few large corporations actually pay that high a rate. General Electric, for example, one of the nation's largest corporations, which made over $14 billion in profit in 2010, paid no taxes that year and, instead received a $3.2 billion tax benefit.[101]

Furthermore, "The Federal Government alone," write Barlett and Steele, "shells out $125 billion a year in corporate welfare."[102] The alleged justification: corporate welfare helps create jobs. However, some corporate tax breaks make it easier for corporations to set up shop overseas. Indeed, many of the corporations subsidized by corporate welfare have been downsizing. "Fortune 500 companies...have erased more jobs than they have created...and yet they are the biggest beneficiaries of corporate welfare."[103] AT&T, Bechtel, Boeing, General Electric, and McDonnell Douglas, all beneficiaries of corporate welfare, have reduced their workforce, in toto, by 38 percent.[104] State and local governments have provided billions of dollars in services and tax breaks to attract jobs to their areas. The value of these services and tax breaks often seems excessive. For example, economic incentives provided to Sears in Illinois amounted to $44,000 per job "saved," and such incentives provided to United Airlines in Indiana amounted to $72,000 for each job.[105]

These are monies that, essentially, are being paid for out of public taxes; yet public outcry has traditionally been vented against the poor. The incongruity is often rationalized by the belief that society as a whole benefits from corporate welfare, but only the undeserving poor benefit from the other kind of welfare. Mark Zepezauer and Arthur Naiman write,

> It's sometimes argued that corporate welfare benefits society as a whole, by recirculating money back into the economy. Of course, that's also true of welfare to the poor, which benefits landlords, supermarkets, variety stores, etc.
>
> What's more, a lot of welfare programs pay for themselves many times over in future savings on health care, prisons, and welfare payments. (Head Start is a perfect example—according to conservative estimates, $1 invested in Head Start saves $3 in future costs to society.)[106]

GLOBAL INEQUALITIES

Much of the affluence found in the North and much of the dire poverty associated with countries of the South have been due to the wholesale exploitation of the South over the past several hundred years. Possessing superior military technology, especially in the way of navies and armaments, European countries established colonies all over the South. The purpose of these colonies was quite simply to enrich the colonizers and their home countries. Wealth was extracted in the form of natural resources and in the form of labor performed by indigenous peoples. Labor was frequently extracted through enslavement or by capturing or destroying alternative means of earning a livelihood. Political scientist Michael Parenti writes,

> The process of extracting the natural resources of the Third World [i.e., the South] began centuries ago and continues to this day. First, the colonizers extracted gold, silver, furs, silks, and spices, then flax, hemp, timber, molasses, sugar, rum, rubber, tobacco, calico, cocoa, coffee, cotton, copper, coal, palm oil, tin, iron, ebony, and later on oil, zinc, manganese, mercury, platinum, cobalt, bauxite, aluminum, and uranium. Not to be overlooked is the most hellish of all appropriations: the abduction of millions of human beings into slave labor.[107]

The extraction of wealth from these countries hundreds of years ago continues to have profound effects on the South today. Parenti continues,

> What is called "underdevelopment" is a set of social relations that has been forcefully imposed on countries. With the advent of Western colonizers, the peoples of the Third World were actually set back in their development, sometimes for centuries.... The enormous wealth extracted should remind us that there originally were very few poor nations. Countries like Brazil, Indonesia, Chile, Bolivia, Zaire, Mexico, Malaysia, and the Philippines were and in some cases still are rich in resources. Some lands have been so thoroughly plundered as to be desolate in all respects. However, most of the Third World is not "underdeveloped" but overexploited. Western colonization and investments have created a lower rather than a higher living standard.[108]

Similar kinds of wealth extraction by affluent countries are still going on today in the South. It has been estimated that at least three-fourths of the known mineral resources in the South are controlled by corporate interests in the North.[109]

Besides the natural resources that are being extracted, as in the past, labor in the South continues to be extracted. The export of labor from the North to poor countries, as we have seen, has had serious negative effects on workers in the North. However, according to popular constructions, it is supposed to play a key role in improving the living standards of the billions of people living in the South. Instead, the evidence indicates that poverty has only been on the rise in the South since the arrival of the manufacturing jobs that left the North. Jobs started leaving the North for the South en masse in the 1970s. Between 1985 and 1990, U.S. corporate investments in the South rose 84 percent, "with the most dramatic increase in cheap-labor countries."[110] In the meantime, standards of living in the South were on the decline.

"Most people in the [South]," writes Walden Bello, "remember the 1980s not as the decade of triumphant capitalism but as the decade of reversal. By 1990, per capita income in Africa was down to its lowest level at the time many African countries achieved their independence in the 1960s. And in Latin America, per capita income in 1990 had not exceeded its 1980 level."[111] The 2000 Mexican census estimates that the number of people living in poverty rose from 49 percent in 1981 to 75 percent in 2000.[112] Between 1980 and 1993, according to World Bank data, low-income countries (except India and China) experienced no growth in their gross national product (GNP).[113] A more recent World Bank report indicates that the number of people living on less than $1 per day is on the increase.[114] According to the United Nations' *2007 Human Development Report,* "There are still around 1 billion people living at the margins of survival on less than US$1 a day, with 2.6 billion—40 percent of the world's population—living on less than US$2 a day."[115] Author Hazel Henderson writes, "Thirty years ago there was a 30-to-1 difference between the richest 20 percent and the poorest 20 percent of humanity. Now, it's 60-to-1. The incomes of the poorest 20 percent have actually declined."[116]

During the 1990s, while the export of labor to the South was increasing exponentially, the United Nations reports,

> Though average incomes have risen and fallen over time, human development has historically shown sustained improvement, especially when measured by the human development index. But the 1990s saw unprecedented stagnation, with the Human Development Index falling in 21 countries.[117]

The International Monetary Fund (IMF) concludes that "in recent decades, nearly one-fourth of the world population has regressed. This is arguably one of the greatest economic failures of the 20th century."[118]

Just as it does in rich countries, extreme forms of capitalism greatly exacerbate inequalities in poor countries. This is perhaps best evidenced by the rapidly accelerating trend in the privatization of state industries and services. If the state were selling off these industries and services at fair market value and distributing the proceeds more or less evenly among its citizenry, then privatization could well be a good thing. However, more often than not, especially in poor countries, corruption comes into play and these industries and services are being sold at fantastic "discounts." Robert Weissman provides such an example in Russia,

> The Russian gas giant Gazprom was privatized for $250 million. Three years later, Gazprom's market valuation was $40 billion. Based on its reserves, if it were valued as a company would be in the United States, where property rights are more secure, it would be worth between $300 billion and $900 billion. Oil, mining, electricity and other companies were privatized at prices sometimes less than a twentieth of their subsequent market value.[119]

Deals much like these create billionaires in the South (though Russia is not in the South) while the rest of the people (already poor) have to pay often exorbitant prices for products and services that were once subsidized by the state. Possibly, the most ominous example of privatization is the privatization of water. The United Nations *Human Development Report* states, "Privatization in water and sanitation has led to much higher fees, sometimes overnight—and sometimes with disastrous consequences."[120]

One of the most formidable impediments to economic progress in the South is foreign debt. "The political economy of debt," write sociologists Frederick Buttell and Peter Taylor, "has become the principal parameter affecting Third World development prospects."[121] Many countries of the South are indebted to creditors in the North for tens of billions of dollars. The debt crisis began in the 1970s when Western banks were glutted with money (much of it deposited by oil-rich nations) and found they could get a good return on their money by loaning to poor countries. In many, but certainly not all, cases, the borrowed money was diverted away from its intended development projects only to line the pockets of the many dictators around at the time. Indebted countries found themselves in a position much like that of the victims of a loan shark: barely able to pay off the interest on their debts, let alone the principal, and often having to borrow more money just to pay the interest on previous loans.

For such loans, they frequently go to the World Bank or the IMF. These agencies often make loans conditioned upon the country's acceptance of a *structural adjustment program* (SAP). SAP conditions often require the country to adopt austerity measures, such as cutbacks in welfare, education, or health-care spending, so that the country will be better able to pay off its debts. These are harsh conditions, given the deprivation and suffering that already afflict these poor countries. Often criticized for serving corporate interests in the North, SAPs may also require a country to open its markets to Northern imports and, thereby, undercut its local economy and the livelihood of its indigenous farmers, craftspeople, and manufacturers. Weissman writes, "[M]ilitary power has receded as the key to ensure multinational corporate access to South resources. The new favorite club of industrialized power brokers is the massive foreign debt of Third World countries."[122]

To the benefit of corporate interests in the North, countries in the South are frequently forced to sell off more of their natural resources to generate the income to service their debts. Weissman writes, "As long as foreign countries are forced to organize their economies toward earning foreign exchange to meet outrageous debt-repayment schedules, they will have almost no choice but to pillage their resource bases."[123]

Moreover, countries in the South are competing with each other for foreign "dollars." They compete with one another on the basis of their labor costs and at the expense of workers' rights and environmental regulations. Thus, the countries with the lowest wages, fewest worker protections, weakest labor unions, and laxest environmental regulations often win out in the competition to attract corporate investments from the North. The effects on working conditions and the environment in the South have been devastating and countries throughout the world are pitted against one another in the "race to the bottom" to see who can cut costs, wages, and regulations faster.

There is growing recognition of the South's need for debt relief. Richard Stevenson writes in the *New York Times*,

> Nearly everyone agrees that it would be a good thing if the world's rich nations could do more to ease the huge burden of debt that is weighing down the poorest countries. Far better, after all, to allow governments of impoverished nations to put what money they have into improving health care and education than to force them to sink as much as a third of their paltry budgets into futile efforts to keep up with loans from governments and international agencies—loans that their creditors have all but written off anyway.[124]

In 1999, leaders from the United States, Britain, France, Germany, Italy, Canada, and Japan agreed on the need to relieve the poorest countries of their foreign debt. They agreed, at least, in principle. Debt relief has been shown to be very beneficial, such as when Zambia was able to introduce free health care in 2006 with the money saved from $4 billion in debt repayment.[125] Sometimes it takes a catastrophe such as the 2004 tsunami to bring about any debt relief. Progress has been slow. Given that foreign debt has provided corporations in the North with leverage over markets and labor conditions in the South, it remains to be seen whether the North can muster any more of the will needed to alleviate the problem.

Corporate Interests and U.S. Foreign Policy

As noted above, poverty in the South has benefitted corporate interests by providing cheap labor and cheap access to important natural resources. We also noted earlier that corporate interests have a profound effect on governmental policies. It should come, then, as no surprise that corporate interests have had a pronounced influence on U.S. foreign policy. In fact, it is the U.S. track record in promoting corporate interests abroad that explains why so many people in the South fear and despise the United States. In a number of cases, when U.S. corporate interests were being threatened, the United States has helped to overthrow democratically elected leaders and replace them with brutal dictators. While espousing the desire to spread democratic principles throughout the world, the United States has continually put corporate interests before those democratic principles and tens of thousands, if not hundreds of thousands, of lives have been lost as a result. Many peoples throughout the Middle East and Latin America are deeply suspicious of U.S. foreign policy, and their suspicions have strong historical origins. Just as the FBI was rooting out leftist elements at home during the 1950s, 1960s, and 1970s, the CIA was rooting out leftist leaders overseas.

In the early 1950s, Mohammed Mossadegh, the democratically elected leader of Iran, decided that the best way to tackle poverty in his country was to nationalize the oil fields that were being operated by British and American oil companies. In 1951, legislation to nationalize the oil fields was passed. Mossadegh knew he was risking retaliation from Western governments and declared that the Iranian people "were opening a hidden treasure upon which lies a dragon."[126] Even though Mossadegh offered to compensate the British and American oil companies, in 1953, with considerable help from the CIA, these companies engineered a coup to topple Mossadegh. If this were not a serious enough threat to Iran's democratic structures and sovereignty, they replaced Mossadegh with Shah Pahlavi, whose secret police were notorious for human rights violations, torture, executions, and "disappearing" any opposition. The Iranian Revolution in 1979, which had and still has strong anti-American elements, was a direct consequence of the Shah's brutal and imperious dictatorship.

Remarkably similar events took place in Guatemala in 1954. Jacobo Arbenz was democratically elected by a large majority of voters and was very popular among the Guatemalan people. At the start of his presidency, 2.2 percent of landowners possessed 70 percent of the land, and the focus of his presidency was land reform[127] (land distribution is one of the most important causes of poverty in many countries of the South). Included in the land he wanted to distribute to the poor was uncultivated land held by the United Fruit Company. He offered them $500,000 in compensation, the value of the land they had provided the government for tax purposes. They would have no part of it. The CIA recruited dissidents within the Guatemalan army to overthrow Arbenz, paying them with money provided by United Fruit. The first attempt was unsuccessful. The CIA trained the next round of subversives, armed them, and provided them with air support. "Soviet-marked weapons were also gathered for the purpose of planting them inside Guatemala to reinforce US charges of Russian intervention."[128] This attempt was successful; Arbenz was forced to flee the country and a military dictatorship, favorable to American corporate interests and responsible for human rights violations, torture, executions, and disappearances, was installed.

Likewise, to understand much of U.S. foreign policy since the 1950s, we need only follow the trail of U.S. corporate interests. The United States supported all sorts of dictatorships as long as they were friendly to U.S. corporate investors (e.g., in Indonesia, the Philippines, El Salvador, Argentina, etc.). The U.S. media played along, providing a great deal of coverage of atrocities committed by left-wing dictators and all but ignoring those committed by right-wing dictators.[129] Meanwhile, the United States made magnanimous claims of spreading democracy around the world, and the right-wing dictators ensured that poverty continued unabated in their countries. In order to understand poverty in much of the South and the animosity many inhabitants of the South have toward the United States, one must understand the history of American corporate involvement in many of these countries.

APPLICATION: THE GROSS DOMESTIC PRODUCT

A recurring theme in this chapter is the paradox of declining and/or stagnating prospects for so many sectors of the American population in the midst of the economic boom that took us into the new millennium. It is time now to look critically at one of the principal measures that goes into popular constructions of the health of the economy, the gross domestic product. Basically, the GDP is a measure of all the money that changes hands in a country. Whenever money is spent, the GDP goes up.

While a rising GDP is taken to be a good sign, the GDP makes no distinction between "good spending" and "bad spending." In other words, if a hurricane devastates an area, money is spent to bring in emergency equipment, for rising medical expenses, and for funerals, so the GDP goes up. When divorce rates rise, former couples spend more money on lawyers, may sell their old home or buy two homes, and get counseling for the kids, so the GDP goes up. When street crime surges, more police are hired, police equipment is updated, more defense attorneys are hired, the prosecutor needs more assistants, more jails are built, more security devices are installed, money is spent on more emergency medical treatment and more funerals, so the GDP goes up. When white-collar crime inflates the price of commodities and utilities, the GDP goes up. When billions of dollars are spent to clean up toxic waste dumps, the GDP goes up. When people spend more time sitting in front of a television, advertisers spend more money to capture their audience, and the GDP goes up. When obesity rates rise because people are buying more and more junk food that they see advertised on television, the GDP goes up.[130] When people require more prescription medicines to lower their cholesterol levels, the GDP goes up. When teen magazines glorifying the sleek physique increase their sales, the GDP goes up. When the girls who read those magazines develop anorexia or bulimia and require counseling, medical treatment, or funeral services, the GDP goes up. When cigarette sales increase, the GDP goes up, as it does when rates of lung cancer are on the rise. Not surprisingly, health-care costs make up a significant contribution to the overall GDP.

Subsistence farming, which is certainly a type of productivity, does not involve the exchange of money and, therefore, is not figured into the GDP. Social behaviors that may improve the health of the family, community, environment, or society but that do not involve the exchange of money are not figured into the GDP. Hence, the amount of money spent manufacturing bombs and building prisons becomes a measure of a country's success; unpaid household work, child care, the preservation of family ties or of forests and water supplies are irrelevant when measuring success. (It is not unlike measuring your value as a person according to the amount of money you exchange in a given year instead of by all of your other attributes.)

As Robert Kennedy eloquently noted in 1968,

> The gross national product does not allow for the health of our children, the quality of their education, or the joy of their play; it does not include the beauty of our poetry or the strength of our marriages, the intelligence of our public debate, or the integrity of our public officials. It measures neither our wit nor our courage, neither our wisdom nor our learning, neither our compassion

nor our devotion to our country. It measures everything, in short, except that which makes life worthwhile.[131]

As a measure of the amount of money changing hands, a rising GDP does indeed suggest that business is good in the United States. However, as we have seen in the examples above, economists' principal measure of the "health" of our economy makes a poor measure of the "health" of our society, although celebratory declarations about a rising GDP implicitly connect the two. It is, of course, an enormous benefit to the corporate world for us to equate the health of corporate interests with that of society's interests. This equation is very powerful in American economic constructions and has a powerful influence on American economic policy. However, if the purpose of the economy is to serve the society (and not simply corporate interests), then this equation can be misleading and perhaps dangerous when it serves to direct the nation's social and economic policies. A statement from the New Economics Foundation reads, "For all our sophistication, modern society still persists in making one huge leap of faith. We blithely assume that if, at the end of the day, one key indicator of economic output—[GDP]—goes up, the quality of life of the citizenry will improve."[132]

Indeed, progressive organizations (e.g., Redefining Progress in the United States and the New Economics Foundation [NEF] in Britain) are working to develop new social and economic indicators that count negative outputs as negatives (to be subtracted) and positive outputs as positives. An NEF publication reads, "New indicators such as these go to the heart of democratic debate, by looking at how we measure the success of politicians, economists, and society. If we continue to ask the wrong questions, we will continue to get the wrong answers."[133] It remains to be seen whether such indicators will ever become a popular alternative or supplement to our current measure of corporate success, the GDP. However, true to critical constructionism, as long as the GDP is taken to be the principal measure of the health of our society and as long as it drives social and economic policy, elite interests are served, often to the detriment of the middle, working, and lower classes.

SUMMARY

The U.S. economy is considered to be among the most capitalist economies in the world. As such, it gives its businesses and corporations more free rein than most or all other countries. A critical examination of the United States indicates that its political system is organized around its economic system, much like that of the former Soviet Union but unlike those of most Western European countries. Unlike the European electoral systems, the two-party system in the United States allows little other choice but the election of procapitalist candidates. Noncapitalist economic ideas that are considered mainstream in Europe and in many countries throughout the world come under formidable attack in the United States. Historically, these attacks have come from the media, the U.S. Congress, the U.S. courts, and the FBI, calling into question whether the United States is indeed the "land of freedom."

During the latter half of the 1990s, politicians, economists, and the media triumphantly proclaimed that the United States was in the midst of an economic boom. However, this was an unusual "boom" in that productivity rates went up, unemployment rates went down, and the lower, working, and middle classes saw almost no improvement in their standard of living. Instead, most of the wealth generated by the boom went to the upper class—corporations, their CEOs, and their shareholders. With the threat of "global competition" dangling over their heads, workers have been forced to accept stagnating wages even when they are working longer and harder. If the chances for the lower and middle classes to improve their fortunes during a booming economy are bleak, then, of course, they are even bleaker in a less robust economy.

The most striking loss for workers over the past few decades has been job security. Once taken for granted throughout most of the workforce, it has become a thing of the past, first for blue-collar workers and then for white-collar workers. The export of work to the South, where labor is cheap, has led to massive downsizing in the United States. Workers who are downsized, if they eventually find new jobs, usually get jobs that pay lower wages and offer fewer benefits. Those who are not downsized often work harder in more stressful work environments, fearing the time when the "axe" will fall on them. Another ominous trend for the American worker is the expansion of the contingency workforce. Across the occupational spectrum, more and more work is being performed by part-time workers who usually work for lower wages, have little or no job security, and have few, if any, benefits. The big winners from these trends are the corporations. The losers are the vast majority of the workforce.

Most European countries, Japan, and many other industrialized countries do far more to moderate the effects of global competition. Some restrict corporations in their ability to lay off workers. Most industrialized countries have far more generous unemployment compensation with fewer eligibility restrictions than the United States. U.S. corporations complain that such policies and programs would limit their flexibility and that they would not be able to compete as well in the global market. However, with the pace of technological and market changes, the harmful effects of globalization will only be exacerbated, and the need for some form of government moderation/ intervention will increase.

In the meantime, the wealthiest country in the world, the United States, has a declining infrastructure and one of the highest rates of poverty among industrialized countries. Officially, in 2010, 15.1 percent of the American population lived below the poverty line; but many critics charge that the method used to calculate the poverty line is obsolete and that a more realistic calculation would produce a much higher poverty rate. In any case, there are nearly 46 million people living below the official poverty line, and the U.S. government does far less to help them than the governments of most other industrialized countries. This can be explained partly by the fact that Americans typically hold the poor in contempt. Believing that the United States is the land of opportunity, they blame the poor for their circumstances. Cross-cultural data, however, suggest that the United States is not exceptional in providing opportunities for upward mobility. Research shows that jobs available to the unskilled poor are not as numerous as many believe. Moreover, the United States compares unfavorably to many other industrialized countries with regard to the rates at which the poor are able to "escape" from poverty.

More than 2 billion people in the South live on less than $2 a day. Many countries in the South are as poor as they are today because of hundreds of years of exploitation by Western imperialist nations. Such exploitation still goes on today, subsidizing lifestyles in the North and corporate profits. Many nations in the South face a foreign debt crisis, forcing them to serve interests in the North instead of using their money, labor, and resources to develop their own infrastructure and improve the prospects of their majority poor. If countries in the North were to forgive these debts, a major obstacle to development in the South would be overcome.

Finally, critical constructionism was applied to an analysis of the GDP. In that the GDP fails to make distinctions between the ways money is spent, it is a better indicator of the health of businesses and corporations than it is of the health of society. Inasmuch as the two are confused by popular constructions, the use of the GDP as the primary economic indicator well serves the interests of the upper class, often to the detriment of the other classes. Nothing, in fact, better suits the interests of the upper class than the frequently held belief that what is good for the upper class is good for the other classes. Holding to this belief, the people willingly approve of economic policies and legislation that enhance the interests of the elite, even when such policies and legislation—as we have seen so often in this chapter—do them more harm than good. Interpreting the GDP as a measure of the health of a society contributes to this phenomenon.

Discussion Questions

1. Politicians who argue for increasing taxes on the rich are often alleged to be promoting "class warfare." What does this allegation mean? Could it be argued that there is already a class war under way? Explain your reasoning.

2. At election time in Fidel Castro's Cuba, voters would go to the polls and they would have a choice of only one candidate for president. Most Americans would consider that a bogus election, signifying the absence of both freedom and democracy. Cubans would likely have responded

that they had both freedom and democracy and they only needed one candidate to choose from because Fidel best represented the interests of the vast majority of Cubans. When Americans go to the polls, they have only two viable choices for president, *both representing the same economic ideology,* capitalism. For most of the past 100 years, political leaders who represented the counterposing ideology, socialism, were persecuted by the U.S. government. So in terms of political freedom, does the United States most resemble Cuba's one-party system or the multiparty systems found throughout Western Europe?

Inequality of Life Chances in the United States

3

L ike Karl Marx, Max Weber was another very influential German social thinker who wrote extensively about inequality. Marx saw inequality as being based strictly on one's relationship to the means of production in society. Weber understood inequality to be more complex and based on a number of more social variables, including wealth, power and prestige. Weber was concerned with how one's social situation affected his or her access to opportunities that sustain or improve the quality of life, or one's "life chances." Race and gender are two social situations that will be considered in this chapter. They are "social situations" because, as we will see, they are socially constructed categories; and the categories in which a person is situated will have a substantial influence on his or her life chances. Access to jobs and a fair wage will be built into our discussions of race and gender.

Two institutions, education and health care, will also be discussed in this chapter, as these have a very strong bearing on one's life chances. These are two institutions specifically conceived to improve our life chances, but access to them is unequally distributed in society.

Race and gender are only two social categories that affect life chances in the United States and education and health care are only two institutions that affect our life chances. The reader is encouraged to think of how the trends and principles discussed in this chapter apply to other categories of people and to other social institutions.

INEQUALITY AND RACE

To begin a discussion on race, we should note that "race" is itself a social construction. We are all descended from the same first human ancestors and have almost all of the same genetic material in common. To select one feature, such as skin color, as distinguishing one race from another is an arbitrary selection; and since there is a continuum of human skin colors, it is another arbitrary decision to judge where one race ends and another begins. "The development of the 'race' doctrine," writes Prince Brown, Jr., "is a social and political process that tells more about the history of relations between people who thought/think of—and define—themselves as different than it tells about what can be known using and practicing science."[1] In other words, genetic or physical features do not establish one's race; society does. Thus, "race" has little or no biological meaning; but in the United States and many other societies, it has tremendous social and economic meaning.

Though the majority of people living in poverty are white, poverty rates are higher among minorities. According to U.S. Census data, rates of poverty among African Americans and Hispanics, year after year, are consistently two to three times higher than the poverty rate among whites. In 2008, over a third of African American children were living in poverty.[2] Research conducted by investigators at Cornell and Washington University found that "nine out of every 10 black Americans, or 91 percent, who reach the age of 75 spend at least one of their adult years in poverty."[3] "African Americans," writes sociologist Martin Marger, "exhibit much higher rates of poverty, unemployment, and low income. They are also under-represented in jobs at the top of the occupational hierarchy and over-represented at the bottom."[4] While many Americans are under the impression that blacks have made considerable strides since the civil rights movement of the 1960s, by at least one critical measure, they have not: the median family income for black families in 1950 was 54 percent of that of the median white (non-Hispanic) family income. By 2008, it had climbed to only 61 percent.[5]

Prejudice and discrimination, despite improvements, remain a stumbling block for millions of African Americans. If we accept what people say in surveys as accurate reflections of their beliefs and attitudes, very few Americans still believe that African Americans are biologically inferior. However, the belief that African Americans are somehow "culturally inferior" is still pervasive among white Americans. Such surveys frequently show that blacks are believed to have a weaker work ethic than their white counterparts. Further, surveys indicate, in the words of sociologists Lawrence Bobo and James Kluegel, "blacks are rated as less intelligent, more violence prone, and more likely to prefer living off of welfare than whites."[6] These qualities are seen as being derived not so much from the biological makeup of blacks as from their environments and upbringing. These attitudes are routinely reinforced by the media in that African Americans are so frequently depicted in stories covering welfare issues and crime.

Whether or not African Americans are disproportionately represented among welfare recipients or violent criminals, these prejudices also afflict the vast majority of African Americans who are law-abiding and motivated to work. Holding such prejudicial attitudes, employers often avoid hiring black applicants, suspecting they will be poor workers. As is always the case with prejudice, a self-fulfilling cycle emerges. Acknowledging the economic gap between blacks and whites, whites are inclined to blame blacks for their lack of motivation; then, perceiving them to be poorly motivated, employers are less likely to hire blacks. Thus, as a consequence of existing prejudices, African Americans are given only limited opportunity to close the economic gap between blacks and whites—and then they are blamed for the gap.

The Great Recession, as devastating as it has been for whites, has hit blacks even harder. Between August 2007 and August 2011, unemployment among whites went from 4.2 percent to 8 percent (a 90 percent increase) while unemployment among blacks, starting almost twice as high as whites, went from 7.7 percent to 16.7 percent (a 117 percent increase).[7]

The poor, as we have noted, are often blamed for their poverty and told that they should go out and get a job—any job. Newman found that job acquisition is not quite so simple for poor blacks, even in the black community. Examining minimum-wage job openings in fast-food restaurants in Harlem, she found, first, that there were far more applicants than there were job openings and, second, that employers frequently opted to hire immigrants from outside the community than blacks who resided in the neighborhood.

> Employers are exercising a preference for applicants who are not African American, even in central Harlem, which is overwhelmingly African American in its residential population.... It is harder for African Americans to get these jobs than for equivalently educated individuals from other racial and ethnic groups."[8]

If resident blacks encounter such adversity finding jobs in their own community, we can imagine that finding employment elsewhere could sometimes be a monumental task.

There is good news, however. In the face of adversity, increasing numbers of African Americans have been making their way into the middle class. The civil rights movement, laws protecting minorities, and *affirmative action* policies have all helped to facilitate the expansion of the black middle class. However, there is one critical difference between the black middle class and the white middle class, and that is wealth. In 2009, the median net worth (wealth) of black households was $5,677 and the median net worth of white households was $113,149, nearly 20 times greater.[9] Black homeowners are more likely than white homeowners to draw all or most of their wealth from their homes because whites are more likely to have other assets. The mortgage crisis that triggered the Great Recession and caused a decline in home values served to widen the already yawning gap between white wealth and black wealth. Between 2005 and 2009 the median wealth of white families declined 16 percent while the median wealth of black families declined a staggering 53 percent.[10]

Throughout the class structure, if we compare black and white families that are similar in income, the white family is likely to possess more in the way of financial assets.[11] Isabel Wilkerson writes,

> [U]nlike the white middle and upper classes, which include 70 percent of all white households and have been a fixture for three generations, the vast majority of the black middle class is starting from scratch....

Perhaps equally important, economists say, black people often enter the middle class with a slight fraction of the financial assets of middle class whites whose parents and grandparents were middle class. So blacks lack the reserve of money and property needed to buy a house, to finance a college education, to weather a personal catastrophe or a national recession.[12]

Wealth brings with it more far-reaching benefits than income, and it accumulates over generations.

Sociologist Dalton Conley has examined the issue of race and wealth in his book *Being Black, Living in the Red*. In the first chapter, Conley asks his reader to imagine two families: one white, the other black. (For the sake of simplicity, I will modify some of the conditions presented by Conley.) The husbands in both families were the main breadwinners. Both were just recently laid off from their manufacturing jobs, which provided the same incomes. Twenty-five years earlier, the white couple was able to borrow $5,000 from their parents so they could make a down payment on a $50,000 home. The black couple was unable to borrow money from their parents, so they had to rent an apartment. The white couple was able to deduct the majority of their house payments from their annual tax bill. They could put the money they saved through these deductions in the bank. The black couple could not deduct their rent payment. When it was time for their son to go to college, the white couple had enough equity in their house (which is now worth three times what they originally paid) that they could get a second mortgage and help him with his tuition. The black couple, of course, had no equity in their apartment and could not afford to help their daughter through college. At the time the two breadwinners were dismissed from their jobs, the white man had enough money in savings (money saved in mortgage interest deductions plus interest) to serve as a buffer while he looked for a new job. The black man had no money in savings and quickly had to take a job far below his skill level that paid less than his former job and had fewer benefits.

Conley, of course, simplified these cases, and I have simplified them even more; but the message is an important one. The grandparents of the black couple described above experienced a great deal of discrimination. The black couple's parents faced a great deal of discrimination a generation later—probably less—but were lucky to earn a living, even though they accumulated no wealth. Because they had no wealth, the parents of the black couple could not afford to lend their children the $5,000 that so improved the fate of their white counterparts. Because of that $5,000 given to them 25 years earlier, the child of the white couple could go to college and the husband could afford to wait for a better job. The child of the white couple will eventually be able to help his own kids out financially because he has a college education and because he will likely inherit more from his parents than the child of the black couple will inherit. Thus, the cycle goes on. Wealth, says Conley, is a far better indicator of one's life chances than is income;

and blacks, in whatever social class they are according to their income, are likely at a disadvantage.

> Since wealth accumulation depends heavily on intergenerational support issues such as gifts, informal loans, and inheritances, net worth has the ability to pick up both the current dynamics of race and the legacy of past inequalities that may be obscured in simple measures of income, occupation, or education.[13]

Affirmative Action

If the disadvantages of being black have been cumulative over generations, then it follows that the advantages of being white have also accumulated over generations. White people in American society today have benefitted and continue to benefit from the fact that their ancestors were given preference over black people in generations past. "[Recognizing] that racism and sexism are systemic inequalities, requiring sustained, long-term, ongoing policy initiatives if they are to be alleviated,"[14] affirmative action policies were developed to counteract cumulative injustice and to give the victims of generations of discrimination a "step up" in the competition for jobs, college admissions, public works contracts, and so on.

Not surprisingly, such policies have always had their opponents; but, in recent years, their opponents have been winning considerable victories, and affirmative action programs are approaching extinction. The fate of affirmative action is, in part, intertwined with many of the processes discussed earlier in this chapter; namely, the declining prospects of the working and middle classes help to explain the frequently bitter reactions to affirmative action policies. When affirmative action policies emerged from the civil rights movement in the 1960s and early 1970s, the United States was prospering and the fortunes of the great majority of Americans were improving. They could afford "sacrifices" in the name of justice and improved race relations. Writes Wilson,

> When affirmative action programs were first discussed in the 1960s, the economy was expanding and incomes were rising. It was a time of optimism, a time when most Americans believed that their children would have better lives than they had. During such times, a generosity of spirit permits consideration of sharing an expanding pie.[15]

Since then, with their economic prospects on the decline or stagnating, many Americans are feeling far less generous.

Critics of affirmative action claim that it amounts to reverse discrimination, that if two equally qualified candidates apply for a job, preference is given to the minority candidate. Further, they claim that when quotas are involved, preference may be given to a less qualified minority applicant. There is validity to these claims, but before discussing them, it might be useful to recount briefly a short documentary segment broadcast on one of the major television network's "newsmagazines" some years ago. In this film, a middle-class black man and a middle-class white man with equivalent educational levels are followed around a mid-western city with a hidden camera for several weeks. Time after time, we witness acts of discrimination directed toward the black man. In the shoe store, a salesperson goes right up to the white man, offering assistance. No one offers to help the black man. In the music store, the white man is assisted; the black man is "tailed" to see if he is shoplifting. At the car dealership, the white man is offered a car at a certain price with a certain down payment; the black man is offered the same car at a higher price with a higher down payment. Responding to job ads, the white man is welcomed and told all about the job; shortly afterward, the black man is told the (still unfilled) job is no longer available. Looking at apartment rentals, again the white man is welcomed and cordially shown around; the black man is told the (unrented) apartment is no longer available.

Certainly for dramatic effect, the segment's producers selectively edited the film clips to show acts of discrimination; we were not shown the times when the two men were treated equally. Furthermore, the city in which the segment was filmed may not be representative of the rest of the country with regard to its race relations. However, there is little doubt that on any given day thousands of African Americans encounter similar acts of discrimination. There are millions of white Americans who, if given the chance, will actively discriminate against blacks. When it comes to jobs and housing, such discrimination is illegal; but *how do we enforce these laws?* Such discrimination is often subtle and could never have been detected without the hidden cameras and microphones. Given that everybody cannot be expected to carry around hidden surveillance devices, "quotas" emerged; not legal quotas but unofficial quotas were adopted by government agencies as a means of directing the enforcement of antidiscrimination statutes. If an employer had 100 employees and only 2 were minority group members, this became grounds for suspicion and further scrutiny. Employers, therefore, felt compelled to hire a given percentage (quota) of minorities to avoid government scrutiny or antidiscrimination lawsuits. Indeed, quotas do mean reverse discrimination; but given that illegal acts of racial discrimination occur thousands of times a day, how, other than hidden surveillance devices or quotas, can antidiscrimination statutes be enforced? (This is not meant to be a rhetorical question.)

Critics of affirmative action argue that discrimination on the basis of race (or gender) is wrong, whether the victim is black or white (or male or female). However, we should remember that these critics are frequently the beneficiaries of generations of discrimination. For the white critics, odds are that their income is higher than the median black income, and part of the reason they are faring better than their black counterparts is that for generations their ancestors have been given preference over the ancestors of their black counterparts.

White critics of affirmative action may also benefit from other preferences that they find less objectionable. Colleges and universities, for example, frequently give admission preference to their "legacies," that is, to children of their alumni. In the past, generations of African Americans and other minorities were less likely than whites to have gone to college, so it is mostly whites who benefit from such admission policies. "A recent study of the nation's ten most selective educational institutions," recounts Deborah Rhode, "found that they have admitted far more whites through alumni preferences than blacks and Hispanics through affirmative action."[16] Interestingly, there has been very little outcry, even from the "victims," concerning legacy preference and the de facto racial discrimination that it engenders.

Another claim of affirmative action's critics is that it does minorities more harm than good. When some minority group members are given preference through affirmative action programs, they argue, the abilities of all minority group members become suspect. Resentful co-workers come to suspect that their minority colleagues are only there because of affirmative action and not because of their abilities. Further, minority group members come to question their own ability, wondering if they got the job only because of affirmative action. These are interesting claims that, again, do not seem to come into play with regard to other preferential selection policies. Over the generations, when whites had been given preferential treatment over blacks, this did not cause them to be held in low regard, nor did it seem to have a negative effect on their self-esteem. College and university legacy entrants do not seem to be held in lower regard by their fellow students, nor do they seem to suffer lower self-esteem. Rhode, a Stanford law professor, writes,

> Affirmative action is not responsible for adverse stereotypes. Racism and sexism are. White males who have long benefitted from preferences by schools, jobs, and clubs have suffered no discernable loss of self-esteem. Nor have the children of alumni who get special treatment in school admissions; they certainly aren't clamoring for policy changes that would spare their children such injuries.[17]

(When Barbara Babcock, an assistant attorney general during the Carter administration, was asked how she felt about getting her job because she was a woman, she replied "It's better than not getting your job because you're a woman."[18])

Given the current economic situation, it is not surprising that critics of affirmative action maintain their opposition, despite many of the contradictions to their arguments, because minority hiring preferences are perceived to have an impact on their ability to earn a living. Like so many of the criticisms of affirmative action, this perception is partially valid but easily exaggerated. Affirmative action often can become the scapegoat of individual failure and of the economy's failure to provide enough job opportunities. For example, if 20 people apply for a job and a minority group member gets hired, all 19 of those rejected can blame affirmative action. If the hiring was indeed based on affirmative action, then it may have, in fact, had an impact on *one* of the white applicants' livelihood; but 18 other white applicants also have affirmative action to blame instead of themselves or an economy that pits 20 applicants against each other for one job.

While the negative impact of affirmative action on majority group members is exaggerated, its successes have been quite significant. In the recent past and in some sectors of the workforce, much of the minority representation in management positions had been achieved through affirmative action. Racial and ethnic diversity in public sectors of the workforce, such as police and fire departments, and public education, was brought about, in part, through affirmative action policies. The expansion of the black middle class over the past few decades has, in part, been made possible by affirmative action. Also, the presence of millions of African Americans, Hispanics, and other minorities on college campuses and faculties, thanks in part to affirmative action, has added a richness and diversity to the college experience that enhances the education of all students, not just minority students. Without affirmative action policies, minorities would not have progressed as far as they have, and the statistics on racial inequality would be even worse than they are today.

Whether or not affirmative action has outlived its usefulness depends on the answers to three questions: (1) Have the accumulated injustices that have been heaped on minorities over generations been sufficiently overcome? (2) Are there still significant numbers of employers, managers, realtors, and others who will discriminate against minorities if left to their own devices? (3) Is there a way to address these concerns other than affirmative action? The answers to these questions can be found in the previous discussion and summarized as follows: (1) at the very least, the wealth inequality between blacks and whites at all class levels indicates that accumulated injustices have not been sufficiently overcome; (2) although beliefs about the biological inferiority of blacks have declined significantly over the past few decades, beliefs about their cultural inferiority (e.g., their lack of work ethic) still abound, and therefore, if left to their own devices, we can expect significant numbers of employers, managers, realtors, and such others to discriminate against African Americans; and (3) affirmative action's critics have proposed no alternative that would adequately address these issues and "level the playing field."

Without hidden surveillance devices or even a desire to know, some of the white majority in America are unable to see how black Americans are still being injured by racism today. They argue that discrimination is not a problem and, therefore, affirmative action is not a solution. They argue that slavery ended with the Civil War nearly 150 years ago and that African Americans need to put that in the past. But certainly there were white Americans saying the same thing just a year after the slaves were emancipated. And, according to Douglas Blackmon, in his recent book, *Slavery by Another Name,* slavery continued in the Southern United States into the 1950s when black men were commonly arrested on specious charges and placed in hard labor camps. They were forced to work in conditions often as or more brutal than the conditions of slavery and they were leased (much as slaves were sold) to labor in various Southern industries. The Southern economy depended on the forced labor of blacks before the Civil War and continued to do so for nearly a century afterward.[19] The injuries of such treatment were significant and persistent in terms of marriage and family and, as we have seen, in terms of African American's ability to accumulate wealth.

INEQUALITY AND GENDER

To begin our discussion of gender inequality, it is important to note the distinction between sex and gender. "Sex" refers to the biological differences between men and women. "Gender" refers to the ways a society treats those differences. Specifically, societies expect girls and boys and women and men to behave differently. These different expectations tend to play themselves out in the ways that girls and boys are raised and in the opportunities made available to them throughout their lifetimes.

People in society tend to conflate the meaning of sex and gender. That is, they tend to confuse the biological fact of sex with the socially constructed reality of gender. The confusion of these two concepts in the popular imagination reinforces gender inequality by making it seem as natural and as immutable as sex. Given that throughout history and throughout most of the world gender inequality has favored men, the confusion of sex and gender also favors men.

That said, over the past century, thanks principally to the courageous activities of women's rights movements, there have been tremendous improvements in the status of women throughout the developed world; and the developing world, also, is poised to see rapid advances. Women throughout the West and in much of the rest of the world have won the right to vote. The violent victimization of women perpetrated by their husbands— once accepted—has been criminalized in the United States and in many other parts of the world. Sexual harassment statutes have been enacted in the United States and elsewhere. Women, today, make up the majority of college students in the United States and in Europe, and their rates of college attendance are going up in many other regions of the world. In the United States, 47 percent of the labor force is comprised of women and women account for a slight majority of people employed in management and professional occupations. Further, the gender wage gap has improved with the median wage of women going from 59 percent of men's median wages in 1970 to 81 percent in 2010.[20]

Despite this progress, gender inequality still persists in most, if not all, regions of the world. And, after all, if you are on the receiving end, 81 cents on the dollar, relative to men, is still hugely significant.

Women in the American Workplace

The fact that the woman's median weekly earnings has always been lower than the man's has almost everything to do with societal expectations of women (gender) and virtually nothing to do with biological differences between men and women (sex). There are a number of factors that have been identified in the literature that explain women's lower earnings. These include active discrimination, male workplace culture, the fact that women are socialized to be less aggressive than men, occupational segregation, and the belief that the care of children and the household are primarily the woman's responsibility. These are all inextricably linked and combined they present a formidable obstacle to women's advancement in the workplace.

Discrimination. As women have moved into the workplace in increasing numbers over the past several decades, the traditional belief that a woman's proper place is in the home and outright antagonism to working women have dissipated considerably. But most women who have been in the workforce for any length of time still have stories to tell about either subtle or blatant acts of discrimination both on and off the job. Psychologist Bernice Lott and her colleagues note, "It is common for women in the United States to nod in recognition when others report having been turned away from, ignored, or put down by men.... [A] woman in conversation with a man may find him staring at her breasts, or he may ignore her positive contributions or attribute them to someone else."[21]

In the higher echelons of the corporate world, gender discrimination manifests itself in what has been called the "glass ceiling," referring to the fact that women are well represented in corporate management, but rarely promoted to executive-level positions. In fact, the Bureau of Labor Statistics reports that women now account for 51.5 percent of all people employed in "management, professional, and related occupations" and some pundits take this to indicate that women have achieved near equality in the American workplace. However, as of this writing, only 12 of the corporations in *Fortune* magazine's top 500 companies were run by women CEOs and women account for only 15 percent of the members of the board of directors of these companies.[22] Further, as seen in Table 3.1, women employed in management positions receive 28 percent less in earnings than their male counterparts.

Male Corporate Culture. Aside from active discrimination, another factor accounting for the glass ceiling is that women often find it difficult to get promoted in the male-dominated culture of the corporate world. Promotions in these ranks often depend on "connections," who you know, weekend golf buddies, and whether an executive will take you under his wing and mentor you or laud your performance during a board

Table 3.1 Women in Selected Management Positions: Earnings
Relative to Men

Women in Management	Earnings Relative to Men
Chief Executive Officers	28% less
Financial Managers	34% less
Marketing and Sales Managers	34% less
Human Resource Managers	20% less
Property/Real Estate Managers	35% less

Source: Household Data, Annual Averages, "Median Weekly Earnings of Full-Time
Wage and Salary Workers by Detailed Occupation and Sex," ftp://ftp.bls.gov/pub/
special.requests/lf/aat39.txt. Retrieved July 17, 2011.

of directors meeting. In other words, too often, advancement depends
on one's progress through what is sometimes called the "good ol' boy"
network. To the extent that gender-role socialization takes place in our
society (that is, to the extent that boys are raised as boys and girls are
raised as girls), men will tend to have more in common with each other
than they do with women. That becomes a problem when men wield more
power than women and women, consequently, find themselves excluded
from positions of power.

Gender-Role Socialization. Throughout history and throughout the world, most
societies have been patriarchal, or male-dominated. It is generally believed
that this is because in prehistoric times brute force was the simplest means
of achieving domination and men were physically stronger than women.
However, as economist Nancy Folbre writes, "Economic development
and technological change have increased the importance of brains—even
women's brains—relative to brawn."[23] Thus, as societies evolved, brute
force became less and less relevant and patriarchal domination has been
maintained principally through gender-role socialization. That is, boys
have been raised to be more assertive, competitive, and controlling; girls
are raised to be more caring, accommodative, and submissive. Salaries and
career advancement often depend upon aggressive behaviors, negotiation,
and self-promotion. Research has shown that women are more likely to
accept initial salary offerings and less likely to negotiate than men. For
example, Babcock and Laschever, authors of *Women Don't Ask: Negotiation
and the Gender Divide,* found that the 57 percent of male professional school
graduates in their sample attempted to negotiate higher salaries than they
were initially offered, while only 7 percent of the female graduates did
so. These authors point out that negotiating a higher salary of only a few
thousand dollars can mean a difference of hundreds of thousands of dollars
over a lifetime career. The problem Babcock and Laschever are careful to
point out is not that women are less likely to negotiate higher salaries and
are, therefore, responsible for the gender-wage gap; the problem is that,

in a patriarchal society, men are socialized to ask for what they want and women are socialized to accept what they are given. They write,

> So we want to be clear: this book is not simply a study of an inexplicable female failing that can be easily corrected. It is not about ways in which women can "fix" themselves. It is an examination of how our culture—modern Western culture—strongly discourages women from asking for what they want.[24]

Negotiation is often best accompanied by self-promotion. Research by Moss-Racusin and Rudman has shown that women are less likely to engage in self-promotion in the workplace than men and are more likely to acknowledge the work of their colleagues. They also found that women are more likely than men to fear a "backlash" if they do engage in self-promotion.[25] This fear is justified because, as Babcock and Laschever note, "[S]tudies have shown that men (and sometimes women) react negatively when women adopt styles or communication patterns expected of men, such as acting assertive and self-confident rather than tentative."[26]

Occupational Segregation. A large part of the gender-wage gap can be explained by the occupational segregation of the workforce. It is self-evident and commonly accepted that some jobs in American society are primarily performed by men, while others are primarily performed by women. Table 3.2 illustrates this fact. Luce and Brenner note that "the occupations that are most common for women workers today are remarkably similar to what they were in the 1940s: nurses, nurses aides, typists, and secretaries."[27] Some would argue that the gender-wage gap is not an indicator of inequality or unfairness because women freely choose to go into occupations that pay less than those that tend to be chosen by men.

The critical constructionist, however, is inclined to acknowledge that to a certain extent, the disproportionate concentration of women in lower-paying occupations is the result of free choice; but that choice is constrained by limited access to better-paying, male-dominated occupations. Furthermore, women's choice of lower-paying occupations is the result of gender-role socialization that functions to perpetuate a patriarchal society. More importantly, argues the critical constructionist, in a patriarchal society, the work typically done by men is likely to be more highly valued than the work typically performed by women. Thus, for example, at the end of the nineteenth century, when most clerical work was performed by men, it was a reasonably well-respected, well-payed occupation; when women became concentrated in clerical work after World War II, it became a "pink-collar job;" persons performing this work came to be called "typists" and "secretaries" and they were awarded less respect and relatively lower pay. Likewise, in countries where women make up the majority of physicians (in Russia, for example) the medical profession tends to be less prestigious and doctors are often paid relatively less than in countries where the profession is dominated

Table 3.2 Percentage of Women in Selected Occupations

Occupation	Percent Women
Preschool and Kindergarten Teachers	97
Childcare Workers	95
Registered Nurses	91
Dental Assistants	98
Host/Hostess Restaurants	85
Bank Tellers	88
Fire Fighters	4
Construction Managers	6
Mechanical Engineers	6

Source: "Employed Persons by Detailed Occupation, Sex, Race, and Hispanic or Latino Ethnicity, 2010," Household data, Annual Averages, Bureau of Labor Statistics, http://www.bls.gov/cps/cpsaat11.pdf. Retrieved July 15, 2011.

by men. With more and more women entering medical schools in the United States and Europe, Doreen Carvajal of the *New York Times* asks, "Will the feminization of medicine lead to losses in income and status?"[28]

The issue of occupational segregation and wages leads us to a discussion of "comparable worth." According to the Bureau of Labor Statistics, in 2010, "janitors and building cleaners" received 20 percent more in weekly earnings than "maids and housekeeping cleaners." Whether or not that disparity is fair depends upon evaluations of the comparable worth of the work done in these two occupations. Do we base such evaluations on education, training, the mental and physical difficulty of the work, value to the employer, or contributions to society? Comparable worth has, thus far, proven a difficult concept to operationalize and as far as legal standards go, that difficulty works in favor of the patriarchal status quo. However, the one and most obvious difference between these two occupational categories is that the higher-paying one is dominated by men and the lower-paying one is dominated by women.

Carework

David Leonhardt of the *New York Times* notes that "[t]he last three men nominated to the Supreme Court have all been married and, among them, have seven children. The last three women—Elena Kagan, Sonia Sotomajor and Harriet Miers (who withdrew)—have all been single and without children."[29] Traditionally, women have strived to be successful homemakers. Today, most strive to be successful at homemaking *and* a career. That is difficult when they compete at work with—and receive little help at home from—men who are focusing more exclusively on their careers.

Societal expectations of women concerning child care and housework are among the most formidable explanations for the gender wage gap. The argument goes that the gender-wage gap exists largely because women are likely to interrupt their careers to take care of children and the home. With this in mind, employers frequently fail to take their female employees' careers seriously because they expect them to leave the job soon or divide their energies between work and home. The result is discrimination. Conflating sex and gender, many consider it "natural" for women to want to do this and, thus, the discrimination is believed to be justified. Further, the argument goes, with women considered to be naturally inclined caregivers, they tend to gravitate toward those jobs that involve helping and caring for others, which usually pay less than male-dominated occupations. Women in the workplace—whether they are married or single, have children, do not have children, or do not even plan to have children—have an uphill battle dealing with such stereotypes, which puts them at a distinct disadvantage from their male counterparts, both at work and at home.

Despite the fact that married women who work outside of the home may be working full-time and may be making more money than their husbands, most women today perform most of the housework and child-care duties. Though there are exceptions, even among better-educated couples with "liberated" husbands, wives tend to do a disproportionate amount of housework. True, today's fathers are more involved in housework than their fathers; but, write Philip Cowan and Carolyn Pape Cowan, "studies in every industrialized country reveal that women continue to carry the major share of the burden of family work and care of the children, even when both parents are employed full time."[30] When a woman gets off from work, she still has to look forward to working what Arlie Hochschild refers to as "the second shift" when she gets home.[31] In their comprehensive study of how family members spend their time, Suzanne Bianchi and her colleagues found that women average 18 hours per week doing household chores and 14 hours per week caring for their children, while men only spend 9 hours per week on household chores and 7 hours caring for their children.[32] While men are doing only about half as much of the household chores, in a Pew Research Center survey, men and women—older and younger, married and single—ranked "sharing household chores" as equally important to a "successful marriage." (Sharing household chores came in third, behind "faithfulness" and "happy sexual relationship," but ahead of "adequate income," "shared tastes and interests," and "children.")[33] As long as working women are disadvantaged at home with the expectation that the second shift is primarily their responsibility, they will be disadvantaged at work.

Working the second shift—taking care of children, performing household chores, maintaining contact with and keeping obligations to extended family—has been traditionally assigned to women and remains far more a part of their domain than of men's domain. This work is critically important, frequently exhausting, usually undervalued and, in fact, receives no value in official accounts of economic productivity. Even when some of these critical responsibilities are outsourced to the private sector—for example, child care and domestic service—the work is usually performed by women and is poorly paid. Given the value our society seems to place on children and their upbringing, the fact that child-care workers are paid so little would seem to be further evidence that "women's work" receives little value simply because it is women's work.

Addressing Gender Discrimination

That women have the capacity to bear children and men do not is a matter of sex. But that this capacity should engender so many disadvantages in the workplace is a matter of gender. Addressing the problem of gender discrimination depends both upon public recognition of the problem and on generating the will to deal with the issue. The problem women face in bearing the brunt of carework takes place in the private sphere of the home and is partly a cultural issue requiring the sensitization and cooperation of men. Indeed, this is occurring slowly as men have been taking on more of the carework over the past several decades—going from an average of 2.5 hours of child care a week in 1965 to 9.6 hours in 2003—but they still only perform half as much as women.[34] The disproportionate burden of carework on women may also be partly alleviated as women gain increasing parity in the workplace. Given that women today tend to be better educated than men, and given that they hold slightly more professional and managerial positions than men, if gender discrimination were to dissipate, then women would more likely be coequal to their husbands in terms of their financial contributions to the family. This would give them more leverage to demand a more equitable distribution of carework.

Such an eventuality depends, in large part, upon the closing of the gender wage gap and the United States uses social policy far less than many other countries to bring this about. Affirmative action policies, as we have seen, whether they target disparities based on race or gender, are very controversial in the United States and have been weakened considerably. Gender discrimination, when it is addressed, is usually addressed in the civil courts and is initiated by individual victims of discrimination. The cases that have the most potential to effect change are typically brought against large corporations with vast legal resources and these have not fared well for the plaintiffs in recent decades. When smaller lawsuits are successful, their effects are usually very limited.

Gender discrimination has been more successfully constructed as a social problem in many other countries of the North and policies addressing the issue have been the result. As we will see in the next chapter, most countries of the North, and many countries in the South, have implemented paid family leave policies. These allow new mothers to take off from work for a specified number of months to care for newborns (or ailing family members) while receiving a substantial part of their salary and without suffering a work-related penalty. Some of these countries also provide for paternity leave, allowing the father the same rights and giving mothers the ability to further limit the effects of childbearing on their career trajectories. Iceland, which scores lowest on the World Economic Forum's gender gap index, has such a paternity leave policy and high rates of men who take advantage of the policy. "Nine in 10 Icelandic men take time off with the babies" reports Katrin Bennhold of the *New York Times*. "A lawmaker, Drifa Hjartardottir," she continues, "described the 2000 law as 'one of the most important steps taken towards gender equality since women's right to vote.'"[35] Many countries achieve similar results by subsidizing day-care services and preschool, relieving the burden on parents, women especially, to stay home and interrupt their career progress. These "family friendly" policies will be discussed at more length in Chapter 4.

Norway is another Nordic country with very progressive policies regarding women's rights. In 2003 Norway implemented a policy requiring the 40 largest Norwegian companies to have at least 7 percent of their boards of directors comprised of women. There are plans to raise this quota to 40 percent. Of course, for reasons outlined in the previous chapter, such a policy would find little support among U.S. capitalists, but in Norway, writes Bennhold, "gender equality is treated as a competitive advantage." Norwegian prime minister Jens Stoltenberg states, "One Norwegian lesson is that if you can raise female participation, it helps the economy, birth rates and the budget."[36] Seeing the advantage, France, Spain, and the Netherlands are phasing in boardroom quotas and the European Union is considering imposing quotas on all member nations.[37]

INEQUALITY AND EDUCATION

The United States was among the first countries in the world to implement mass education with many national and community leaders feeling that a healthy democracy depends upon the education of its citizenry. Implementation depended upon location, but by the end of the nineteenth century most American citizens were guaranteed the right to an education paid for by public taxes. A socialized educational system was accepted as necessary in almost all sectors of American society. The concept of socialized mass education has since been embraced by almost all countries in the world.

However, the United States stands apart from most modern nations in that the right to an education is not written in its national constitution, but in each state constitution. This makes the education of the American citizenry largely a state responsibility and not the responsibility of the federal government. And that makes the American educational system prone to all sorts of inequalities. For example, reacting to the 1954 U.S. Supreme Court ruling that separate schools for black and white students were unconstitutional, Alabama amended its constitution in 1956 to read "nothing in this Constitution should be construed as creating or recognizing" a right to an education. "This was done," writes Erwin Chemerinsky, "to allow Alabama public schools to close rather than desegregate."[38] In defiance of modern court rulings Alabama's constitution still provides for separate schools for black and white students. More specifically, the document reads, "Separate schools shall be provided for white and colored children, and no child of either race shall be permitted to attend a school of the other race"[39]—an unenforceable provision with seemingly a good deal of symbolic importance.

Popular constructions hold that education is the key to success in American society and that the universal accessibility of primary and secondary education in the United States compensates for the disadvantages of birth in the lower class, making it possible for anyone to succeed in American society. The decentralized control of the American educational system, however, makes room for substantial disparities that depend on where a child is raised and that are more likely to maintain economic inequalities over generations rather than alleviate them. To the extent that schools are funded by local city and town taxes (as opposed to federal and state taxes) educational systems are further decentralized and this increases economic inequalities often to extraordinary levels. After describing the strikingly inadequate conditions of Alliyah's elementary school in New York City, with mostly minority students, renowned educator and author Jonathan Kozol notes,

> At the time I met Alliyah...., New York's Board of Education spent about $8,000 yearly on the education of a third grade child in a New York City public school. If you could have scooped Alliyah up out of the neighborhood where she was born and plunked her down within a fairly typical white suburb of New York, she would have received a public education worth about $12,000 every year. If you were to lift her up once more and set her down within one of the wealthiest white suburbs of New York, she would have received as much as $18,000 worth of public education every year and would likely have had a third grade teacher paid approximately $30,000 more than was her teacher in the Bronx.[40]

Children of affluent parents more often have access to better schools (both public and private) and are, therefore, qualified for better colleges and then better jobs, while children of poor parents often have access only to inferior schools that inadequately prepare them for college and the workplace. Thus, while popular constructions see schools as the path to success for rich and poor alike, critical constructionists see schools as serving primarily to perpetuate inequality in society. Rather than helping students overcome the disadvantages of poverty that are concomitant to a capitalist economy, the schools reinforce those disadvantages.

The American educational system has often risen to our definition of a social problem, attracting the attention of significant numbers of people and numbers of significant people. Few Americans are satisfied with the quality of education in the United States. Corporate capitalists focus not on inequality, but upon the poor performance of American schools, focusing, for example on the United States' ranking on various international scores. American 15-year-olds recently ranked 25th in mathematics among over 70 countries surveyed by the Organization for Economic Cooperation and Development's Program for International Student Assessment; U.S. students were ranked 15th for reading literacy.[41] The concern is that the U.S. economy will become less competitive as students graduate with inadequate preparation for jobs in a global economy.

This is a valid concern, but the critical constructionist is inclined to suggest that the mediocre U.S. rankings in international comparisons are due to inadequately funded public schools, most especially those schools in jurisdictions where there are high rates of poverty. Due in large part to the decentralized nature of American public education and the localized funding of education, the United States spends more educating its affluent (mostly white) children than its poor (mostly minority) children. "White and Asian children score just above the average for the European OECD nations in each subject area," writes Linda Darling-Hammond of Stanford University, "but African-American and Hispanic students score so much lower that the national average plummets to the bottom tier." Recent research has indicated that if we consider only the test scores of students who attended schools where less than 10 percent of the students lived in poverty, the United States ranked first in the world. It was, in fact, the test scores of students who attended schools where 50 percent or more of the students lived in poverty that dragged the U.S. rankings down so far.[42] Thus, it appears that rich kids and most middle-class kids are being well prepared for work in a global economy; but schools in which we underinvest are unable to compensate for the disadvantages of growing up in poverty.

Nonetheless, corporate capitalists have seized upon these international rankings as an opportunity to expand capital markets, often blaming teachers, frivolous government spending, and capricious government regulations, while offering up privatization and market-based solutions to the problem. With the hundreds of billions of dollars spent on public education every year, private organizations and corporate entities stand to make huge profits in a recession-wracked economy where there are few other such opportunities. John Bellamy Foster argues, "The corporate-driven onslaught on students, teachers, and public schools…is to be explained not so much by the failure of the schools themselves, but by the growing failure of the capitalist system, which now sees the privatization of public schools as central to addressing its larger malaise."[43]

The charter school movement and school vouchers are two initiatives particularly appealing to those who want to see market-based solutions to the problems in American education. Charter schools are paid for by public taxes, but are managed by private entities and they are free from many of the regulations that apply to other public schools. Today there are some 5,000 charter school with 1.5 million students enrolled.[44] Though the charter school movement has very strong supporters, the data showing their effectiveness are less than impressive. Diane Ravitch, a former appointee in the

George H. W. Bush administration, and a former advocate of "choice" initiatives in education, reports,

> The only major evaluation of the national charter sector was carried out by economist Margaret Raymond at Stanford University. Her study was funded by the staunchly pro-charter Walton Family Foundation, among others; yet she found that only 17 percent of the charters outperformed a matched public school. The other 83 percent were either no better, or they were worse. On the NAEP [National Assessment of Educational Progress] exams in reading and mathematics, students in charter schools perform no better than those in regular public schools, whether one looks at black, Hispanic, or low-income students, or students in low income districts.[45]

Reports that often appear in the media or are presented by charter school supporters detail students' experiences at one or a few nonrandomly selected stellar schools and such accounts almost always neglect to mention some important facts that an audience needs in order to evaluate charter schools' relative effectiveness. "[O]ne," writes Ravitch,

> the charters select students by lottery, and thus, attract motivated students and families; two, charters tend to enroll a smaller proportion of students who are limited-English proficient, students with disabilities and homeless students, which gives them an edge over neighborhood public schools; and three, charters can remove students who are "not a good fit" and send them back to the neighborhood school. *These factors give charters an edge, which makes it surprising that their performance is not any better than it is.*[46]

Almost all public schools have unionized employees and almost all charter schools are nonunionized. So reports showing the effectiveness of charter schools are used in the media to suggest that government regulations and teachers' unions are the two major causes of problems in American education. More balanced media reportage, however, would certainly point out the difficulty in comparing charter schools to public schools when charter schools are able to cherry-pick the best students from the poor neighborhoods and they can remove the least able students from their ranks with relative ease. Undoubtedly many poor students benefit from being picked by the charter schools, but when public resources are diverted to charter schools, the lowest-performing poor students are left behind in even worse schools and comparisons become even less valid.

School vouchers are another initiative in the market-based solutions menu. Jurisdictions that implement such a program issue vouchers to low-income students that can be used toward tuition at a private school. The idea is to expand educational choices for poor families and to pressure the public schools to improve themselves so that they may compete effectively with private schools. (Some supporters would like to see such programs expanded to include middle-income or all kids.) Since the majority of private schools in the United States are religiously affiliated,[47] many critics are concerned that such programs are a violation of the First Amendment separation of church and state, with public taxes supporting the religious education of students receiving vouchers.

Like charter schools, school vouchers divert public taxes toward private entities and like the charter schools such programs leave the most in need in worse circumstances. Vouchers often do not cover the full costs of attending a private school (e.g., books, uniforms, transportation, etc.). The neediest students—students from families unable to afford the extra costs or with parents unwilling or unable to apply for vouchers—are left behind in the worst schools which, on top of everything else, have had their funding cut to pay for the vouchers of the students who left. Public taxes, thus, are being diverted from the schools most in need to mostly religiously affiliated private schools who are educating mostly middle- and upper-class students.

From the perspective of critical constructionism, the hundreds of billions of dollars paid in taxes every year to support public education are both an affront to the antitax capitalists and an attraction to their corporate counterparts. As Naomi Klein argues in her book *Shock Doctrine: The Rise of Disaster Capitalism*, problems in government services are often seized upon by elite corporate interests, exaggerated in the public imagination, often to the point where a crisis seems imminent, all as a pretext for privatizing these services and/or introducing market-based solutions and then collecting huge profits at the taxpayers' expense.[48] Because education is seen as a necessity by the American public and most are willing to pay taxes to support education, to the extent that privatization takes hold, a secure supply of profits is ensured to those private entities that get a share of the business. The result, to paraphrase economist John Kenneth Galbraith, is socialism for the rich and capitalism for the poor. That is, the rich reap government-insured public resources, while the poor fend for themselves.

INEQUALITY AND HEALTH CARE

As we have already seen, though the United States is farther on the capitalist extreme of the continuum than most other nations, it is not purely capitalist. Among other things, its police departments, fire departments, and public schools are socialized. Almost all Americans would agree that everyone has a right to police protection, fire protection, and an education paid for at public expense. However, the United States is the only advanced industrialized nation that does not feel the same way about health care; it is the only one without a nationalized ("socialized") health-care system. Fire departments, police departments, and schools are considered essentials and it is, therefore, considered necessary for them to be provided at public expense. Certainly, it could be argued that publicly provided health care is at least as essential as public education. After all, what good is an education if one is too sick to learn, or apply what he or she has learned—or dead.

The U.S. Census Bureau estimates that in 2010, 50 million Americans were uninsured, with blacks and Hispanics uninsured at higher rates than whites.[49] Figure 3.1 shows the results of a survey by the Centers for Disease Control indicating that blacks are about 1.5 times more likely than whites to be uninsured and Hispanics are 3 times more likely than whites to be uninsured. Vernellia Randall, a law professor with a degree in nursing, reports, "In fact, a disproportionate number of racial minorities have no insurance, are unemployed, are employed in jobs that do not provide health care insurance, are disqualified for government assistance programs, or fail to participate because of administrative barriers."[50] The lack of health insurance is not just a problem of the poor minorities. A 2009 report from the Kaiser Family Foundation estimates "nearly a quarter of the nation's 45 million non-elderly uninsured are middle class."[51] According to Elizabeth Warren and Amelia Tyagi, the number of personal bankruptcies due to serious illness rose more than 2,000 percent over the two decades prior to the 2003 publication of their book *The Two-Income Trap: Why Middle-Class Mothers and Fathers Are Going Broke.*[52]

As for the poor, eligibility for Medicaid benefits varies from state to state. Eligibility rules are tightening and benefits are being cut as states across the country are dealing with budget cuts. While many of the poor do qualify for Medicaid benefits, there are many who do not. It is often the working poor and their families who do not qualify, earning wages that put them just above the poverty line and above the eligibility threshold in their state.

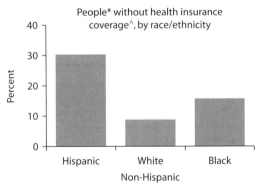

* People of all ages, age-sex-adjusted percentage
^ At time of interview (January–March 2008).
United States

Figure 3.1   People without health insurance coverage, by race/ethnicity

Source: "People without Health Insurance Coverage, by Race and Ethnicity," Centers for Disease Control and Prevention, http://www.cdc.gov/Features/dsHealthInsurance/. Retrieved November 7, 2011.

At the Health Center
Source: www.blackcommentator.com.

When the poor do receive health care, it is typically substandard, frequently in underfunded, understaffed, overcrowded "charity hospitals" or state or county hospitals.[53] The poor typically do not have a regular family physician who is familiar with their medical histories. Poor children frequently go without immunizations, poor women frequently go without regular gynecological checkups, and poor pregnant women frequently go without prenatal or postnatal care. This lack of care would be unconscionable to our counterparts in most other industrialized countries.

Not surprisingly, research has shown a correlation between social class and life expectancy in the United States. Those of lower social classes have lower life expectancies.[54] The rich live an average of 7 years longer than the poor.[55] In large part, as a result of its lack of a nationalized health-care system, the United States ranks poorly in some of the more critical international standards (see Table 3.3). A report from the World Health Organization ranked the U.S. health-care system 37th out of the 191 countries that they studied, even though the United States spent more per capita on health care than any other country.[56] In 2011, the CIA *World Factbook* ranks the United States 50th among nations for life expectancy.[57] A study published in the prestigious *New England Journal of Medicine* found that, for most age groups, death rates in Harlem were higher than those in rural Bangladesh.[58] As for the

Table 3.3 Cross-National Statistics on Health and Health Care

	WHO Ranking	Infant Mortality	Maternal Mortality	Life Expectancy
France	1	3	8	81
Italy	2	3	5	82
Spain	7	3	6	81
Austria	9	4	5	82
Norway	11	4	7	80
Portugal	12	5	7	79
Greece	14	5	2	80
Netherlands	17	5	9	80
United Kingdom	18	5	12	80
Ireland	19	4	3	80
Switzerland	20	4	10	81
Sweden	23	3	3	81
Germany	25	4	7	80
Finland	31	3	8	79
Denmark	34	4	5	79
Average Above		*3.9*	*6.7*	*80.3*
United States	37	6	24	78

Sources: Life expectancy and infant mortality data from *CIA World Factbook,* 2011 estimates, https://www.cia.gov/library/publications/the-world-factbook/rankorder/2102rank.html and https://www.cia.gov/library/publications/the-world-factbook/rankorder/2091rank.html. Retrieved September 24, 2011. Maternal mortality data from *Trends in Maternal Mortality: 1990–2008*, World Health Organization, UNICEF, UNFPA, and The World Bank. The World Health Organization, 2010. http://whqlibdoc.who.int/publications/2010/9789241500265_eng.pdf. Retrieved April 29, 2012.

period people live in "good health," the average Japanese citizen lives 4 more healthy years than the average American, and the average French citizen lives 3 more healthy years than the average American.[59]

Perhaps the most embarrassing ranking for the United States is for its infant mortality rate. This statistic measures the chances that a baby will die in its first year of life. In 2011, the U.S. rate was 6 deaths per 1,000 live births, which was higher than at least 40 other countries and twice as high as Japan's rate of 2.9.[60] Indeed, the infant mortality rate varies among the states between 4.9 (in Washington state and Utah) and 10.6 (Mississippi); and the District of Columbia has an astonishing rate of 12.8.[61] Researchers at the Centers for Disease Control have found that much of the variation in infant mortality rates within the United States is indeed due to social class. They found that the rate for children born to low-income women was 60 percent higher than the rate for children born to women of higher incomes.[62] The maternal mortality rate is another statistic for which the United States does not fare too well compared with its industrialized counterparts. This rate refers to the chances of a mother dying from complications due to childbirth. It is very strongly related to poverty and the quality of medical care provided; consequently, 99 percent of maternal mortality occurs in the countries of the South.[63] The United States, however, ranks high in the industrialized world, with a rate of 24 maternal deaths per 100,000 live births, compared with rates of 5 per 100,000 in Italy, Austria, and Denmark (see Table 3.3).

As with many of the problems associated with the U.S. government's failure to control private industry, it is not only the poor who suffer. "The United States," reports *USA Today*, "is the only industrialized nation in the world that doesn't control the prices of prescription drugs."[64] As a result, Americans typically pay much higher prices for most of their prescription drugs. The elderly are hit with a double whammy: very often living on fixed incomes, Medicare pays a limited amount of the costs of their prescription medicines (whereas the health-care systems throughout the rest of the industrialized world pay all or most of the costs) *plus* their medicines are priced much higher. Poor, elderly Americans who are not poor enough to qualify for Medicaid (remember, eligibility varies from state to state) face difficult choices between food, medicine, and other necessities.

In 1993, the Clinton administration was considering health-care reform. The most often talked about reform would have been a move in the direction of Canada's "single-payer" plan. (All citizens of Canada are covered by its national health insurance, which is paid for by public taxes.) Of the interest groups that were most threatened by health-care reform in the United States, the multibillion-dollar health insurance industry, of course, figured most prominently as people would no longer need private health insurance. The health insurance industry mounted a multimillion-dollar advertising campaign designed to discredit any move toward a national health-care plan. Among the misinformation propagated by the health insurance industry, and the media in general, were the following messages: (1) under a national health-care plan, people would lose their choice of physicians; (2) a national health-care plan would require an enormous increase in taxes; and (3) national health-care plans like Canada's can only function by "rationing" medical treatments. These can all be characterized as exaggerations or distortions because (1) most Americans who are insured are covered by health maintenance organizations that limit the policyholder's choice of physicians, and consequently, most Canadians have more choice of physicians than their American counterparts;[65] (2) in between Americans and their medical treatment are the multibillion-dollar insurance companies, which spend money to keep themselves in business and their shareholders happy that could instead be paid in taxes to support national health insurance; and (3) all health-care systems ration their services: in Canada, rationing is based on need, while in the United States, it is based on social class (i.e., the patient's ability to pay).

Almost all of the criticisms of a national health-care plan that appeared in various media could have been systematically refuted by the news media, but they were not. Why not? You may have noticed a great deal of advertisements from pharmaceutical companies and health-care providers in magazines and on nationally broadcast (ABC, NBC, CBS) evening television, especially on the news broadcasts. These represent a substantial source of revenues for the media and it is not in their best interests to alienate one of the largest sources, if not their largest source, of profit. More balanced coverage of the issues, countering the claims of their advertisers, would not have been good business.

In his discussion of the "myths about health care around the world," journalist T. R. Reid concludes,

> [T]he most persistent myth of all [is] that America has "the finest health care" in the world. We don't. In terms of results, almost all advanced countries have better national health statistics than the United States does. In terms of finance, we force 700,000 Americans into bankruptcy each year because of medical bills. In France, the number of medical bankruptcies is zero. Britain: zero. Japan: zero. Germany: zero.[66]

In the most recent move to reform the U.S. health-care system, the health insurance industry went into battle formation, contributing tens of millions of dollars to political campaigns, deploying hundreds of lobbyists to Washington, DC, and meeting with White House officials. In just a few months before the Senate Finance Committee developed its recommendations for reform, the health-care industry spent $380 million dollars on lobbying, advertising, and campaign contributions, with the largest contribution of $1.5 million going to the chairman of the committee.[67] The result was not a "public option" to compete with private insurance companies that surveys showed most Americans favored, but new laws mandating that all adults purchase health insurance, an obvious boon to the insurance industry. "What the bill has done," said cofounder of Physicians for a National Health Program and Harvard medical professor Steffie Woolhandler, "is use the coercive power of the state to force people to hand their money over to a private entity which is the private insurance industry. That is not what people were promised."[68] Not surprisingly, a large segment of the American population is dissatisfied with the recent health-care reform. The law mandating people buy health insurance is probably the most contentious aspect of the legislation. But the critical constructionist is concerned with how political pundits and the corporate media have focused the public fury on the overreach of the federal government and *not* on the influence of corporate capitalism on the federal government. Therein lies the heart of the power of capitalism. With enormous resources at their disposal to influence perceptions of social problems and, in this case, discredit socialized medicine, the interests of corporate capitalists prevail and the majority of Americans will continue to pay more for their health care and receive less than their counterparts in other industrialized nations.

APPLICATION: IMMIGRATION

Elementary school children in the United States are proudly taught that the United States is a nation of immigrants. Textbooks beam with pride in how the decision to immigrate to America improved the life chances of tens of millions of people over the generations. The pride in our immigrant origins is shown to the world by the Statue of Liberty whose base is inscribed with the following passage by Emma Lazarus,

"Keep ancient lands your storied pomp!" cries she
With silent lips. "Give me your tired, your poor,
Your huddled masses yearning to breathe free,
The wretched refuse of your teeming shore,
Send these, the homeless, tempest-tost to me,
I lift my lamp beside the golden door!"

Despite this legacy and this integral part of our national identity, Americans are today, and frequently have been in the past, ambivalent about immigration.

Inequalities between nations frequently serve as a powerful incentive for people to emigrate from poorer countries to wealthier ones. Impoverished immigrants are quite often not welcome and, like other groups discussed in this chapter, are often deprived of equal access to society's resources; in particular, they are deprived of many of the rights afforded to the society's citizens. While societies cannot necessarily be expected to provide the full rights of citizenship to everyone who wants to cross their borders, the role played by race in American immigration issues makes immigration relevant to other issues of inequality. There have always been racial groups deprived of citizenship rights in the United States. Blacks were deprived as slaves and Native Americans as a conquered people. Americans were *legally* justified in subjecting racial minorities to these deprivations. But it took many generations before most Americans realized that we were not *morally* justified. Later, the Chinese were persecuted through immigration quotas and today much of the consternation over immigration concerns Latino immigrants. Again, we are as legally justified in depriving noncitizen Latinos of citizenship rights as we were of blacks, Native Americans, and the Chinese in the past. But will we one day come to see it as morally wrong?

Problems associated with immigration tend to cycle with the economy. Capitalist economies are well known to cycle between booms and busts, with some booms and busts being more pronounced than others. Immigration has been disappearing and reappearing on the social problems radar screen for well over a century, usually reappearing during economic downturns when workers are feeling less secure in their jobs and when taxpayers resent being taxpayers more than usual. That this problem surfaces and subsides is not surprising, given the critical role immigration has played in American history. Writes, Justin Akers Chacón, "The particular history of the United States as a nation consciously populated with foreign labor has meant that, at any given point, foreign-born workers can comprise between 8 percent and 20 percent of the population, while another significant portion is made up of the children of immigrants."[69]

During the last few decades of the nineteenth century, there was enormous industrial expansion, and capital required a much larger labor force. Thus the floodgates were open to massive immigration, mostly from Europe. Labor historian Kitty Calavita writes,

> By 1880 more than 70% of the population in each of America's largest cities were immigrants or children of immigrants....The foreign born increasingly made up the bulk of the industrial labor force [so much so that] Samuel Lane Loomis noted that "Not every foreigner is a working man, but in the cities, at least, it may almost be said that every working man is a foreigner."[70]

When the labor market becomes saturated, the welcome mat is removed. It is more than just a matter of who will or will not be let in during economic downturns; but immigrants who were once welcomed with open arms (or gracelessly permitted to come in) are now resented for their presence and often come to be demonized. Demonizing them makes it easier to deprive them of social services when the economy turns sour. "By shifting the blame for poverty onto impoverished workers," writes Chacón, "capital absolve[s] itself of the need to sustain a large surplus population of workers during times of downturn."[71]

Critical theorists point out that the capitalist elite benefit from the ensuing hostilities, pitting workers against each other, diverting their attention from their exploitative working conditions. Native workers can blame immigrants for job scarcity, job insecurity, and low wages when, in fact, these conditions would likely be the same even if there were far fewer immigrants competing with native workers. Further, employers benefit considerably by the illegal status of vast numbers of undocumented aliens who are often compelled to take jobs without any government protections, that is, jobs that pay less than minimum wage, offer no overtime, no benefits, and might not meet minimum government safety requirements. Undocumented aliens cannot blow the whistle on their employers without drawing the attention of the authorities to themselves and facing dismissal, imprisonment, or deportation. Lacking legal protections, undocumented aliens can ill afford to demand higher wages and better working conditions. In this regard, undocumented immigrants may indeed be more attractive to employers than those who are here legally and this "competitive edge" would be diminished by the legal empowerment of undocumented aliens. Thus, the working class, as a whole, would benefit by documenting the undocumented and employers would have to improve their working conditions.

In the past, there have been times when we need more immigrant labor than at other times. It may well be that conditions have shifted such that we will need more and more immigrant labor in the future. The population of the United States is aging, meaning that the ratio of working-aged people to retirement-aged people is getting smaller. In 1935, when Social Security was first conceived, there were 16 workers for every beneficiary, while in 1999 there were only 3.3 workers per beneficiary, and by 2030 it could be as low as 2 workers for every beneficiary.[72] This trend is not likely to be sustainable. But an alternative to slashing Social Security and letting the elderly fend for themselves would be to allow, or even encourage, more young people to immigrate to the United States and tax their earnings as we do all other workers.

In short, critical constructionists (1) are concerned about the contradiction between Americans taking pride in their immigrant origins while, at the same time, trying to close the gate on new immigrants; (2) question the role of race as it is played out in immigration issues in U.S. history; and (3) see the timing and substance of immigration issues as reflecting the interests of the capitalist elite more than those of the average worker and taxpayer.

SUMMARY

This chapter begins with a brief discussion of the Weberian concept of "life chances" and how one's social situation affects the opportunities that are available and his or her chances of success. The case is made that, despite the abatement of blatant racism, race still has a very substantial bearing on a person's income and, just as or more importantly, a family's wealth. Wealth determines a person's access to opportunity and ability to weather economic downturns and it is usually accumulated over generations. This cumulative quality of wealth means generations of prejudice and discrimination are reflected in the enormous gap between black wealth and white wealth that exists today.

One increasingly unpopular remedy for generations of racial prejudice has been affirmative action. Affirmative action programs emerged as a means of enforcing antidiscrimination policies and laws and became unpopular as they were seen to be a form of reverse discrimination against whites. However, affirmative action was effective in countering racial discrimination and the problem of reverse discrimination has been greatly exaggerated in the popular imagination. The number of white victims of discrimination has been infinitesimally small relative to the number of black victims there would have been had there been no affirmative action programs. Affirmative action is/was an essentially flawed but effective means of addressing the very real problem of racial discrimination and the effects of accumulated racism over past generations—problems that are decreasingly acknowledged in today's political and economic climate.

From race, the chapter proceeds to a discussion of gender inequality. Popular constructions often hold that problems of gender inequality have been successfully addressed and indeed the gender income gap has been closing over the past few decades. However, women's median income is still only 81 percent of men's median income and women are finding it more difficult than men to make it into the upper echelons of the corporate world. These

98 / SOCIAL PROBLEMS

inequities are explained by a number of factors, including active discrimination, the male corporate culture, the occupational segregation of women along with the lower value assigned to "women's work." Perhaps the most formidable obstacle to women in the workplace is the popular construction of gender that makes parenting and housework the primary responsibility of women. This construction places a heavier burden on women at home and impedes their advancement at work whether or not they are married and whether or not they have children.

Access to education and health care are specifically addressed as critical factors in assessing life chances. Free access to primary and secondary education is popularly constructed as a remedy to other inequalities in society. Unfortunately, the quality of public education varies tremendously in the United States—from state to state, town to town, and neighborhood to neighborhood—with affluent kids having access to better schools and poor kids having access to inferior schools. Thus, the critical constructionist is inclined to see the public school system as reinforcing and perpetuating inequalities in society rather than helping to overcome them. Corporate capitalists offer privatization as a solution to problems in education in the form of charter schools and school vouchers. Because hundreds of billions of dollars in public monies are spent on education, corporate entities stand to make huge profits from privatization. Evidence of the effectiveness of charter schools and school vouchers is less than convincing. But such programs leave the schools most in need of improvement with their funding cut and the children most in need of improved educational access are left behind in such schools.

In the United States, few question the rights of citizens to an education paid for at public expense. That is, almost everyone accepts the idea of socialized education. The United States, however, is among a very few industrialized countries in the world where the right to health care at public expense is not popularly accepted. While the United States spends more per capita on health care than any other nation, it receives less than dozens of other countries as measured by U.S. rankings on various international indicators. As with education, the United States' subpar rankings on international scores appears to be primarily due to the lack of access to decent health care for the poor. Efforts to reform U.S. health-care policies and bring them into closer alignment with the rest of the industrialized world threaten the profits of the health-care industry and have been confounded by the enormous resources brought to bear by the industry to influence public perceptions of the problem and its possible solutions.

The chapter concludes with a discussion of the issue of immigration in the United States. The critical constructionist is concerned about the contradiction between the pride that Americans take in being an immigrant nation and the simultaneous anti-immigrant fervor that frequently takes hold of the popular imagination. The corporate elite benefit from this fervor in that it distracts the public's attention away from the problems inherent in corporate capitalism and focuses their attention on poor, powerless immigrants, usually minorities. The elite also benefit in that the illegal status of many immigrants means that they are effectively lacking in legal protections and that allows employers to exploit their labor virtually at will. Thus, helping to foster anti-immigrant sentiments in the United States works to the benefit of elite interests.

Discussion Questions

1. In matters related to employment and housing, discrimination on the basis of race or gender is illegal. So, given that there are thousands of instances of discrimination every day, what is your answer to the question posed earlier in this chapter: How, other than hidden surveillance devices and quotas, can antidiscrimination laws be effectively enforced?

2. Of the following services, the first four are already socialized in the United States and the last two could be:

   Police

   Fire Fighting

   Primary Education

   Secondary Education

   Higher Education

   Health Care

   Was it right to socialize the first four services? And, if you think so, should the latter two services be socialized as well? Explain your reasoning.

Problems of the Family

THE FAMILY IN HISTORICAL PERSPECTIVE

T he family is such a basic institution—and so near and dear to us all—
that a great variety of problems in society are often believed to ema-
nate from problems in the family. Social problems as varied as poverty,
drug abuse, crime, and deficiencies in educational achievement are often
blamed on the "breakdown" of the family. While there are many who think
the family is on the verge of extinction, it has been and continues to be one
of the most enduring institutions throughout the world and throughout history. Many people think the family is undergoing dramatic changes today.
They are right. However, many think that these changes have begun only
relatively recently and that they spell the doom of the family and of civil
society. They are wrong. The family in America has been undergoing change
since the first settlers arrived, and the colonists—much like their modern-
day descendants—prophesied the downfall of the institution.[1] "The 'crisis
of the family,' " writes Arlene Skolnick, " . . . is a national tradition, and not
just in America: historians of the family in other countries have made much
the same discovery."[2] The "crisis of the family" argument is not just typical
throughout the world; it has been typical throughout history. Historian of
the family Stephanie Coontz writes,

> [F]or thousands of years people have been proclaiming a crisis in marriage
> and pointing backward to better days. The ancient Greeks complained bit-
> terly about the declining morals of wives. The Romans bemoaned their high
> divorce rates, which they contrasted with an earlier era of family stability. The
> European settlers in America began lamenting the decline of the family and
> the disobedience of women and children almost as soon as they stepped off
> the boats.[3]

In 1966, Clark Vincent noted that "[s]ince the earliest writing available,
changes occurring in the institution of the family have been used and interpreted to support either an optimistic or a pessimistic premise concerning social change, and the pessimists have consistently outnumbered the
optimists."[4]

Thus, significant numbers of people have always felt the family to be on
the verge of collapse when, in fact, history has demonstrated that it was not.
Problems of the family, then, are a prime subject for a critical constructionist

analysis because there is a considerable discrepancy between perceptions of reality and objective conditions. Popular constructions of problems of the family are based on some dubious assumptions.

Notions about the breakdown of the family, almost by definition, make assumptions about the history of the family. The words *breakdown, extinction,* and *collapse* suggest a process going from some reasonably healthy state in the past to a relatively unhealthy state in the present and/or future. Those who argue that the family is breaking down assume a knowledge of the state of the family in the past and that that former state was better than that of today's family. These are questionable assumptions. To put these assumptions in critical perspective, we need to know something about the history of the family. Writes John Demos,

> To study the history of the American family is to conduct a rescue mission into the dreamland of our national self-concept. No subject is more closely bound up with our sense of a difficult present—and our nostalgia for a happier past. How often, in reference to contemporary problems, does the diagnostic finger point in the direction of family life?[5]

Not until relatively recently have a good many historians begun systematically studying the history of the family. More has been learned about the history of the family in the past four decades than in the previous two centuries.[6] Demos's review of the history of the family reveals, "First and definitely foremost, there is no Golden Age of the Family gleaming at us from far back in the historical past. And there is no good reason to construe recent trends in terms of decline and decay."[7] Every family pattern that has developed and then faded has had its own advantages and disadvantages. Many problems associated with the family today are either exaggerated or falsely dissociated from the family of the past. For example, while divorce rates are inordinately higher today than they have been in the past, we cannot assume that marriages were more successful in the past. Demos notes that "[i]n earlier times, countless marriages were ended by simple, and legally unrecognized, desertion."[8] Besides those opting for desertion ("the poor man's divorce"), there were many more people trapped in loveless marriages, who were spiritually and emotionally separated, with little hope of moving on to a better marriage in a world where divorce was severely stigmatized. The proportion of marriages "invisibly" separated in the late nineteenth century may not have been much different from the proportion visibly separated today.[9]

Many of those who fear the breakdown of the family identify the changing role of women as the principal source of the family's decline. They long nostalgically for the "breadwinner/housewife" form of family that, writes Coontz,

> produced a sentimental, almost sacred, domestic sphere whose long-term commitments and nurturing balanced the pursuit of self-interest in the public arena. Recent social problems, they argue, stem from a self-defeating

superegalitarianism that denies men's and women's differing needs and abilities and desanctifies family relations.[10]

Many believe this traditional division of gender roles to be part of the "natural order" of things and that departures from the breadwinner/housewife model are unnatural. However, the breadwinner/housewife model did not emerge as the dominant family form until the nineteenth century. Before that, in an agrarian society, the family—mother, father, and older children—made up an economic unit, with each member contributing to production (harvesting, making clothes, milking cows, churning butter, etc.). Not until the Industrial Revolution did father go off to work and become the "breadwinner," leaving mother at home to become the "housewife" and perform unpaid housework. It is questionable, then, just how natural and traditional the breadwinner/housewife form of family is. In cross-cultural and historical perspectives, it seems to be an unusual and transient form of family. The breadwinner/housewife model is, according to sociologist Kingsley Davis, an "aberration that arose in a particular stage of development and tends to recur in countries now undergoing development."[11]

It should also be noted that the breadwinner/housewife model that emerged in the nineteenth century appeared as the dominant form of family only in the middle and upper classes, only among those who could afford it.[12] Popular constructions blame the problems of the poor on their departure from the breadwinner/housewife model, yet the poor have never been able to afford such a lifestyle in significant numbers.

While some believe the family that is based on "traditional" gender roles to represent the natural order of things, it produced some unnatural and disaffecting results. In the nineteenth century, men were perceived to have uncontrollable sexual desires, while women were supposed to have none. This could hardly have been conducive to satisfying sexual relations. Studies in the history of gynecology have uncovered an "astonishing number of cases" in which women sought clitorectomies in order to control their sexual desires.[13] Prostitution was rampant in the nineteenth century. Many married men sought prostitutes as a sexual outlet, in part because they had been socialized to believe their sexual appetites were uncontrollable and because their wives had been socialized not to enjoy sex. Writes Demos,

> But sex was merely an extreme case of a pattern that affected every sort of contact between men and women. When their appropriate spheres were so rigorously separated, when character itself appeared to be so gender-specific, what was the likelihood of meaningful communication? ... [It] was a new mode of partnership—formal, self-conscious and contrived.[14]

Divorce rates began to rise in the middle of the nineteenth century, and the "tramp phenomenon" emerged with, eventually, hundreds of thousands of disaffected men who had run away from their wives, wandering the cities and countryside.[15] The nineteenth century also saw the rapid proliferation of "voluntary," often single-sex, organizations, such as the Elks, the Mother's Association, and the Women's Christian Temperance Union. These, according to Demos, signaled a "deficit in family life" and a search for companionship "preferable to what could be found at home."[16]

Though the conditions described above may be grim, there certainly were happy families in the nineteenth century; but this could hardly be thought of as the "golden age" of the family. Following World War II came a brief, but unusual, period in the history of the American family, which still plays a pronounced role in the American psyche and continues to affect popular constructions of problems relating to the family. This new and historically odd family was the postwar family, or the "'50s family."

The Family of the 1950s

Today, those who glorify the breadwinner/housewife form of family do not harken back to idealized images from the nineteenth century but to idealized images from the 1950s. If they had a television in the 1950s, they likely had a steady dose of idealized images of the family broadcast into their house through such programs as *Ozzie and Harriet, The Donna Reed Show, Father Knows Best*, and *Leave It to Beaver*. Some of these shows, *Leave It to Beaver*, for example, continue to be broadcast in syndication. However, if you are too young to have caught these on television, you can be sure that a great many of the baby boomers—a large proportion of today's parents, grandparents, teachers, professors, and legislators—grew up watching the 1950s construction of the ideal family on TV. There were usually two or three kids, the division of labor among father and mother was quite specific, and gender roles were mutually exclusive. Father worked 9–5, mother was the homemaker/nurturer, and when father came home from work, he took charge of the family. Other family patterns were rarely, if ever, seen on television.

Today, many social problems are seen as the result of deviations from this family form, the so-called traditional family. Mary Ann Mason and her colleagues write,

> The current debate starts from the idealized American family of the 1950s—middle class, two biological parents, a breadwinner husband and homemaker wife, and two or three biological children—and assumes that any departure from that pattern is negative. Since most contemporary families do depart in one way or another from this pattern, most commonly because the wife and mother is in the paid work force, the fifties norm implies by definition that the family is in decline or in trouble.[17]

The family of the 1950s—both on and off television—however, was far from traditional. It was, in fact, most unusual and, historically, almost freakish. Men returned home from the war, and a great many of the women who had been in the workforce during the war left their jobs (either willingly or not so willingly). New families were being formed at an astonishing rate, and the baby boom was under way. "In fact," writes Skolnick, "the decade stands out as an unusual one for twentieth-century family life, whose historical trends have been falling birth rates, rising divorce rates, and later ages of marriage."[18] Also, according to Coontz,

> [T]he "traditional" family of the 1950s was a qualitatively new phenomenon. At the end of the 1940s, all the trends characteristic of the rest of the twentieth century suddenly reversed themselves: for the first time in more than one hundred years, the age for marriage and motherhood fell, fertility increased, divorce rates declined, and women's degree of educational parity with men dropped sharply. In a period of less than ten years, the proportion of never-married persons declined by as much as it had during the entire previous century.[19]

"Domestic bliss" was supposed to be the principal goal of everyone, especially of women. The home became a sanctuary and was to be the primary source of self-fulfillment, especially for women. "The legendary family of the 1950s...," writes Elaine Tyler May, "was not as common wisdom tells us, the last gasp of 'traditional' family life with deep roots in the past. Rather, it was the first whole-hearted effort to create a home that would fulfill virtually all its members' personal needs through an energized and expressive personal life."[20]

From the turn of the century until the 1950s, women had been steadily gaining new freedoms, more independence, and increasing parity with men. Such progressive steps came to a screeching halt with the family of the 1950s. In the first half of the century, more women were going to college and planning to establish a professional career. "But in the 1950s," notes Skolnick, "most women who attended college had no career plans and dropped out in large numbers to marry."[21] Women had always been at a disadvantage, but in the 1950s in the United States, with "a birthrate that approached that of India, the insistence that marriage and motherhood take up the whole of a woman's identity, and the increased emphasis on gender difference," women's social and economic status began moving backward rather than forward.[22]

Perhaps most women would have testified that, like their television counterparts, they found all of the fulfillment they needed as housewives and mothers. However, there were signs of widespread despair that were never depicted on television and rarely brought to the public's attention through any other medium in the 1950s. According to Coontz, "The hybrid idea that a woman can be fully absorbed with her youngsters while simultaneously maintaining passionate sexual excitement with her husband was a 1950s invention that drove thousands of women to therapists, tranquilizers, or alcohol when they actually tried to live up to it."[23] Women who had difficulty accepting their domestic roles were sometimes diagnosed as schizophrenic, then institutionalized, and sometimes administered shock treatments to force them into submission.[24] Psychiatrists introduced a new term to their diagnostic regimen, *housewife's blight*; and doctors began prescribing record numbers of antianxiety drugs. A favorite prescription drug was called *Miltown*. By 1957, with the drug out for just 3 years, 1.2 million pounds of these pills had been consumed in the United States.[25] When magazines did recognize the plight of the 1950s housewife, by printing articles such as "The Plight of the Young Mother" and "The Mother Who Ran Away," their sales often increased dramatically. When *Redbook* asked its readership to submit examples of "Why Young Mothers Feel Trapped," 24,000 people replied.[26] In the 1960s, commentators, nostalgic for the 1950s, noted the resurgence of increasing divorce rates; but they failed to note that a great many of those getting divorced in the 1960s had gotten married in the 1950s.

In the 1950s, nobody heard much about marital strife, wife abuse, child abuse, or incest. The fact that nobody heard about these phenomena did not mean that they did not occur at rates comparable to those of today; it means only that these phenomena had not surfaced in the public consciousness. They had not been constructed into social problems. Yet, it is quite likely that these incidents occurred as or more often then as they do today because the family was much more shielded from public scrutiny in the 1950s than it is today. Wife abuse was dismissed as "nobody else's business";[27] incest involving a daughter, if it did come to anybody's attention, was quite likely to be defined as female "sex delinquency";[28] and evidence of child abuse was more likely to be shrugged off by emergency room physicians as being the result of an "accident" than it is today.[29] Family violence has received a good deal of public attention in recent years from both professionals and the media; law enforcement officers have been alerted, and neighbors have been sensitized. Consequently, there is less opportunity to perpetrate such acts with impunity than there was in the 1950s.

Television in the 1950s showed us only the middle-class families who could afford a particular standard of living. In the 1950s, 25 percent of the U.S. population was poor.[30] Yet, television never showed poor families that could not afford the kitchen appliances and vacuum cleaner that made June Cleaver's life so much more tolerable. It did not show us the families that could not afford the breadwinner/housewife model because both parents had to work to eke out a living.

It also showed nothing about social inequality or about the diversity of American society. Television families, writes Coontz, "were so completely white and Anglo-Saxon that even the Hispanic gardener in *Father Knows Best* went by the name of Frank Smith."[31] Yet, during the 1950s, the United States was undergoing major changes with regard to its racial and ethnic composition. Prior to that decade, most African Americans and Mexican Americans lived in rural areas and most African Americans lived in the South. By the end of the decade, most African Americans and Mexican Americans lived in the cities, and the majority of African Americans had moved to the North. Puerto Ricans were immigrating in such large numbers that by 1960 there were more Puerto Ricans living in New York than in San Juan.[32] Such demographic changes must have been unsettling to many in the white majority, who likely found comfort in the virtually all-white world depicted on television.

Finally, for those who believe many of society's problems would disappear if only we could return to the 1950s-style family—when people were independent, self-sufficient, and able to manage without government subsidies—we should be mindful of the fact that middle-class families of the 1950s were the recipients of some of the most generous government subsidies in U.S. history and would likely not have existed without such assistance. Through the GI Bill, World War II veterans were eligible for generous benefits, including educational subsidies and extremely low-interest housing loans subsidized by the government. With the help of these benefits, people were able to marry earlier in life than in times past; they bought their houses in the suburbs, and millions improved their lot in life. Sylvia Ann Hewlett and Cornel West note,

> More than any other government program before or since, the GI Bill helped a broad spectrum of Americans—blue-collar as well as white-collar workers, black as well as white workers—attain the American Dream....In...an age of disillusionment with government, it is hard to comprehend that the conservative 1950s, that golden age of the American family, was largely a creation of public policy....Contemporary conservatives who espouse family values but attack social spending seem unaware of the degree to which the families of the 1950s were subsidized by public programs....[33]

Furthermore, the federal government pumped billions of dollars into highways, sewage systems, and other projects that made middle-class suburban life all the more attractive. Enormous amounts of government monies went into the subsidizing of middle-class suburban family life. Meanwhile, the conditions of the cities were being ignored. Cities became increasingly dilapidated and dangerous, spurring a further exodus from them; those who could afford it moved out to the suburbs, leaving the poor behind to face a host of social problems for decades to come.

In summary, popular constructions that hold to the view that the family is breaking down and that the decline of the family is the cause of numerous other social problems are based on the belief that the family was once a healthier institution and, consequently, engendered fewer social problems. An examination of the history of the family provides little basis for such a belief. Throughout American history, there have been significant numbers of people or numbers of significant people who believed the family was on the brink of disaster, blamed then-current social problems on the woeful condition of the family, and waxed nostalgically for the golden age of the family. Today, substantial numbers of people wax nostalgically for the family of the 1950s, which (1) was a very unusual family pattern brought about by a unique set of historical conditions; (2) had its own problems as well as many of the problems experienced by today's families; (3) was inaccessible to millions of poor families; and (4) to the extent that it was a healthy institution, derived much of its strength from government subsidies, often at the expense of the poor.

THE CURRENT STATE OF THE FAMILY

Historically, there have always been people alarmed about the state of the family because the family has always been undergoing changes. One of the most significant changes taking place in the past few decades, the one that has had a pronounced effect on millions of families, causing considerable concern, has been the movement of women into the workplace. Since the Industrial Revolution, lower-class women have always worked in as well as outside the home. Until relatively recently, most middle-class women did unpaid work within the house but did not do paid work outside of the house. Today, they do both. This change has had momentous effects on women, on children, on men, on marital relations—on families.

After World War II, most jobs in the labor force were in manufacturing; since the 1970s, the economy has depended increasingly on service sector jobs (i.e., providing services, such as word processing, teaching, computer repair, social work, etc.). The demand for high-paying blue-collar workers, in automobile and steel manufacturing, for example, began to shrivel; and the demand for low-paying "pink-collar" workers, sales clerks and secretaries, for example, began to expand. With several economic recessions in the 1970s, men faced unemployment and stagnating wages. Women moved into those pink-collar jobs and into other jobs as well; and though their wages were lower, they were able to offset the declining financial situation of their husbands.

In that women demanded less in terms of salary, they began competing with men for jobs, driving down wages for men and making it even more difficult for a man to support his family without the help of a working wife. In fact, many company owners and managers came to prefer hiring women because they were "better adapted, cheaper, more reliable and more easily controlled" than men.[34] In 1960, 32 percent of married women were in the labor force. By 1985, this figure had climbed to 54 percent, and in 2007, it stood at 62 percent. Even more striking is that the proportion of working married women with children under the age of 6 rose from 19 percent in 1960 to 62 percent by 2007.[35]

Today, millions of middle-class wives must work outside of the household if their family is to maintain a middle-class lifestyle. Of course, securing middle-class status for their families is not the only reason for women to work outside of the home. "Economic necessity, the traditional reason for women working," write W. Norton Grubb and Marvin Lazerson, "has increasingly come to coexist with positive assertions of choice: work allows women to become independent, to develop a career, and to terminate unsatisfactory marriages, and it gives them greater power both outside the family and within it."[36]

Does a woman working outside of the family increase a couple's likelihood of divorce? The research data are inconclusive but do suggest that dual-earner families are indeed more likely to divorce.[37] There are a number of possible explanations for this correlation. For one thing, most women working outside of the home basically have two jobs because, as we have seen in Chapter 3, they also do most of the housework. This undoubtedly causes stress and resentment and decreases marital satisfaction among many women. Another part of the correlation between dual-earner families and divorce is explained by the fact that a woman earning an income has greater independence and is better able to exit a failed marriage and live on her own.

Stress in the Modern-Day Family

We should keep in mind that divorce rates today are also quite high among breadwinner/housewife couples. Both dual-earner and breadwinner/house-wife marriages face considerable challenges in today's society. Cowan and Cowan write,

> The challenge to juggle the demands of work, family, and friendship presents different kinds of stressors for men and women, which propels the spouses even farther into separate worlds. When wives stay at home, they wait eagerly for their husbands to return, hoping the men will go "on duty" with the child, especially on difficult days. This leaves tired husbands who need to unwind facing tired wives who long to talk to an adult who will respond intelligibly to them. When both parents work outside the family, they must coordinate schedules, arrange child care, and decide how to manage when their child is ill. Parents' stress from these dilemmas about child care and lack of rest often spill over into the workday—and their work stress, in turn, gets carried back into the family atmosphere.[38]

Cowan and Cowan refer to the modern couple as "pioneers" because they are crossing uncharted territory. "[A] brief survey of the changing context of family life in North America suggests the transition to parenthood presents different and more confusing challenges for modern couples creating families than it did for parents of earlier times."[39] Today's family, they argue, must get along with less support than families of the past. Parents today are more isolated from their parents and siblings, who in the past were more available to help out in child-rearing. People today are less likely to know their neighbors, who otherwise might be able to help them. Even if they do know their neighbors, their female neighbors are more likely to be off working during the day. "Many women who stay at home to care for their babies find themselves virtually alone in the neighborhood during this major transition, a time when we know that inadequate social support poses a risk to their own and their babies' well-being."[40]

Further, they argue that today's family must deal with more ambiguity than families of previous generations. In the past, the family's life was more tightly scripted. The purpose of the family was to produce and raise kids. The father had his specified role and the mother hers; there were few acceptable choices available to them with regard to how they played their roles. Consequently, there was less ambiguity. Today's parents have "more choice about whether and when to bring children into their lives...will the mother return to work, which most were involved in before giving birth, and, if so, how soon and for how many hours?"[41] Such ambiguity leads to anxiety, and this is one of the many sources of stress families face in today's society.

In addition to these stressors, which are relatively new to today's parents, real wages have stagnated, men and women are working longer hours on the job, and their jobs have become less secure. The restructuring of the global economy and corporate downsizing have placed untold pressures on families, depriving them of both their job security and the time they had to spend together. Writes David Elkind, "The postmodern global economy makes unceasing demands on adults to constantly update their skills or to change occupations, and has robbed postmodern parents of their sense of vocational security."[42] Not only are jobs less secure but people are putting in longer work hours than they did 20 years ago. According to Juliet Schor's research, the average worker puts in an additional 163 hours of work on the job per year, or the equivalent of about an extra month's work.[43] This work increase cuts across the occupational spectrum to include assembly-line workers, hospital orderlies, and Wall Street attorneys. Parents, consequently, have less time to spend with their children. This is a primary source of concern both for those who would like to see the return of the 1950s family and for those couples who feel they cannot afford to have the wife stay home to care for the children.

Bankruptcy and the Family

The number of personal bankruptcies in the United States has increased steadily and alarmingly over the past two decades. Even before the Great Recession, Elizabeth Warren and Amelia Warren Tyagi, authors of *The Two-Income Trap: Why Middle-Class Mothers and Fathers Are Going Broke*, wrote,

> Bankruptcy has become deeply entrenched in American life. This year, more people will end up in bankruptcy than will suffer a heart attack. More adults will file for bankruptcy than will be diagnosed with cancer. More people will file for bankruptcy than will graduate from college. And, in an era when traditionalists decry the demise of the institution of marriage, Americans will file more petitions for bankruptcy than for marriage....The number of car repossessions has doubled in just five years. Home foreclosures have more than tripled in less than 25 years, and families with children are now more likely than anyone else to lose the roof over their heads.[44]

Before the Great Recession, most of those filing for bankruptcy were in middle-class families with two working parents. To stay in the middle class, most families require two incomes; and while popular wisdom may hold that two incomes make a family more secure, Warren and Tyagi argue that two incomes make a family more vulnerable to financial collapse. In the past, when most mothers stayed at home most of the time, they acted as standby reserves who could go into action should an emergency arise. If the father lost his job, became bedridden for an extended period, or indeed died, the mother could go to work and make up for a significant part of the lost income. Today, families depend on the incomes of both mother and father, and there is no one standing by in case of an emergency.

Furthermore, with two-income earners, families are twice as likely to be beset by an emergency. The chances of financial disaster befalling the family due to job loss, serious illness, or death are doubled because now both father *and* mother are vulnerable. Should either parent lose income over an extended period, there is no one to take up the slack and financial ruin, then bankruptcy, become very likely.[45] This is not an argument in favor of mothers staying at home because if most mothers did so, besides the fact that women would not be able to fulfill their career goals, millions more families would not be able to own their own home or to send their kids to college, and the number of families able to afford a middle-class lifestyle would be only a small fraction of what it is today.

Research shows that most bankruptcies are not the result of foolishly incurred debt as some would argue. According to the Harvard-based Consumer Bankruptcy Project, almost 90 percent of those who file for bankruptcy do so because of job loss, medical problems, or divorce or separation.[46] The myth of the foolishly spending debtor, however, is propagated by creditors who do not want to see their debtors protected by bankruptcy law. The myth was also cultivated by members of Congress who passed legislation in 2005 making it tougher for families to file for bankruptcy. It is probably no coincidence that lending institutions spent $5,000,000 lobbying for the bill and over $20,000,000 in contributions to both political parties and to individual legislators.[47] A congressional staff member who helped craft the legislation chided, "If this were NASCAR, the members [of Congress] would have to have the corporate logos of their sponsors sewn to their jackets."[48] MBNA, a major lending institution, was also the largest contributor to George W. Bush's 2000 presidential campaign.[49] Cracking down on credit card abuse, the public was told, would lower fees and interest rates. Instead, what we saw was credit card companies' profits rise 30 percent the first 2 years after the legislation, no decrease in fees and interest rates, and more families suffering financial crises, experiencing much more stress than they would have before the legislation was passed.[50]

The myth of the foolishly spending debtor also persists today, argue Warren and Tyagi, because blaming the victim allays the financial fears of the rest of us. We can take comfort and feel less vulnerable if we tell ourselves that "they" went bankrupt because of their lack of discipline.[51] Meanwhile, in a country where downsizing can lift stock values, health care is not viewed as a basic right, and two incomes are required for membership in the middle class, most of us are indeed vulnerable.

Warren and Tyagi warned us of the rising vulnerabilities to bankruptcy even before the subprime mortgage crisis which triggered the Great Recession. This crisis was brought on by reckless financial institutions that required little or no proof of income or assets from borrowers and by legislators who looked the other way while receiving campaign contributions from the very same institutions.

CHILDREN: OUR MOST PRECIOUS RESOURCE?

We often hear politicians, religious leaders, and pundits refer to children as "tomorrow's leaders," "our nation's future," and "our most precious resource." One would think that such phrases indicate the importance of our country's investment in children. Yet, in the United States, the wealthiest country in the world, our government invests very little in the welfare of its children relative to other Western industrialized countries and many other countries around the world. The message from today's legislators to American parents is fairly clear: "you do the investing because we won't." Consequently, the United States has higher rates of child poverty and lags behind other Western industrialized nations in terms of day care and parental support programs.

Child Care

Most middle-class mothers must remain in the workplace if their family is to maintain their standing in the middle class. It was the goal of welfare reform in the 1990s to move more and more lower-class mothers as well into the workplace. The Personal Responsibility and Work Opportunity Reconciliation Act of 1996 that "ended 61 years of guaranteed aid to poor children"[52] was designed to force poor "welfare mothers" out of the home and into the workplace. Oddly enough, some people that would like to see middle-class mothers leave the workplace and return home to their children also want to see lower-class mothers leave their children at home while they go to work. This might not be such a glaring contradiction if these people also supported adequate government funding for child-care services and facilities.

Consistent with its insubstantial antipoverty programs, the United States ranks miserably in the world in terms of providing for the care of young children with working parents. Part of this is explained by the belief that mothers should be at home caring for the kids. (A Baptist church in Berryville, Arkansas, for example, closed its day-care center in the belief "that working mothers too often neglect their children and set bad examples."[53]) However, adding to our list of contradictions, despite the desire of many to see mothers do more "mothering," the United States provides very little in the way of leg-islation that allows working mothers to spend time at home caring for their children. Every Western European nation, for example, guarantees paid maternity leave, ranging from 14 weeks in Germany to 64 weeks in Sweden and from 50 percent of the woman's average wage in the United Kingdom to 100 percent of the average wage in Norway and at least half a dozen other countries.[54] The United States guarantees leave only, *without* pay, and only to women working in organizations with more than 50 employees. In Sweden, even fathers are allowed up to 10 "daddy days" to stay at home and help care for their newborn, and they are compensated at 90 percent of their regular income. Swedish law also allows parents with children under the age of 8 to opt for a 6-hour workday instead of the usual 8-hour day, with a propor-tional reduction in pay.[55] A sample of family leave and wage replacement policies can be found in Table 4.1 below. With some 30 countries reporting to the International Network and Leave Policies and Research, the organization announced in its 2011 review, "Australia introduces a universal paid leave entitlement—now only the USA is without."[56]

Recognizing that mothers often have to work outside the home, most Western European countries offer state-subsidized day care. Danish public policy, for example, ensures that parents have to pay no more than 30 per-cent of operating costs of day-care facilities; low-income families pay no fees at all. The vast majority of Western European countries provide child care for children from the age of 2½ or 3 until primary school. In most of these countries, such care is part of an educational system that allows parents to start their kids in the system at such early ages, but only if they choose to do so. Many countries are cutting back on the provision of child-care serv-ices. Sheila Kamerman and Alfred Kahn estimate that "these countries meet about 67 to 75 percent of the 'need,' not enough, but far more than in the United States."[57] Though the United States does allow child-care tax credits and subsidizes child care for some low-income families, child care remains a tremendous financial burden for most families with young children.

The U.S. government does little to nothing to regulate the quality of child care provided by day-care centers, while its European counterparts set strict standards for the training of staff members and for limiting staff-to-child ratios. Of course, one of the best means of maintaining quality is by offering providers a decent salary. Yet, in the United States, day-care providers are often paid at minimum wage, and their jobs often do not include benefits. A *U.S. News and World Report* article sums up the problem, "the warped dynamic of the child-care market is all too plain: There are too many par-ents chasing too few day-care openings in settings where there is too much turnover of providers who receive too little training and pay.[58] The median annual wages of a child-care worker in 2008 was just under $20,000 (only about $3,000 above the poverty threshold for a family of three) and more than 40 percent of workers in the industry have only a high school educa-tion or less. The Bureau of Labor Statistics reports that "[m]any child daycare

Table 4.1 Maternity and Parental Leave Policies

Country	Duration of Leave	Percentage of Wage Replaced
Austria	16 weeks	100%
	2 years	Partial
Belgium	15 weeks	75–80%
Canada	1 year	55%
Denmark	1 year	60%
	+2 weeks paternity	60%
France	16 weeks for first 2 children including compulsory 6 weeks before birth; 26 weeks for 3rd child; post-birth leave applies to adoption as well	100% for Maternity and paternity leaves; flat rate for parental leave
Germany	14 weeks	100%
	+2 years	Flat rate/Income tested
	+3rd year	Unpaid
Greece	16 weeks	50%
Hungary	24 weeks	70%
Iceland	6 months	Flat rate + dependent benefit
Ireland	18 weeks	70%
Italy	5 months	80%
Japan	14 weeks (6 pre and 8 post Birth)	60%
Mexico	12 weeks	100%
Norway	52 weeks parental leave (or 42 weeks at 100%)	80%
Poland	16 weeks for first child 18 weeks for subsequent births	100%
United Kingdom	18 weeks	6 weeks at 90% 12 Weeks at low flat rate
United States	12 weeks family	unpaid

Source: The Clearinghouse on International Developments of Child, Youth and Family Policies at Columbia University, http://childpolicyintl.org.

workers become dissatisfied with their jobs' stressful conditions, low pay, and lack of benefits and eventually leave. The proportion of child daycare workers who need to be replaced each year is much higher than the average for all occupations."[59]

A study of child-care centers conducted by a team of researchers from a number of prominent universities throughout the country found, among other things, that (1) "child care at most centers in the United States is poor to mediocre"; (2) "children's cognitive and social development are positively related to the quality of their child care experience"; and (3) "states with more stringent licensing standards have fewer poor-quality centers." They also found that the centers that offered higher-quality care depended less on parent fees for their operating costs, paid higher wages and provided more benefits to their staff members, had higher staff-to-child ratios, and had staff members who were better educated, better trained, and had longer tenure at the center.[60] These happen to be many of the features that distinguish child care in European and many other countries from that in the United States. While many argue that the United States cannot afford to ensure that high-quality care is available at reasonable costs to all those in need, Kamerman and Kahn write, "most of what we have urged also is done in many countries and is popular with citizens and a range of political parties. Their economies have not collapsed, and their families thrive."[61]

Again, the critical constructionist is concerned with the disjuncture between perceptions of reality and objective conditions. If Americans think that children are "our most precious resource" and "our nation's future," then there is a considerable discrepancy between these beliefs and the priority given to children on our national agenda.

Children in Poverty

> What is not on the table, and perhaps most significant, is a set of social arrangements that allows children to be the most poverty-stricken group in America. There is no concept of justice or virtue that justifies our willingness to allow millions of children to suffer in poverty.
>
> (Paul Wellstone)[62]

As mentioned earlier, critical constructionists are concerned with alternative ways various problems can be explained. Also, as mentioned in Chapter 2, popular American constructions place the blame for poverty on those individuals suffering the condition rather than on current economic arrangements. This construction of the problem suggests that the solution lies in changing the behavior of those individuals rather than changing the economy. This construction, therefore, works to the advantage of those who have an interest in keeping the economy just the way it is, namely, of those benefitting the most by current economic arrangements: the elite. However, what about the children of the poor? If we are to believe that poor adults have only themselves to blame and, therefore, deserve to suffer from poverty, do their children deserve the same? Are the children of the poor counted among "our most precious resource"?

There were more than 12.3 million children living at or below the U.S. Census Bureau's conservative poverty threshold in 2005;[63] 7 in 10 of these children live in families with at least one parent working.[64] That was before the Great Recession. By 2010, the number of children living in poverty had risen to 16.4 million, or 22 percent of all children. In 2010, a significant proportion of the children living in poverty—more than 40 percent—live in families with incomes that amount to less than half the poverty threshold.[65] Instead of using the official U.S. poverty threshold, Table 4.2 below looks at relative poverty, setting the poverty line at 50 percent below a country's median family income. As this table indicates, the United States tolerates

Table 4.2 Children in Poverty (Percent of Children Living Below 50% of the Median Income)

Australia	15.8
Austria	7.8
Belgium	6.7
Canada	14.9
Finland	2.8
France	7.9
Germany	9.0
Italy	16.6
Netherlands	9.8
Norway	3.4
United Kingdom	15.3
Average Above	*10.0*
United States	21.9

Source: Mishel et al., *The State of Working America, 2006/2007.* Ithaca, NY: Cornell University Press, Economic Policy Institute, 2007, 350.

double the average rate of child poverty and levels greater than all other OECD countries indicated.

Especially at risk are children under the age of 3, who experience the highest poverty rate of any age group.[66] Dr. David Hamburg, former director of the Carnegie Corporation, a foundation dedicated to the study of children's well-being, states,

> Early childhood is clearly one of the most crucial periods of development. It is characterized by rapid growth, specific environmental needs, maximal dependence on caretakers, great vulnerability, and long-term consequences of failure in development. It is a dramatic period, with great changes and striking contrasts. First, the nine months of pregnancy—from a single cell to a very complex organism. Next, the critical transition from living inside the mother's body to living in the world outside. Then the period of forming the initial human attachments that shape so powerfully the possibilities for human relationship and social skills. So this initial phase has a strong bearing on a child's entire life. Especially in poor communities, the risks of permanent—and largely preventable—damage are formidable.[67]

Contrary to popular constructions about poverty, three in five poor children are white, one in three lives in suburban America, one in three lives in a family with married parents, and most live in a family with a parent(s) who works.[68] However, minorities do, indeed, account for a disproportionate number of the poor. Black and Hispanic children are more likely to be living in families without fathers, and their mothers are more likely to be unemployed; but they are also more likely than white children to be living in poverty *whether or not* their mothers are working. About 20 percent of white children under the age of 3 are living in poverty; most of them are living with single, unemployed mothers.[69]

Thus, there is reason for some of the traditionalist alarm about the breakdown of the breadwinner/housewife family. High rates of out-of-wedlock births, as well as of divorce, do indeed have a negative impact on the economic status of millions of families, especially minority families. With regard to the welfare of children, however, it makes no difference whether out-of-wedlock birth and divorce rates are the result of individual decisions or grander structural and economic factors; the children of the poor still suffer for reasons beyond their control. Furthermore, it must be noted that even having a working father living at home is certainly no guarantee that a family will rise out of poverty. "Thirty-two percent of all men between twenty-five and thirty-four when working full-time now earn less than the amount necessary to keep a family of four above the poverty line."[70] According to Rebecca Blank, "The emphasis in this country on encouraging the poor to work harder ignores evidence that the vast majority of the poor either cannot participate in the labor market, are already looking for more work and not finding it, or are already working full-time."[71]

The Consequences and Costs of Child Poverty

Poverty can affect virtually every aspect of a child's life. Poverty increases the likelihood of marital instability, alcoholism among parents, and child abuse.[72] Compared to nonpoor children, poor children are one-third as likely to have had adequate prenatal care, almost twice as likely to be born prematurely, almost twice as likely to be of low birth weight, twice as likely to repeat a grade in school, and about three and a half times more likely to be expelled from school.[73] State health officials in Kansas report that low-income children are three times more likely to die before reaching age 18 than higher-income children. According to the same report, before reaching age 18, low-income children are four times more likely to die from fires and five times more likely to die from infectious diseases and parasites.[74]

Recent research in the neurosciences reveals that children growing up in poverty are more prone to high levels of stress hormones that can permanently impair their neurological system that "literally disrupt the brain architecture." These effects are more likely to occur among children between the ages of 6 months and 3 years and these effects are beyond "the damage caused by inadequate nutrition and exposure to environmental toxins."[75]

Poor children tend to score lower on IQ tests and on tests of their cognitive abilities. Such correlations help to explain their lower school achievement and suggest that poverty is, to an extent, self-perpetuating. If it is more difficult for poor children to succeed in school, then there is an increased likelihood that they will fail to generate higher incomes than their parents. Some would argue that correlations between test achievement and poverty can be explained by inadequate parents, inadequate parenting, or a number of other variables. Research cited by Arloc Sherman of the Children's Defense Fund indicates "that poverty's ill effects *cannot be explained away* as mere side effects of single parenthood, teen parenthood, race, or parents' low IQs or lack of education"[76] and that poverty is correlated with IQ irrespective of growing up in a single-parent family or of the mother's education.[77] Therefore, it seems that poverty itself generates an environment that produces these effects. Poor families are less able to afford an adequate diet necessary for a child's proper mental development; a poor child's environment is less likely to be filled with books and educational toys that might better facilitate the child's intellectual development; and a poor child's home life is characterized by a variety of deprivations, distractions, and "setbacks" that make achievement extremely problematic. Box 4.1 illustrates the problems posed by such setbacks.

Poverty does not have costs and consequences just for poor children and their families but, of course, for society as well. With the help of University of Michigan researchers Mary Corcoran and Terry Adams, the Children's Defense Fund estimates that each year of childhood lived in poverty reduces future earnings for young men by 2.5 percent and for young women by 1.65 percent. They argue that reduced earnings result in reduced consumption

---

BOX 4.1. PROBLEMS THAT ADD UP AND INTERACT

Picture a seventh grader struggling to do well in school. Perhaps child poverty means she cannot concentrate properly on her homework one night because the power company has shut off the lights. The next night she cannot concentrate because she's hungry. The night after that she cannot concentrate because people are shouting and arguing in her crowded apartment building. The next night she cannot concentrate because her brother's asthma has flared up and the family must make a long nighttime trip to the emergency room by bus. By the end of the week, she is tired and has fallen further behind in her studies.

The number and breadth of problems assailing poor children wears down their resilience by forcing them to fight battles on many fronts at once. A child with a wealth of resources can absorb a minor illness or other setback and then compensate or catch up. But for poor children who are faced with more setbacks than other children, the cumulative weight of assaults can be overwhelming....Some experts believe that the number of setbacks a child suffers often matters as much or more than what the setbacks are.

Source: Arloc Sherman, *Poverty Matters: The Cost of Child Poverty in America*. Washington, DC: Children's Defense Fund, 1997, 27, 9.

and, therefore, reduced production. They conclude that "for every year 14.5 million American children continue to live in poverty...society will lose a total of $130 billion in future economic output."[78] Poverty also costs citizens and taxpayers. Poor children are more likely to repeat a grade in school and/ or to need special education. Poor children are more likely to grow up and become violent, costing citizens in terms of their potential for victimization and in terms of taxes spent controlling the poor through the criminal justice system. As Sherman states, "A nation that does not invest to end child poverty now will inevitably pay for its consequences later."[79]

As we have seen, European countries invest far more in the welfare of their children and they do so, according to sociologist James Russell, based on the principle "that all adults, including those without children, should share to some extent in the costs of raising society's children because society as a whole benefits from having children adequately reared."[80] As we begin to think of children in terms of their potential contributions and/or costs to society, we approach a *human capital perspective*. From this perspective, children are seen as future assets or future liabilities to society, depending upon how society invests in them. Children are, in the words of Kamerman and Kahn, "an investment good, not merely a consumption frill. They are society's future."[81] The phrases "our nation's future" and "our most precious resource" imply a human capital perspective and an appreciation for the importance of investing in children. Yet, the United States invests relatively little in its children.

Responding to the Problem

The way the causes of a social problem are constructed will affect the way the solutions to the problem are constructed. In the United States, the causes of poverty are often believed to be laziness and a lack of moral fortitude among the poor. While such constructions undoubtedly apply to some poor persons, they do not apply to most. The media, however, on those rare occasions when they do attend to the problem of poverty, rarely portray anything other than the stereotypes.

William Scarborough sums up typical constructions of poverty and the problem with such constructions.

> There are many commonly held stereotypes about poor families with children in the United States. For example, many believe that all poor families are alike—that they are lazy (in that their parents do not work), that they are persons of color, that they are uneducated, that they have many unrelated members, and that they have been poor all of their lives. The facts are that many of these families are white, are composed of relatively small numbers of related individuals, and the adults in the families generally work and have high school educations....The problem is that these and other important facts rarely receive adequate media attention, thus perpetuating the stereotypes.[82]

By their effect on public policy, constructions of the poor as lazy and undisciplined have severe effects on poor children, even though no one actually believes that poor children are themselves to blame for their poverty. As mentioned earlier, many of the negative consequences poverty has on poor children occur irrespective of the parents' marital status, educational attainment, or parenting abilities. In other words, the principal cause of these negative consequences is a lack of family income. This suggests that the best remedies would be policies targeting the enhancement of family income, such as income subsidies, minimum-wage increases, and programs boosting the number and availability of employment opportunities. If family values and the welfare of children are indeed primary policy concerns, then these should be the focus of our efforts. This is not a new argument, but it seems to have been lost in much of the debate about the family.

Responding to child poverty is largely a matter of priorities. Priorities are such that, for example, every 66-year-old in the United States is entitled to health care at public expense but not every 6-year-old because many of the poor do not qualify for Medicaid. Few take issue with providing Medicare to the elderly, many of whom may have a hard time taking care of themselves; but what rationale could legitimate depriving children of the medical care they need? The answer is that it is not so much a matter of rationale as it is the fact that the health care needs of poor children have not been successfully constructed into a social problem. They have not been made a priority. Meanwhile, "every six days we spend more on the military than we do annually on Head Start, which still serves only one in three eligible children."[83] President Eisenhower himself (a Republican and former five-star general) recognized the woeful priorities that placed child welfare below military expansion when he stated, "Every gun that is made, every warship launched, every rocket fired signifies...a theft from those who hunger and are not fed, those who are cold and not clothed. This world in arms is not spending money alone. It is spending the sweat of its laborers, the genius of its scientists, and the hopes of its children."[84]

Despite the U.S. view of itself as being "child-centered," the United States is one of only two countries in the world that has not ratified the U.N. Convention on the Rights of Children. (The other country is Somalia, which does not have an internationally recognized government.) Having been ratified by 198 countries, it is the most widely accepted of all U.N. conventions. Among other rights, the document includes access to food, shelter, and health care. The convention best represents an ideal to which its signatories pledge they will aspire. Many of these countries, of course, have a worse record on child welfare issues than the United States. However, most of these are themselves poor countries that might argue that they cannot afford to assure every child access to food, shelter, and health care. The United States, though, is among the wealthiest countries in the world and cannot make such an argument.

It may seem astounding to most Americans, but all Western European countries provide some form of family allowance programs. These initially began as a way to offset the costs of having children in the face of declining birthrates. Finland, for example, subsidizes families nearly 85 percent of the cost of raising a child. More generally, most European countries subsidize the costs by an average of "10 percent of wages per child."[85] In contrast, the United States only offers a tax credit of $600 per child. These countries' family welfare policies are based on the human capital perspective discussed above, viewing children as

> a societal good, a societal investment, rather than only a private "consumption" pleasure for the individual family. The family's economic situation is a major factor in how children fare and develop. Therefore, society should share some of the costs of child-rearing as a matter of justice, solidarity, and societal self-interest.[86]

In Sweden, for example, as in the United States, absent parents are expected to contribute financially to the child's welfare; however, if the parent fails to do so in Sweden, the government provides a "maintenance advance" to the child. "The parent responsible for paying child support," writes Ruth Sidel, "is required to repay the amount advanced, but in the meantime, the child will not have to suffer because of nonpayment."[87] Such progressive policies reflect very different priorities than those seen in U.S. policy. Consequently, it is not surprising to find that in European countries, as Kamerman and Kahn report, "[i]nfant mortality rates are consistently lower than those in the United States, fewer babies have low birth weights, childhood immunization rates are higher, and therefore certain disease rates are lower than in the United States."[88]

Table 4.3 compares poverty rates among children in selected countries before and after taxes and transfers. ("Transfers" refer to government payments to the poor in the form of welfare, tax credits, food stamps, etc.). The "Proportional Reduction" column shows how much each country's "welfare system" effectively reduced rates of child poverty. As we can see, some countries reduced their rates of child poverty by as much as 70 or 80 percent or even greater. Before taxes and transfers, France and the United Kingdom had child poverty rates comparable to the United States. But, through taxes and transfers, France reduced its child poverty rate by more than 70 percent, the UK by nearly 40 percent, while the United States reduced its rate by less than 18 percent. The only country with a lower proportional reduction than the United States in Table 4.3 is the Netherlands; but note that it started with a child poverty rate considerably less than half of the U.S. rate. From these data, it appears that, relative to its peers, the antipoverty system in the United States is quite insubstantial.

Child welfare and antipoverty programs are expensive but not as expensive as many of the programs to which the United States has historically given priority, such as the military. Many European countries are cutting back on their child welfare and antipoverty programs, but these programs remain a much higher priority than in the United States. The constructions

Table 4.3 Percentage of Children Living in Poverty Before and After Taxes and Transfers

	Before	After	Proportional Reduction
Austria	17.7	10.2	42.3
Belgium	16.7	7.7	53.9
Canada	22.8	14.9	34.6
Denmark	11.8	2.4	79.7
Finland	18.1	2.8	84.5
France	27.7	7.5	72.9
Germany	18.2	10.2	44.0
Netherlands	11.1	9.8	14.4
United Kingdom	25.4	15.4	39.4
Average Above	*18.8*	*9.0*	*52.1*
United States	26.6	21.9	17.7

Source: Data obtained from Lawrence Mishel, Jared Bernstein, and Sylvia Allegretto, *The State of Working America: 2006/2007,* Economic Policy Institute, 351. Authors cite Miles Corak. 2005. "Principles and Practicalities of Measuring Child Poverty in Rich Countries." LIS working paper no 406. Luxembourg Income Study.

of children as "our most precious resource" and "our nation's future" do not correspond with where children rank in our nation's list of investment priorities. A critical constructionist analysis calls for a reexamination of these priorities, keeping in mind that countries not as wealthy as the United States have done much more to improve the lot of their children and, therefore, the prospects for their nations' futures.

CAPITALISM VERSUS THE FAMILY

It is generally agreed that the two principal ingredients in a capitalist economy are (1) the pursuit of individual self-interests and (2) a free market. Under these conditions, according to Adam Smith, the best possible products and services will be made available at the lowest possible prices. According to Smith, there is no better way to ensure the efficient production and distribution of goods and services in society. A free market is one in which the government does not intervene. The less government intervention, the freer the market and the more capitalist the economy. As was mentioned in Chapter 2, the United States is among the most capitalist societies in the world; but it does not represent a pure form of capitalism because the U.S. government does intervene in the production and distribution of goods and services in a number of ways. Some of these interventions include the minimum wage, Social Security, unemployment compensation, and state-funded educational, police, and fire-fighting services. Note that in one way or another, each of these "interventions" serves to ensure the well-being of millions of families. So while most Americans have been socialized to take a negative view of the phrase *government intervention,* virtually all of us benefit from one or another interventionist policy.

A great many countries provide far more in terms of government policies ("interventions," in capitalist terminology) that ease economic strain on family life than does the United States. While some may argue that the United States is the financial powerhouse that it is today because of its relatively anti-interventionist/capitalist policies, we should note—as mentioned above—that the most profamily program in U.S. history was the GI Bill, which made the American Dream a reality for millions of families, which was implemented during American economic ascendancy throughout the world, and which helped to prolong that ascendancy for decades to come.

Whether or not one subscribes to the belief that poor adults are to blame for their own poverty, few people believe that poor children are to blame, yet capitalist anti-interventionism means that higher proportions of our children suffer from poverty than those in other Western industrialized nations. While providing children with substandard nutrition, substandard housing, and substandard education would be unthinkable in many of the less capitalistic Western nations, such provisions are tolerated in the United States.

As we have seen, economics plays a crucial role in the well-being of the family. While it may be preferable to have a stay-at-home parent (mother or father), especially in the early years of a child's life, most families can ill-afford the loss of wages involved. Efforts to enable more parents to spend more time at home with their children—such as family leave legislation—are often opposed by powerful constituencies as unwelcome government intervention. (Often, these are the same constituencies that are heard bemoaning the decline of the breadwinner/housewife couple and calling for the return to "traditional family values.")

In short, "family values" and capitalist values are often antithetical. Capitalists, write Hewlett and West,

> undermine family life because they fail to see the ways in which market values destroy family values. Committed as they are to free and unfettered markets, they forget that values are the "black hole of capitalism," to use Lester Thurow's memorable phrase. Indeed, market capitalism leans on some of the least attractive human traits—avarice, aggression, self-centeredness.[89]

Americans who identify themselves as conservatives are typically against both government regulation of the economy and government assistance to families. However, it is the scarcely regulated economy that so frequently disrupts families. As we saw in Chapter 2, the lack of government regulation does indeed make business more flexible and competitive; at the same time, it allows for social change to take place at such a rapid pace that millions of families have been, are, and will be devastated. For example, Edward Luttwak writes of the deleterious effects of deregulation in the airline industry,

> From a strictly economic point of view, the greater efficiency brought about by unregulated competition justifies all. But from a social point of view there is no such compensation. With its stable well-paid jobs, the regulated airline industry of the past enhanced the stability of employees' families and their communities as well as those of the aircraft industry that supplied the airlines.
>
> Today's chaotically unstable airlines are by contrast very disruptive, as they rapidly expand or drastically shrink over a matter of months or even weeks, as they abruptly shift "hubs" and maintenance bases from one place to another, each time hiring and firing employees in their constant maneuvering. It would be a nice bit of sociological research to calculate the number of divorces...caused by deregulation-induced economic stress on the families of airline employees.[90]

Of course, the airline industry is just one among thousands of industries and its employees among tens of millions workers (and parents) who have and/or will undergo the effects of "creative destruction" as the United States drags the world's economy toward an even more extreme mode of capitalism.

In the meantime, other democratic but less capitalist societies are mindful of the effect free markets can have on families, and they have enacted policies to prevent or reduce the kinds of family devastation that have been seen in the United States. While their economies may or may not be less competitive, their families are arguably much healthier. If unemployed, parents have generous unemployment compensation available to them. If employed, parents are more secure in their jobs and can rest assured their children are being well cared for in government-subsidized child-care centers. Further, government policies ensure that they have more time to spend with their children, especially when they are newborn or very young, without serious reductions in their incomes. These policies, far more than the policies found in the United States, do indeed seem to reflect "family values."

SAME-SEX MARRIAGE

One of the most divisive issues in American politics in recent years has been whether or not gay and lesbian couples should be allowed to marry. At issue is whether gay and lesbian unions should be recognized by law and accorded the same rights and privileges as heterosexual couples. For members of the gay community these rights and privileges amount to more than a matter of tax returns, employment benefits, and the rights of survivorship, but also to the respect of equals and, in the words of the Declaration of Independence, "Liberty and the pursuit of Happiness"—because for most

Americans growing up, a happy marriage is a goal for which, we are told, everyone should strive. Philosopher Martha Nussbaum writes,

> Marriage is both ubiquitous and central. All across our country, in every region, every social class, every race and ethnicity, every religion or non-religion, people get married. For many, if not most people, moreover, marriage is not a trivial matter. It is a key to the pursuit of happiness, something people aspire to—and keep aspiring to, again and again, even when their experience has been far from happy. To be told "You cannot get married" is thus to be excluded from one of the defining rituals of the American cycle of life.[91]

The exclusion of gays and lesbians from the defining ritual of marriage almost certainly seems to stem from centuries of prejudice against homosexuality in the Judeo-Christian world because few other explanations seem to apply. Ian Robertson writes, "The traditional sexual values of American society in general have their roots in a particular interpretation of ancient Judeo-Christian morality.... [The] Old Testament, which urges the faithful to 'be fruitful and multiply,' censures those who 'waste' their seed, and imposes severe penalties for non-reproductive sexual acts."[92]

Groups that are opposed to same-sex marriage are often forthright in acknowledging that their objections are based on their religious beliefs and usually argue that marriage is for the purpose of procreation. Indeed this is most likely the reason for the origin of marriage, but "nonprocreative" marriages have long been tolerated. No one objects to marriages of sterile people or of people too old to have children. Nussbaum notes,

> Impotence, lack of interest in sex, and refusal to allow intercourse may count as grounds for divorce, but they don't preclude marriage....Convicted felons, divorced parents who fail to pay child support, people with a record of domestic violence or emotional abuse, delinquent taxpayers, drug abusers, rapists, murderers, racists, anti-Semites, other bigots—all can marry if they choose. Indeed, they are held to have a fundamental constitutional right to do so—so long as they want to marry someone of the opposite sex.[93]

Other than religious grounds, alternative objections to same-sex marriage are rarely articulated in public forums. The battle over same-sex marriage, with one side wanting to see its religious beliefs enforced by law and the other side wanting the law to reflect its secular beliefs, is not dissimilar to ongoing strife in the Middle East between the Islamists and the secularists. In fact, the social constructionist is inclined to see the issues of same-sex marriage as a symbolic flashpoint between liberals and conservatives in the so-called culture wars. The modern usage of the term *culture wars* stems back to the 1960s when student protests, Vietnam, and civil rights marches were frequently in the headlines. But an example more similar to the same-sex marriage issue can be found in events leading to Prohibition in the 1920s.

At the turn of the twentieth century the white Anglo-Saxon Protestant majority comfortably held the reins of power in the United States. The coming decades saw a large flow of immigrants into the country, and most of these immigrants settled in the nation's large urban industrial centers. Many of these immigrants were Catholics from Ireland and Italy and many were Jews from Eastern Europe. The Protestants traditionally eschewed alcohol, while alcohol was well integrated into Catholic and Jewish traditions. According to Joseph Gusfield in his classic sociological analysis, the largely rural Protestants felt their lifestyles and their position of power were being threatened by the new immigrants and alcohol became symbolic of their differences. This cultural conflict resulted in the passage of the Volstead Act in 1919, outlawing the nonmedicinal consumption and distribution of alcohol. But since the law was rampantly and flagrantly violated, says Gusfield, this was more of a "symbolic victory," demonstrating that Protestants had so much power they could even make a part of Catholic and Jewish cultures illegal.[94]

Similarly, same-sex marriage has become symbolic of the differences between religious conservatives and secular liberals, especially of their different attitudes toward sexual diversity. As we will discuss in Chapter 5, it was not that long ago that large segments of the U.S. population thought that homosexuality was sinful, perverse, and and/or a manifestation of psychological pathology. It was not surprising that most gays and lesbians stayed in the "closet." In the aftermath of the civil rights movement, when many gays and lesbians started "coming out" and proudly declaring their sexual orientation, it was to the shock and horror of many religious conservatives. In recent decades, when civil rights protections have been extended to the gay and lesbian community, many on the religious right have objected, feeling threatened, feeling their lifestyles undervalued.

The extension of antidiscrimination laws and the extension of partner benefits in the workplace to gays and lesbians have been little victories in what may be seen as a larger war between religious conservatives and secular liberals. In this case, the symbolism of same-sex marriage probably does not escape either side in the debate; but when one side's objections are based almost exclusively on religion, it may well be fighting a losing battle in a nation constitutionally bound by the "establishment clause"—what most people know as the "separation of church and state."

History suggests a certain inevitability of victory for the cause of same-sex marriage. An easily discernable trend in United States' history is toward the extension of equal treatment to disenfranchised groups who organize and fight for their rights. Women and racial minorities have fought for and gained the rights to equal treatment under the law. Gays have fought for and won recognition and respect from large segments of the American population. As we will see in Chapter 5, in the 1970s the gay community successfully fought to have homosexuality dropped from psychiatry's handbook of mental disorders. They fought for and won the right to serve in the U.S. armed forces.

As this book is being written don't-ask-don't-tell has been repealed. The most recent surveys show that the majority of younger Americans favor the abolition of laws banning same-sex marriage and, reports the *Los Angeles Times,* "the gradual shift in public acceptance occurred as younger people entered the voting population and older ones died."[95] If the gay and lesbian community stay organized in their opposition to these laws—which they almost certainly will—then it is not a question of *if* they will succeed, but *when.*

APPLICATION: CHILDREN HAVING CHILDREN

President Bill Clinton once called teenage parenthood the nation's "most serious social problem." The problem was reignited when Jamie Lynn Spears, teen star on the Disney Channel, revealed her pregnancy and again when the daughter of Sarah Palin, the Republican vice presidential candidate in 2008, revealed hers. Indeed, teen parenthood is often assumed, without question, to be a negative social condition. Reactions to the concept of teen pregnancy and/or parenthood are so universally negative that its mention elicits an almost knee-jerk response, and its detractors rarely have to state what is wrong with it. Some think it is a principal cause of poverty, some are concerned that the mother (as it is usually the mother who is implicated) is not mature enough to raise a child, others argue that she is not physiologically ready, and still others are concerned because teen pregnancy is indicative of trends in teen sexual behavior that they find alarming. However, those who express alarm are rarely called upon to specify their concerns. British researchers Sally MacIntyre and Sarah Cunningham-Burley note similar concerns with the construction of the problem in the United Kingdom.

> This failure to specify why we should be worried often proves particularly irritating because it leads to a lack of precision about the nature of the perceived problem of adolescent pregnancy. It is often simply taken for granted that conceptions (or births or abortions) occurring in the teenage years are problematic. For whom they are problematic, and in what ways, are topics that are too infrequently discussed. But unless we are clear in our definition of the problem, how can we analyze its features or proper solutions to it?[96]

Teen pregnancy/parenthood did not become part of popular discussions of social problems until the early 1970s.[97] The issue did not suddenly become a matter of public concern because of increases in adolescent fertility at that time or just before that. In fact, rates of childbirth among teenagers were declining between 1957 and 1983.[98] The construction of the phenomenon as a problem persisted; in 1993, Annette Lawson and Deborah Rhode commented, "Contrary to much alarmist rhetoric, neither the United States nor the United Kingdom is experiencing an epidemic of 'children having children.' The frequency of teenage childbirth has varied considerably over time and culture, and current levels are by no means unprecedented."[99]

Yet, popular concern had been unprecedented. Thus, because of the lack of correspondence between public perceptions and objective realities, the problem is particularly amenable to a critical constructionist analysis. Such an analysis starts with the fact that teen parenthood has not always been held in such disregard and goes on to examine the reasons, other than the ostensible ones, that account for its recent status as a social problem.

Many people's concerns about teen pregnancy have to do with their moral objections to premarital sex. Though proscriptions against premarital sex have always been prevalent in American culture, the historical evidence from the seventeenth and eighteenth centuries indicates a certain tolerance for premarital sex and teenage pregnancy as long as the couple was willing and financially able to marry. In the latter half of the eighteenth century, it is estimated, almost 30 percent of first births were premaritally conceived.[100] At the end of the nineteenth century, 23 percent of the babies born in the United States were conceived out of wedlock, mostly to young, urban, working-class women who were less subject to the oversight of their family or community. (To the extent that there was opprobrium, most of the wrath of family and community was focused on women who engaged in premarital sex, not their male partners.) Rates of out-of-wedlock births were also high among lower-class black families, especially among tenant farming families for whom child labor was an economic asset. These children were cared for by extensive kinship networks, a system that still survives in parts of the black community today.[101]

In addition to the concern about premarital sex, many people object to the notion of teenagers bearing children, whether married or not. However, this too, is a relatively new concern. Teenage childbearing has been common throughout American history and was far more common in the 1940s and 1950s, for example, than it is today. Of course, most of the teenage mothers were married; yet they experienced far less stigma than the married teenage mothers of today. Popular constructions of teen pregnancy/parenthood, then, include prevailing notions of childhood ("children having children"), youth, adolescence, and the appropriate age at which people can engage in sexual relations and begin families. It is important to note that the vast majority of teenage mothers are in their late teens: two-thirds of them are 18 or 19 and only a small fraction are below 16.[102] It should also be noted that such notions of age-appropriate behavior are themselves social constructions. "The appropriate age for sexual relations and parenthood has always been a matter of cultural definition, and in the United States it has varied considerably across time, region, class, race, ethnicity, and gender."[103] Diana Pearce writes,

> In the strictly physiological sense, "children having children" is an oxymoron. In fact, in our national history and in much of the world today, marriage and childbirth for teenage women are the norm. Thus the definition of teenagers who become pregnant as children reflects a cultural construction of the ending of childhood that is considerably later than the actual physical transition.[104]

If not in terms of physiological maturity, then in what ways do popular constructions suggest teenage mothers are different from older mothers? Many associate teenage pregnancy with unplanned pregnancy. Yet, about three-fourths of all unplanned pregnancies are to women beyond their teens.[105] Another common perception associates teen parenthood with out-of-wedlock births. Yet, 69 percent of births out of wedlock are to women over 20.[106] As McIntyre and Cunningham-Burley point out, popular constructions do not recognize that

> many women over 20 have unplanned or unwanted pregnancies and may be unmarried or unsupported. It is also worth pointing out that no one expresses much concern about older mothers—for example those having children when they are 35 or 40—even though they may face obstetric and social hazards and may often be unsupported, and even though the rates of pregnancy among these age groups are increasing.[107]

Popular constructions also question the motives of a teenager who decides to have her baby, while they do not question the motives of her older counterpart, even though they might be the same motives. MacIntyre and Cunningham-Burley write,

> Of the first it is often said that her motives...are suspect because she seeks an object to love and to return her love, that she desires to achieve adult status, or that she wants to gain independence from her parents. But a 26-year-old might have identical motives, which in her case are taken to be normal and possibly admirable.[108]

It is also believed that the teenager will have fewer supports available to help her with her child than her older counterpart. Yet, she is more likely to be living at home with her parents than her older counterpart, and more government-assistance programs are available to her than to her older counterpart. The implication of most constructions about teen motherhood is that the teenager will live to regret her choice of having a baby, but there is little empirical evidence to suggest that this is the case any more for the teen mother than for her older counterpart.[109]

Race and Class

Much of the attention focused on teen parenthood emphasizes its occurrence within the black community. The media portray teen motherhood as largely a problem of the black community. Ann Phoenix writes,

> The issue of teen motherhood provides an excellent example of the intersection of the negative constructions of teenage mothers with those of people of color. Although teenage motherhood is stigmatized generally...concern about black teenage mothers is expressed more frequently and is often more heightened than that about their white peers.[110]

Indeed, teen motherhood does occur disproportionately in the black community. However, there are far more white teen mothers than black teen mothers in the United States, and the rate of teen motherhood is increasing much faster among whites.[111] The rates among white women in the United States are also far higher than they are among white women in most other industrialized countries.[112]

Singling out black single mothers became a popular exercise in the 1960s, with the release of Daniel Patrick Moynihan's report blaming much of the plight of the black poor on the increased incidence of female-headed families in the black community. Poverty is indeed one of the more frequently cited objections to teen motherhood. The problem, as it is popularly constructed, is that if a teenager decides to have a baby, she is forgoing education and training that would otherwise allow her to achieve financial success. Teen motherhood, especially black teen motherhood, usually comes to the attention of the public when calls for welfare reform heat up. Welfare critics charge that teenagers are having babies just so that they can live on the dole, thus attacking the motives of teen mothers and accusing the welfare system of encouraging teen motherhood. There is little evidence substantiating these claims, however. In fact, teen motherhood rates are frequently higher in the states that provide the least amount of public assistance.[113]

The relationship between poverty, teen motherhood, and race is far from obvious. However, to the extent that it can be delineated, a good deal of research indicates that being black in the United States increases one's likelihood of being poor and that being poor increases the likelihood of teen motherhood. "Teens from low-income or poor families," writes Jane Mauldon, "…are nine times more likely than teens from higher-income families to have a child."[114] As for teen mothers forgoing their education in favor of having a child, studies indicate that a great many of them dropped out of school *before* becoming pregnant.[115] In other words, teen motherhood was not the cause but often the result of forgoing an education, and the young woman's inability to succeed in school may explain both her decision to have a child while in her teens as well as her remaining poor into her later adulthood. Among poor teenagers who have a child while still in school, the odds of finishing high school or obtaining a GED are comparable to those of poor teenage women who do not have children.[116]

Further, if a young woman from a low-income family does indeed drop out of school—"forgo" her education—to have a baby, research indicates that she will likely be in no worse shape in her adulthood than her peer who delayed maternity. Joseph Hotz, Susan Williams McElroy, and Seth Sanders compared poor women who had babies in their teens to an interesting control group, poor women who had miscarriages in their teens and had their first child at the age of 20 or 21; they found that the former group worked more, earned more, and received less public assistance in their later adulthood than the women who delayed maternity.[117] This seemingly paradoxical finding is explained fairly easily. The poor women who had children in their teens were likely still living at home and still linked to a social support network that could help them raise their children. On the other hand, the poor women who delayed maternity were less likely to be living at home, more distant from such a support network, and therefore, less able to leave their children to go to work and more in need of public assistance. In other words, having their children in their teen years may actually be adaptive for low-income women, especially poor black women. Mauldon writes,

> While by most people's standards few of the teenagers who become parents are well equipped to raise a child, these women might not be in a much better position if they waited. These young women probably have greater claim on familial resources (however limited) if they are teenage parents than if they give birth in their twenties. They may also have greater claim on social resources, in the form of specialized education programs for teenage parents, health care, or counseling. The employment picture for them could also favor childbearing: they probably cannot find good jobs as teenagers, but by the time they are in their mid-twenties, when employers might be more inclined to hire them, they will have completed their childbearing and their children will be in school full time.[118]

Frank Furstenburg, who has studied teen pregnancy extensively, writes, "the advantages of delaying parenthood are not so great for black [women]. . . . The cruel fact is that for blacks delaying childbearing has relatively low payoff. They are damned if they do and damned if they don't."[119] He further argues that "[d]iminishing teen pregnancy is not, as claimed by many social scientists and policymakers, the silver bullet that, if properly aimed at the right target population, could make a huge dent in the level of poverty and disadvantage in our nation."[120]

The "obvious" drawbacks of teen motherhood become less than obvious from the viewpoint of critical constructionism. As we can see, a critical constructionist analysis illustrates the fact that many of the assumed disadvantages of teen pregnancy are often exaggerated or unsubstantiated. Nevertheless, the way the problem of teen motherhood has been popularly constructed serves to reaffirm the ideology of abundant opportunity in the United States and, in doing so, remains an effective scapegoat for the problems of the poor, especially the black poor, blaming them rather than the social structure for their impoverishment. This is not to suggest that there are no drawbacks to teen motherhood or that teens should be encouraged to have children, but such an analysis does challenge us to reconsider where this problem is placed on our list of priorities. If poverty is more often the cause rather than the effect of teen motherhood, then perhaps poverty and its structural causes should be placed higher on that list.

SUMMARY

Popular constructions of the breakdown of the modern-day family are based upon idealized impressions of the family of the past. Yet, there has never been a "golden age" of the American family. Even in colonial times, people were bemoaning the decline of the family. While divorce rates are quite high today, in the past, when divorces were rare, it was not uncommon for people to be trapped in loveless marriages, to be unofficially separated, or to opt for the "poor man's divorce," separation. Today, those who are the most alarmed about the state of the family often identify the "working mother" as the source of the problem. Yet, the breadwinner/housewife form of family is a relatively new pattern that did not emerge until the Industrial Revolution; and when it did emerge, it was common only in the middle and upper classes and made possible only through the labor of the lower classes.

The breadwinner/housewife form of family reached its apotheosis in the 1950s, following World War II. The baby boomers—that is, many of today's parents, writers, politicians, and political pundits—grew up on a steady diet of idealized images of the 1950s family, which made up a substantial proportion of television programming. Those images inform a good deal of the rhetoric in current debates about the family. References to the "traditional family" often allude to this form of family. The family of the 1950s, however, was far from traditional. It in fact represented a setback in a long-standing and continuous progression in the status of women. Women were marrying younger, having more babies, and giving up career ambitions; and the educational gap between men and women began to widen. Women were suddenly supposed to find all of their happiness within the confines of the family. Many did not. Of those who did not, their frustration was indicated by the new psychiatric diagnosis of "housewife's blight" and by the thousands upon thousands of women being prescribed antianxiety drugs. When the divorce rates did increase in the 1960s, "traditionalists" often failed to recognize that a substantial proportion of those couples getting divorced were the ones who had gotten married in the 1950s.

The family of the 1950s was also far from traditional in that it was very heavily subsidized by government monies. Traditionalists—who proclaim the values of independence and self-sufficiency and who are often the fiercest opponents of welfare—also fail to recognize that the family of the 1950s was made possible by some of the most generous government subsidies in U.S. history. The GI Bill enabled World War II veterans to establish themselves, marry early, support their wives and children, and achieve the American Dream with relative ease.

Since the 1950s, married women have taken jobs outside the home in substantial and increasing numbers. A series of recessions, wage stagnation, and a rising cost of living have made it necessary for families to have both husband and wife working in order to maintain a middle-class lifestyle. So, while the traditionalists argue that mothers should be at home with their kids and not out working, the lost income would represent far more sacrifice today than it would have in the 1950s.

While "family values" are often proclaimed to be the country's first priority when election time rolls around, the United States has fewer policies and programs to support the family than a great many countries around the world. Many other countries have far more generous laws providing for maternity leave (usually paid), and some even provide for paternity leave (often paid). Relative to other industrialized countries, the United States also ranks poorly in the provision of child-care services. As a result, many poor single mothers feel the need to stay at home with their children, and many middle-class children receive inferior child care.

When the family is identified as a serious social problem, children are usually considered the most important casualties. Of those problems facing children, the critical constructionist is most concerned with those associated with poverty. While Americans often speak of children as "our most precious resource," the United States is willing to tolerate child poverty rates that would be unconscionable in Western Europe and other parts of the globe. The belief that individuals are to be blamed for their poverty and not the social system accounts for the American tolerance of high poverty levels. Yet few, if any, actually believe that children are to be blamed for their poverty. Minimal efforts to resolve this contradiction are to be found in U.S. social and economic policies.

From child poverty and a lack of social supports for poor families, we turned our attention to the issue of same-sex marriage. Most of the opposition to the legalization of marriage is found among Christian conservatives and the issue has become a symbolic flashpoint in the so-called culture wars. But the trend in American history is toward equality and with the gay and lesbian community achieving success in many recent battles, history seems to be on the side of victory in this one.

One popular method of blaming poverty on individuals has lain in the identification of teenage pregnancy as a social problem, especially when it occurs in the black community. Teen pregnancy has only relatively recently been constructed as a social problem. Today, it has such negative connotations that its detractors rarely feel compelled to say what is wrong with it; but it is generally regarded as irresponsible behavior that leads to the diminution of the mother's life chances and to the perpetuation of poverty, especially within the black community. Research, however, reveals that poverty is more the cause of teen pregnancy than the effect. Further, there is evidence indicating that teen pregnancy may well be an adaptive behavior for poor women.

In summary, throughout this chapter, a critical constructionist analysis reveals numerous inconsistencies in the way problems of the family are popularly conceived. Popular constructions about the current state of the family often work from false assumptions about the history of the family. Popular constructions usually place blame on individuals, whereas there are grander social and economic forces accounting for many of the problems facing the family. In placing blame on individuals, popular constructions reinforce the status quo and offer inadequate remedies relative to the remedies found in countries that implement policy based on a human capital philosophy.

Discussion Questions

1. What is meant by the assertion in this chapter that the family of the 1950s was perhaps the most heavily subsidized generation of families in American history?

2. Could the U.S. government develop more family-friendly policies than it has? And would the costs of such policies outweigh the benefits?

3. If it was agreed that teen pregnancy is a serious problem in the United States, what policies or programs can you think of that would minimize the incidence and/or the deleterious effects of teen pregnancy?

5

Crime and Deviance

O f all the social problems considered in this and other texts, crime and deviance consistently rank among the more serious in the minds of most Americans. Because we are constantly being bombarded with images and accounts of murder, random violence, drug abuse, and various other signs of "moral decay," millions of us alternate between feelings of concern, fear, disgust, and outrage. As we shall see in this chapter, however, those feelings often stand in the way of a sociological understanding of crime and deviance.

UNIVERSALITY AND RELATIVITY

Crime is certainly not new to the United States, nor is it unique to the United States. Crime is universal. All societies have had, do have, and will always have crime. Therefore, according to Emile Durkheim, crime is not a sign of social pathology. That is, crime is normal, and it is not an indication that there is something wrong with a society. Furthermore, since crime occurs in all societies, Durkheim postulated, it must be functional; it must serve some purpose.[1] Besides providing society with millions of jobs—as law enforcement officers, defense attorneys, prosecuting attorneys and their assistants, judges, bailiffs, court recorders, prison guards, counselors, people who build the prisons and the courts, probation and parole officers, people who sell insurance, those who make and sell security devices, criminologists, crime writers and their publishers, and the list goes on—crime also provides members of society with a common purpose. Crime, though disruptive, also has a unifying effect, uniting society against a common enemy. Crime and deviance provide the opportunity for mutual moral outrage. Rarely, in fact, do social problems produce such a unifying effect.

Crime and deviance are not only universal but also relative. Conceptions of crime and deviance vary from time to time and culture to culture. Behavior that is normative in one culture may well be deviant in another. For example, it is often stated that the incest taboo is universal. Though there is truth to this statement, it is also misleading. It is true that all societies have *an* incest taboo. However, different societies define incest differently. Hence, some societies may permit sexual relations between certain family members that are prohibited in other societies and vice versa. Likewise, behavior that is normative at one time may be deviant at another time in the same culture. For example, before the turn of the century in the United States, large segments of the population regularly consumed opiates (derivatives of the opium poppy). Shortly after the turn of the century, these drugs became strictly regulated and their consumption came to be considered deviant.

The relativity of crime and deviance suggests that there is nothing inherent in an act that makes it "wrong," "criminal," or "deviant." Instead, sociologists emphasize that the "wrongfulness" of an act is extrinsic to that act. That is, whether or not an act is considered wrongful, criminal, or deviant depends upon the norms of the society and the perceptions of the audience, not upon the evil that resides in the act or upon the harm caused by the act.[2]

EXAMPLES OF THE RELATIVITY OF CRIME AND DEVIANCE

Homosexual Behavior

Not long ago, homosexual behavior was vigorously condemned in the United States. Until the 1960s the subject was rarely mentioned in polite conversation or in the media. When it was recognized, it was generally seen as a sign of moral depravity or mental illness. So deviant was homosexuality that it was extremely rare that an individual would openly admit to his or her own homosexual orientation. Today, while there are still those who would like to return to previous times, most people would agree that homosexuality is far less deviant than it was in the not-so-distant past. Most of us are aware of friends, relatives, or public figures who have openly acknowledged their homosexuality and some of us may have done the same. This marked change in public attitudes toward homosexuality—the fact that homosexuality is far less stigmatized today than it was, for example, in the 1950s—illustrates the temporal relativity of deviance.

Homosexuality also provides a very good example of the cross-cultural relativity of deviance. Though the deviant status of homosexuality has lessened considerably over the past few decades in the United States, there are other societies in which homosexual behavior is quite normal. In their classic study of sexual behavior in preindustrial societies, Clellan Ford and Frank Beach write, "Our own society [the United States] disapproves of any form of homosexual behavior for males and females of all ages. In this it differs from the majority of human societies. Some peoples resemble us in this respect, but a larger number condone or even encourage homosexuality for at least some members of the population."[3] In some societies—the Siberian Chukchee, for example—the homosexual may assume the role of shaman, a religious figure who enjoys considerable power and prestige. Among the Siwans of Africa and the Keraki of New Guinea, boys routinely engage in anal intercourse. Likewise, in some Latin American countries, such as Brazil and Nicaragua, where machismo is highly valued, it does not compromise a male's manhood to play the insertor role in same-sex anal intercourse.[4]

Thus, the cross-cultural and historical relativity of the deviant status of homosexuality suggests that there is something external to the behavior—something in the culture—that makes it deviant, rather than something inherent in the behavior itself.

Drug Consumption

Another example of the relativity of crime and deviance can be seen in the variable attitudes and laws regarding the consumption of different mind-altering drugs across time and across cultures. Today, most Americans take the regulation of various drugs for granted. Few people question whether such drugs are inherently harmful; therefore, few question the right of the government to restrict them. However, such attitudes did not come to represent the majority of Americans until the twentieth century.

Before the turn of the last century, the consumption of mind-altering substances in the United States and in Europe was widespread and generally accepted. Opiates were especially popular, advertised in newspapers and available over the counter at the general store. There were likely hundreds of thousands of addicts.[5] In Britain, opium was rubbed on the gums of babies to ease teething pain. Morphine was used in the treatment of pain. In the United States, thousands of Civil War veterans were addicted to it, having had their war injuries treated with morphine. Various patent medicines were laced with opium. One in particular, laudanum, was especially popular among upper-class women. Also, during the latter part of the nineteenth century, preparations from the coca leaf (from which cocaine is derived) achieved some popularity in the United States and Europe. At first, it was mixed in wine, and its developer received a medal of appreciation from Pope Leo XIII; later, another coca preparation was developed, and it was named Coca-Cola.[6] (Eventually, of course, the coca had to be removed from the cola, and it was replaced by a more socially and legally acceptable drug, caffeine.)

All of this drug consumption went on with very little negative attention from the press or the public. Writes Troy Duster,

> From 1865 to 1900, then, addiction to narcotics was relatively widespread.... In proportion to the population, addiction was probably eight times more prevalent then than now.... It is remarkable, therefore, that addiction is regarded today as a problem of far greater moral, legal, and social significance than it was then.[7]

With regard to the cultural relativity of attitudes and laws affecting drug consumption, there is surely no shortage of data. The consumption of mind-altering drugs is normative behavior in many, if not most, societies throughout the world. Such drugs often play an integral role in the performance of important rituals in these societies. For example, in the United

States, wine is consumed during the Catholic mass and almost all weddings involve the provision and consumption of alcohol. Peyote, a hallucinogenic drug, plays a critical role in religious rituals among some Native Americans in the western United States and Mexico. Another hallucinogen, *ebene,* is used in the rituals of the Yanomamo Indians of northern Brazil. The Rastafarians of Jamaica consider marijuana to be an important part of their religious experience. While alcohol is strictly forbidden in Yemen, consumption of the stimulant *qat* is quite popular. And coca leaves are appreciated for their stimulating qualities among numerous peoples in the Andes.[8]

Since drug-consumption patterns vary so tremendously across cultures, it is not surprising to find considerable variations in the way societies regulate drug consumption. In some countries—Malaysia and China, for example—drug traffickers may be executed. In the Netherlands, coffee shops are allowed to sell small quantities of marijuana and hashish. In Liverpool, England, a clinic has been established where drug addicts can receive prescriptions for the drug of their choice—for example, heroin or crack cocaine—and redeem them at the local pharmacy. In the United States, the official stance on illegal drugs is quite punitive relative to other Western industrialized countries. In the 1980s, the American incarceration rate doubled, becoming one of the highest in the world, largely due to the "war on drugs."

The Significance of Relativity

The fact that crime and deviance are relative to time and culture is extremely significant to the sociologist because it demonstrates the importance of history and social structure to the understanding of these social problems. Historical changes in attitudes toward homosexuality and drug consumption suggest important changes in institutions, values, beliefs, and norms—all of which make up a social structure and its culture.

Changes in the deviant status of homosexuality, for example, were the result of changes in social structure and culture. During the civil rights movement of the 1950s and 1960s, momentous changes took place in society's institutions, values, beliefs, and norms. Disenfranchised minorities were demonstrating, writing, marching, boycotting, and rioting, demanding equal rights. Institutions were forced to become more inclusive of women and racial and ethnic minorities. Attitudes, values, and stereotypes began to change. People's beliefs about the differences and abilities of minority groups began to change. Gays and lesbians were among those organizing to demand equal rights.

In addition to the civil rights movement, values, beliefs, and norms with regard to sexual behavior and sexuality began to change. People, especially younger people, became more free and open with the expression of their sexuality. Together, the civil rights movement and the "sexual revolution" led to increasing tolerance and increasing demands for tolerance. The most probable turning point in the struggle for the acceptance of gay and lesbian lifestyles in the United States was the Stonewall Riot on June 28, 1969, in New York City. A few days later, the Gay Liberation Front was founded, and ever since, more and more gays and lesbians have come out of the closet to fight for inclusion.

The conflict theorist would emphasize that another lesson to be learned from the relativity—especially the historical relativity—of crime and deviance is that these phenomena, as well as all other social problems, are very political in nature. Politics is the arena in which different groups fight to uphold their own interests. Gays and lesbians entered this arena to fight against discrimination and for their acceptance into mainstream society. As late as 1972, homosexuality was classified by the American Psychiatric Association (APA) as a psychiatric disorder. Gay groups, including the Gay Psychiatric Association, organized and entered the arena to fight this classification. They lobbied the APA's leadership, and they picketed and caused general mayhem at the annual meetings of the APA. Eventually, under considerable pressure, the APA took a vote among its members as to whether homosexuality should be dropped from the official classification manual. With a vote of 58 percent to 37 percent, the classification was deleted.[9] This series of events provides a prime example of the political nature of deviance. Thanks to the political maneuverings of gay activists, strides were made in making homosexuality less deviant.

Likewise, the laws that eventually criminalized various types of drug consumption were the result of political processes. Among the first antidrug laws passed in the United States was the law prohibiting opium smoking passed in California in the 1870s. Although there were various forms of opiates used throughout the state, smoking opium was done almost exclusively by the Chinese immigrants of the time. It has been argued that this legislation was aimed primarily at the Chinese (as were many other legislative efforts in California at the time). Chinese immigrants competed with the white majority for jobs working on the railroads. The white majority was able to use the new law to persecute their Chinese competitors. In other words, the white majority entered the political arena and fought for the exclusion of the Chinese from the labor market, and they won.[10]

This series of events set a precedent for much of the drug legislation that was to follow. That is, much of the legislation was preceded by public images and debate that associated the target drug with a given minority that, at the time, was the object of public scorn. Addressing this historical trend David Musto writes,

> The most passionate support for legal prohibition of narcotics has been associated with fear of a given drug's effect on a specific minority. Certain drugs were dreaded because they seemed to undermine essential social restrictions which kept these groups under control: cocaine was supposed to enable blacks to withstand bullets which would kill normal persons and to stimulate sexual assault. Fear that smoking opium facilitated sexual contact between Chinese

and white Americans was also a factor in its total prohibition. Chicanos in the Southwest were believed to be incited to violence by smoking marijuana. Heroin was linked in the 1920s with a turbulent age group: adolescents in reckless and promiscuous urban gangs. Alcohol was associated with immigrants crowding into large and corrupt cities. In each instance, use of a particular drug was attributed to an identifiable and threatening minority group.[11]

In other words, according to the conflict theorist, antidrug legislation resulted when representatives of the white majority entered the political arena and fought for and won control over the offending minority group.

In the more recent past, crack cocaine was of particular concern to the criminal justice system and the public imagination. It was associated with poor, young, urban black males, whom the press and the public associated with much of the street violence in urban centers. Consequently, whites stepped into the political arena to fight for what they believed to be their safety. For decades, sentences for crack cocaine were far more severe than they were for powder cocaine, which is largely associated with upper- and upper-middle-class whites. An understanding of history and social structure helps to account for these differences.

Thus, the critical constructionist asks, Why is it that alcohol and tobacco are viewed benignly relative to heroin and crack when, in fact, they are relatively more harmful, both physiologically and societally? Alcohol use is implicated in thousands of murders and thousands of drunken driving deaths each year. Tobacco use is implicated in hundreds of thousands of lung disease deaths every year. There are tens of millions of alcohol and tobacco addicts. All of these figures arguably add up to more harm than the combined effects of heroin, crack and methamphetamine.[12] Yet, heroin, crack and methamphetamine are illegal while alcohol and tobacco are not. The reason, states the critical constructionist, is that the advocates of alcohol and tobacco have more political power than the advocates of heroin and crack. Alcohol and tobacco are the drugs of choice among those in power, and the alcohol and tobacco industries have more political sway than the heroin and crack industries.

The Case of Marijuana

Most of the experts agree that marijuana is the least harmful of the drugs mentioned above, including alcohol, tobacco, cocaine, and heroin. Yet, in terms of severity, the penalties for possession, growing, or distributing marijuana approach those for heroin and cocaine-related offenses and sometimes exceed those for rape and murder. Most of us have heard about successful efforts to decriminalize marijuana, stories about the police "looking the other way," and stories about celebrities or their children being punished lightly when they were caught with the drug. However, in many parts of the country it would be foolhardy to assume that smoking marijuana involves minimal risks with regard to the criminal justice system. Arrests for marijuana offenses increased from 327,000 in 1997 to over 850,000 in 2007. The FBI reports 46 percent of all arrests for drug violations in 2010 were for marijuana possession.[13] Penalties can be severe. For example, possession of less than an ounce of marijuana is punishable by up to 20 years in Louisiana. Journalist Eric Schlosser, author of *Reefer Madness,* reports a number of marijuana cases that resulted in severe penalties. One such case is reported as follows:

> Douglas Lamar Gray purchased a pound of marijuana from a government informer at an Econo Lodge in Morgan County, Alabama. After paying $900 for the pot, which seemed like a real bargain, Gray was arrested, charged with trafficking in cannabis, tried, convicted, fined $25,000, sentenced to life without parole, and sent to a maximum security prison.[14]

Many states provide sentences from decades to life in prison for distributing marijuana, and possession of more than an ounce can be taken as evidence of intent to distribute. In Virginia, a defendant can be imprisoned for up to 30 years for cultivating a single marijuana plant.[15] "On top of fines, incarceration and forfeiture [of property]," writes Schlosser,

> a convicted marijuana offender may face the revocation or denial of more than 460 federal benefits, including student loans, small-business loans, professional licenses, and farm subsidies. Americans convicted of a marijuana felony, even if they are disabled, may no longer receive federal welfare payments or food stamps. Convicted murderers, rapists, and child molesters, however, remain eligible for such benefits.[16]

Despite the severity of the penalties that are dispensed for marijuana offenses, the evidence of its harmfulness is sketchy at best. In 1972, President Nixon established the National Commission of Marijuana and Drug Abuse to examine the problem. The commission noted the importance of "desymbolizing" the drug and, much to Nixon's displeasure, recommended that marijuana be decriminalized. The commission argued that "[c]onsidering the range of social concerns in contemporary America, marijuana does not, in our considered judgment, rank very high."[17]

The commission's effort to desymbolize marijuana in 1972 closely resembles a critical constructionist approach to the problem. The commission was implying that the severity that many attached to the problem of marijuana did not correspond to the objective effects of the drug but could indeed be better explained by what the drug symbolized to its opponents. In the 1920s, marijuana symbolized the "invasion" of Mexican immigrants into the country, and it was also associated with the controversial new form of music called "jazz." In the 1960s, the drug came to symbolize the "radical liberalism" of American youth. Many young people, especially college students, grew their hair long, protested in favor of civil rights, protested against the Vietnam War, and smoked marijuana. Many who had a stake in the established order were appalled by these activities. The police often reacted violently to the student protests, and lawmakers reacted by strengthening the laws against the drugs that were associated with the student movement. Following the commission's report, many of the drug laws were relaxed. However, in 1980, Ronald Reagan was elected president, and his conservative platform blamed many of society's problems on the "liberal excesses" of the 1960s and 1970s. A major plank in his platform was his war on drugs. That war made little distinction between marijuana and the "harder" drugs because marijuana symbolized the liberal excesses of the past and was, consequently, viewed as just as serious a social problem as the drugs that produced more deleterious effects on the mind and body of the user. One might have expected the laws against marijuana to be relaxed under the Clinton administration, but Clinton was on the defensive because he had admitted to smoking marijuana (but not inhaling); he could not risk being associated with the liberal excesses of the past by appearing "soft" on drugs. Thus, the enforcement of tough antimarijuana laws continued unabated, as it does to this day.

THE CULTURAL PRODUCTION OF KNOWLEDGE ABOUT CRIME

The social problems perspective emphasizes that crime constitutes a social problem primarily because the public defines it as such, while most people are inclined to think that crime is a social problem because it is harmful and there is so much of it. Citizens are mostly concerned with street crime or stranger-to-stranger violence. Despite recent declines in crime rates, relative to most other industrialized societies in the world, the United States does indeed have high rates of violent crime, especially homicide. However, it should be noted, first, that crime rates are very difficult to measure and, second, that public concern about crime and crime rates are not directly related.

Measurements of Crime and Deviance

Crime and deviance are difficult to measure because their perpetrators want to keep their activities secret. The "official" criminal statistics are generally considered to be the *Uniform Crime Reports*, published every year by the FBI. This is a compilation of reports from thousands of local law enforcement agencies across the country. Generally speaking, the crime rates are comprised of those crimes that are reported to the police. They do not include the so-called *dark figure of crime*: those crimes that do not come to the attention of the authorities. Some types of crime are more likely to be reported to the police than others. For example, murder rates are highly reliable because when a homicide occurs it is almost always reported to the police (i.e., the dark figure is minuscule). However, drug offenses are less likely to be reported because they usually involve willing participants (hence, the dark figure would be quite large). Likewise, certain crimes may be more likely to be reported at certain times or in certain places than in others. For example, a date rape that occurred in the 1950s was probably less likely to be reported than one that occurs today because in the 1950s the victim was more likely to be blamed for her own victimization than she is today. By the same token, a rape occurring in a rural area may be less likely to be reported than one occurring in an urban area because in the rural area the victim and the rapist are more likely to be known by everyone in the community and each one's guilt or innocence may become a source of contention throughout the community for years to come.

All such factors that affect the "reportability" of crime affect the dark figure of crime. Consequently, it is very difficult to interpret official crime rates—so difficult that rising crime rates may actually be a good sign with regard to the crime problem. Rather than indicating that more crimes are being committed, rising crime rates may indicate that the crimes that are being committed are more likely to be reported than they were in the past.

Most criminologists would agree that the best way to analyze the *Uniform Crime Reports* is in conjunction with *victimization surveys*. The largest and most renowned of these are conducted by the Bureau of Justice Statistics, in which tens of thousands of people are selected randomly every year and interviewed about whether they have been victimized by crime in the past year. Criminologists generally consider victimization surveys to be more accurate indicators of crime trends because they take into account both crimes that are reported to the police and those that are not. Consequently, these surveys show that a good deal more crime occurs than is indicated by the *Uniform Crime Reports*. But both measures show that crime has been decreasing over the last decade.

The early to mid-1990s saw an explosive increase in media coverage of crime. One of the major networks regularly began its evening news with a screen behind the anchor reading "America the Violent"; another began its evening coverage with a screen reading "America under Siege." In 1993, for example, the three major television networks broadcast 1,632 crime segments on their evening news shows, up from 785 the previous year—more than a 100 percent increase. There had been no corresponding increase in crime during those years. In fact, the crime rate actually decreased between 1992 and 1993. In 1992, 104 segments focused on homicide; this figure rose to 329 the next year—more than a threefold increase.[18] Meanwhile, the homicide rates fluctuated only slightly upward from 9.3 to 9.5 (per 100,000 population) between 1992 and 1993. Crime had been constructed into a full-blown social problem. The public had been led to believe that crime was exploding in the United States, even though homicide rates were relatively high, there had been no corresponding increase in measurements of crime. This was not the first time that constructions of the crime problem were grossly misleading, and the critical constructionist remains circumspect whenever the public is whipped into a frenzy over the problem of crime. As we will see in our discussion of crime scares later, the exaggeration of crime problems usually serves some interests other than the public interest.

Images of Crime and Justice from the Media

While most people have little or no personal experience of serious criminal victimization,[19] they nevertheless are often very fearful and have some strong opinions about the nature of crime in the United States and what to do about it. If the fear of crime does not come from personal victimization, then it must come from other sources. It may be that those who are fearful know others who have been personally victimized or, quite possibly, that they have been exposed to a steady regimen of television news coverage, cop shows, and crime dramas.

It has long been recognized that crime news sells. Not only does it sell, but it is cheap to produce. Local news stations often make the most of crime news. Steven Beschloss writes,

> Television stations, armed with polls that place drugs and crime at the top of people's fears, are feeding the perceived public appetite for these stories. And as the federal government has pushed its war on drugs, news organizations— hungry for ratings and determined to cover the news for less—often provide a willing outlet and heighten the fevered pitch.[20]

All that is really needed is a camera on the scene; the gorier the images, the better they sell (as the old news adage goes, "If it bleeds, it leads"). Today, with the video camera and the help of a police scanner and perhaps a helicopter, news coverage of crime has become more and more immediate and graphic. The news emphasizes violent crime when, by far, the most frequent crimes are property offenses. With crime taking up a large portion of TV programming,[21] the viewer can easily get the sense that violent crime is skyrocketing and is taking place everywhere, all of the time, in spite of the fact that violent crime has been trending downward for the past decade. Combined with the oftentimes alarmist rhetoric of the newscasters, the public can come to feel that it is under siege by violent, ruthless criminals.

News coverage is usually so immediate that the viewer has little chance to understand the context of the crime. The criminal incident is the news; the reasons for the crime are not newsworthy. A crime is news as, or shortly after, it occurs. An understanding of why the crime took place usually does not come about until after the crime has lost its newsworthiness. Random violence is emphasized, and a lack of context makes almost any violent crime seem like a random and senseless act, which makes it seem all the more threatening to the general public and makes a punitive response seem all the more appropriate.

"Reality-based" cop shows were among the most popular shows on television during the 1980s and '90s when sentencing got more punitive and when U.S. prison populations began to grow at unprecedented rates. These shows tend to emphasize violent and drug-related crimes. What many in the audience may not realize is that, despite their "reality," they depict inaccurate accounts of unrepresentative cases. The problem lies in their selectivity. It is best to think of what is portrayed in such shows as a sample of what goes on in the real world of crime. In fact, that is how these shows present themselves.

However, all social scientists would agree that the most important feature of a sample is that it be representative of the world that it is supposed to portray. The best way to ensure a representative sample is through random selection. The images presented in these shows are far from randomly selected. They are selected, first, on the basis of their entertainment value. Another important consideration is that the images shown do not present the police in a bad light. These shows depend upon the cooperation of the authorities, and their producers must keep in mind that if the police are not presented in a positive light, then they will not get their cooperation for future broadcasts.

The cases selected in reality-based crime shows do not represent the real world of crime, nor do the images even represent the cases that are selected. Much of the reality of crime is edited from reality-based shows. The following was written by Debra Seagal, a former story analyst for the now-defunct show *American Detective*:

> I'm developing a perverse fascination with the magic exercised in our TV production workshop. Once our supervising producer has picked the cases that might work for the show, the "stories" are turned over to an editor. Within a few weeks, the finished videos emerge from the editing room with "problems" fixed, chronologies reshuffled, and, when necessary, images and sound bites clipped and replaced by older filler footage from unrelated cases.[22]

In an article entitled "Tales from the Cutting-Room Floor," Seagal describes some of the material edited out from the show's broadcast, "While an undercover pal negotiates with a drug dealer across the street, the three detectives survey an unsuspecting woman from behind their van's tinted windows...." The footage includes the following conversation:

DETECTIVE 1: Check out those volumtuous [*sic*] breasts and that volumtuous [*sic*] ass.

DETECTIVE 2: Think she takes it up the butt!

DETECTIVE 1: Yep. It sticks out just enough so you can pull the cheeks apart and really plummet it. [*Long pause*] I believe that she's not beyond fellatio either.

[Zoom to close-up of Detective 1]

DETECTIVE 1: You don't have true domination over a woman until you spit on 'em and they don't say nothing.

[Zoom to close-up of Detective 3]

DETECTIVE 3: I know a hooker who will let you spit on her for twenty bucks....

[Direct appeal to camera]

Can one of you guys edit this thing and make a big lump in my pants for me?

[Zoom to close-up of Detective 3's crotch, walkie-talkie between his legs.][23]

The most notable thing about this footage is that the detectives dared to make these outrageous statements in front of the camera, obviously quite confident that they would be edited out. This suggests a degree of collusion between the police and the videographers that severely diminishes any claim they might have to objective reporting. Seagal reports that it usually required the editing of 50 or 60 hours of "mundane and compromising" video footage in order to produce one episode. The result was a highly distorted image of crime and law enforcement.

Another problem with both news coverage of crime and reality-based programming is their emphasis on crimes committed by poor minorities. Many, if not most, of the images of crime that are presented involve minorities. "The pictures we tend to show are white officers arresting black people," says one television news director in Texas. "[I]t creates the impression that it's all black people who are using drugs." He goes on to explain, "The problem is that the police don't tend to raid white middle-class people and pull them out of their homes. Is that because it's not there—or the police are afraid of losing their jobs?"[24] Whatever the answer, the disproportionate representation of minorities in crime reports is sure to reinforce prejudices that already exist in society, especially given the failure of the news and reality-based programs to provide context. Without a context—an explanation—for the crime being covered, viewers may come to attribute the crimes committed by a particular minority group to something inherent—or genetic—in that group rather than to their position and experiences within the social structure (i.e., context). This is a form of biological determinism that is the essence of racial bigotry.

In short, nonfictional and fictional accounts of crime on television do very little to promote an understanding of crime. This is disturbing because, as voters, the viewing public can and does affect policymaking. "If people are operating with theories of crime that are derived from television," write Craig Haney and John Manzolati, "and these theories are *wrong*, then real world decisions will be made and actual consequences follow from these unreal perspectives."[25] To the extent that the public internalizes the misleading images of crime provided through television, appropriate solutions to the crime problem may be ignored, avoided, evaded, delayed, or condemned.

CRIME SCARES

Earlier, the point was made that, in contrast to public perceptions, crime and crime rates are not directly related. At certain times, crime in general, or certain types of crime, receives a great deal of attention from the media, politicians, and the public, though this attention is unwarranted, given the data. That is, suddenly crime, or certain types of crime, becomes a heated social problem, even though the evidence suggests that there has been no sudden surge in criminal activity. The media and the public are whipped into a frenzy; many come to think that social life is very dangerous and/or that society is on the verge of a moral breakdown. We might call this phenomenon a "crime scare." The infamous Salem witch trials provide a classic example of a crime scare. Following are some examples of crime scares that have taken place in more recent history.

The Missing Children Scare

Beginning in the early 1980s, Americans were besieged by reports of missing children. Although the phrase "missing children" actually includes runaways, children taken by a parent who lost legal custody, and abduction by strangers, the public was given the impression that stranger abductions represented the preponderance of the problem. This followed a couple of well-publicized stranger abductions that resulted in the child's death. Most notable was the case of Adam Walsh, who was abducted and whose dismembered body was later found on a riverbank in Hollywood, Florida. His father, John Walsh, subsequently became a leading activist for the cause of missing children and is renowned as the television host of *America's Most Wanted*.

Activists and politicians began describing a social problem of immense proportions. Joel Best describes the situation:

> The crusaders described a stranger-abduction problem of astonishing dimensions. Then U.S. Representative Paul Simon offered "the most conservative estimate you will get anywhere"—50,000 children abducted by strangers annually. Child Find, a leading child-search organization, estimated that parents recovered only 10 percent of these children, that another 10 percent were found dead, and that the remainder—40,000 cases per year—remained missing. In short, the crusaders described a large number of stranger abductions with very serious consequences.[26]

The social problems perspective defines a social problem as a phenomenon recognized as such by a significant part of the population. By the mid-1980s, stranger abduction easily met this definition. The National Center for Missing and Exploited Children had been established, pictures of missing children were showing up on the sides of milk cartons, talk shows devoted considerable air-time to the issue, the estimate of 50,000 stranger abductions per year became popular wisdom (although some estimates went as high as 400,000), and the press played its role in perpetuating the scare. Best reports that ABC's first news story about the problem stated, "By conservative estimate, 50,000 children are abducted each year, not counting parental kidnappings and custody fights. Most are never found. Four to eight thousand a year are murdered."[27] Meanwhile, surveys showed a growing concern, some might say "paranoia," among parents and children.[28] Parents became ever more watchful of their children, sometimes going so far as to keep identification files with photographs and dental records (in case they should be needed to identify their children's dead bodies). And children were encouraged to be fearful of strangers.

In 1985, however, the 50,000 figure began to be questioned. The *Denver Post,* which later won a Pulitzer Prize for its coverage of the issue, drew attention to the fact that the FBI investigated only 67 cases of stranger abductions in 1984. A *Post* editorial suggested that there are more "preschoolers who choke to death on food each year" than are abducted by strangers.[29]

In actuality, the FBI figure is probably way too low (because they do not investigate all stranger abductions), and the 50,000 figure claimed by the crusaders is certainly way too high. According to Best and extrapolations made by other researchers, the figure is probably in the neighborhood of 500 to 1,000 children abducted by strangers every year.[30] When confronted with the outrageousness of the 50,000 estimate, crusaders would often respond that "one missing child is too many."

As sociologists interested in social problems, we need to look more carefully at this statement. Yes, it is true, one missing child is a tragedy. However, there are millions of tragedies that take place in the world each and every day; few of them are successfully constructed into "social problems." People have a limited amount of time and emotion to attach to social problems, and they cannot do this for the millions of tragedies that take place every day. Potential social problems compete for the public's attention. The public needs accurate information in order to set rational priorities with regard to social problems. Suppose there were "only one" missing-then-murdered child per year but thousands of deaths resulting from worker safety violations every year. More people might rationally assess worker safety to be a greater threat to themselves and their families. Then, worker safety would become a heated social problem, and public policy might be implemented that would improve the safety conditions of millions of workers. This rational prioritization of social problems is preempted by much of the heated rhetoric and inflated statistics that are often used by activists, capitalized on by politicians, and parroted by the media.

And while the missing children scare took place decades ago, its repercussions continue to affect our culture today. Children, then, were likely raised by parents who were overly-alarmed by the prospect of stranger abduction and who took precautions to protect them from this very unlikely event. Children were taught to fear strangers and many were fingerprinted in case they (or their remains) had to be identified at a later date. These children are today's parents and today's children are allowed far less opportunity to play outside unsupervised than they were in the generations before the missing children scare.

The Serial Murder Scare

In the 1980s and 1990s, serial murder came to occupy the public imagination in a big way. This was thanks largely to some highly publicized cases (e.g., Ted Bundy, Henry Lee Lucas, John Wayne Gacy, and later, Jeffrey Dahmer), as well as some very popular fictional books and movies (most notably, *Silence of the Lambs*). The FBI's Behavioral Sciences Unit was also highly instrumental in spreading fear of serial homicide. In the early 1980s, it estimated that approximately one-fifth of all American homicides were cases of serial murders; their estimates went as high as 4,000 or 5,000 cases per year. These estimates were based on the assumption that when the police reported an *unknown* circumstance in a homicide case, that case must have been the work of a serial killer. Phillip Jenkins writes,

> ...this interpretation of the data is quite unwarranted. In effect, it suggests that an *unknown* circumstance equates to *no apparent motive,* which in turn means that the murder is *motiveless,* or "with no apparent rhyme, reason, or motivation." This is unpardonable. All that can be legitimately understood from an *unknown* circumstance is that, at the time of completing the form, the police agency in question either did not know the exact context of the crime, or did not trouble to fill in the forms correctly.[31]

Nevertheless, in 1983, the U.S. Justice Department held a news conference about the alarming increase in the serial murder phenomenon. At the conference, Justice Department officials reiterated that there were likely several thousand cases of serial murder each year and "that there might be thirty-five such killers active in the United States at any given time."[32] The juxtaposition of these two figures—4,000 victims and 35 serial killers—meant that the average serial killer must have been responsible for over 100 killings per year. Interestingly, there is no confirmed case on record in which a serial killer was responsible for so many murders. At least one of the two statistics was in need of serious readjustment.

According to Jenkins and, indeed, more recent FBI estimates, there may indeed be more than 35 serial killers operating in the United States at any given time, but the annual number of victims, rather than being in the neighborhood of 4,000, is more likely to be in the range of 50–70.[33] This latter estimate amounts to considerably less than 1 percent of all U.S. homicides. Writes Jenkins,

> In reality, serial homicide accounts for a very small proportion of American murders, and the claims frequently made in the 1980s exaggerated the scale of victimization by a factor of at least twenty. Moreover, such offenses are far from new, and the volume of activity in recent years is little different from conditions in the early part of the present century, while the phenomenon is by no means distinctively American.[34]

Much as in the case of stranger abductions of children, discussed above, misleading statistics and images concerning serial murders captured the public's attention and fostered a deeply ingrained fear of strangers among millions of Americans, even though statistically their chances of being murdered by an acquaintance or loved one were enormously greater than their chances of being murdered by a serial killer. In fact, 70 serial killings per year in a country of over 300 million people means that any person's chances of being murdered by a serial killer are infinitesimally small. As with the missing children scare, one has to wonder the degree to which the fear of strangers among today's parents and children is a vestige of these misleading statistics propagated a generation ago.

Thus, in the case of serial homicide, the perceived, or subjective, reality of the problem bore little resemblance to the objective reality. We can say, then, that serial homicide was a socially constructed problem. This leads us to the question, Why was this social problem so successfully constructed? Why were such misleading statistics accepted and internalized by so many? The answer, according to Jenkins's constructionist analysis, lies in the fact that a diverse number of interest groups found it to their advantage to perpetuate exaggerated statistics.

The FBI had an interest in perpetuating the myth that there were thousands of victims of crazed killers who roamed the country. They claimed part of the problem lay in the lack of communication between law enforcement agencies, as well as their inability to make the connections between similar crimes happening in very different locations. By exaggerating the extent of these crimes and the extent to which serial killers actually "roam" and by establishing themselves as the experts who could link these disparate killings, the FBI was able to enhance both its jurisdiction and its prestige. Prior to the serial homicide scare, the FBI's jurisdiction was quite limited, restricted to federal crimes and/or crimes that involved the crossing of state lines. However, thanks to the serial homicide scare, the Behavioral Sciences Unit managed to portray themselves as supersleuths, and the public and other law enforcement agencies came to welcome their help rather than resent the intrusion of federal powers, as they might have prior to the scare.

Jenkins argues that the serial killer scare also fit neatly into the ideological framework of the conservative Reagan administration. Conservative ideology places blame for society's problems on weak, immoral, or depraved individuals rather than on the social structure. The serial homicide scare diverted attention away from other crimes—the vast majority of crimes—that can be more readily associated with the social structure. The vast majority of homicides, for example, occur within the lower class and can, therefore, arguably be linked with poverty and similar structural determinants. Serial homicides, on the other hand, are less readily linked to the social structure; they appear to occur randomly, and they seem to be committed by crazed, pathological, immoral individuals who are, quite simply, "evil." Consequently, by shifting society's focus on crime to serial killings, conservatives were able to perpetuate their view that crime has more to do with the moral breakdown of our society than with poverty, inequality, and the dismantling of social welfare programs.

Paradoxically, liberal groups also found an interest in perpetuating the inflated statistics. When the victims were black, as were many of Jeffrey Dahmer's and John Wayne Gacy's victims, black leaders could blame the problem on a lack of concern on the part of law enforcement agencies and their neglect of cases involving missing African Americans. When the victims were gay, similar complaints could be lodged by gay activists. When the victims were female, feminists could blame the patriarchal criminal justice system for its lack of concern for female victims, in which case serial homicide could be "contextualized together with offenses such as rape, child molestation, and sexual harassment."[35]

Ironically, the serial murder scare also served the interests of those serial murderers who were convicted or were in jail awaiting trial. They received extraordinary amounts of media attention and their exploits, some would say, were "glorified" by the media. Their murderous activities and their perverse "skills" were recounted in numerous books and movies, both fiction and nonfiction. At least one of these convicted murderers, Henry Lee Lucas, even got to escape the drudgery of imprisonment and fly around the country confessing—probably falsely—to unsolved murders.

In other words, the myths surrounding serial homicide were successfully constructed because many parties had an interest in perpetuating these myths and few had an interest in uncovering the truth. Once again, we can see a connection between crime—in this case, perceptions of crime—and politics. Once again, different groups entered the political arena fighting for their interests and allowing certain misperceptions to reign because it suited them to do so.

The Drug Scare

Beginning in 1986 and continuing for several years, the American public was hit with a barrage of news stories about the problem of drugs, especially crack cocaine. Arnold Trebach refers to "The Scared Summer of '86," while Craig Reinerman and Harry G. Levine refer to the phenomenon as "The Crack Attack." Reinerman and Levine note that while there have been numerous drug scares in the United States, probably none has paralleled in intensity this crack attack.[36] Erich Goode and Nachman Ben-Yehuda write, "It is possible that in no other decade has the issue of drugs occupied such a huge and troubling space in the public consciousness."[37]

Powder cocaine is a stimulant that is usually inhaled through the nose (i.e., "snorted"); it is quite expensive, and the "high" that it induces is generally a subtle one. Crack cocaine, however, is crystalline; it is smoked; it is considerably less expensive; and the high it induces is quite intense, though relatively brief. Crack's effects are considerably harsher than those of powder cocaine, and its appeal seems, more or less, limited to residents of impoverished inner-city neighborhoods, the same people, note Reinerman and Levine, who have traditionally gravitated toward heroin.[38]

While a smokable and more intense form of cocaine (namely, "freebase") had been around since the 1970s, crack did not appear on the scene until the mid-1980s. When it did appear, it was portrayed by the media, politicians, and many in the drug treatment community as being one of the worst scourges ever to hit America. Numerous stories in the press referred to crack as "instantly addicting."[39] Terms such as *epidemic* and *plague* were popularly used to describe the phenomenon. Crack's popularity in the inner-city ghettos was usually noted, but then news stories went on to explain how the "epidemic" was spreading into middle-class high schools and suburbs. A full-page editorial in *Newsweek,* written by the editor-in-chief and entitled "The Plague among Us," reported that "[a]n epidemic is abroad in America, as pervasive and dangerous in its way as the plagues of medieval times. [The epidemic] has taken lives, wrecked careers, broken homes, invaded schools, incited crimes, tainted businesses, toppled heroes, corrupted policemen and politicians."[40] The CBS television weekly newsmagazine *48 Hours* aired an episode entitled "48 Hours on Crack Street," which attracted the highest viewer audience for a show of its kind in the five and a half years previous. Write Reinerman and Levine,

> In July 1986 alone, the three major TV networks offered 74 evening news segments on drugs, half of these about crack. In the month leading up to the November elections, a handful of national newspapers and magazines produced roughly 1,000 stories discussing crack. Like the TV networks, leading newsmagazines like *Time* and *Newsweek* seemed determined not to be outdone; each devoted five cover stories to crack and the "drug crisis" in 1986 alone.[41]

In 1987, a nonelection year, drug coverage began to subside; then in 1988, it began to pick up again. On September 5, 1989, President George H. W. Bush went on the air with a speech from the Oval Office about the drug crisis in the United States. During the speech, he held up a plastic bag labeled "EVIDENCE" that contained crack, and he announced that it was "seized a few days ago in a park across the street from the White House." It was revealed a couple of weeks later by the *Washington Post* and by National Public Radio that the bag of crack President Bush had held up was little more than a theatrical prop:

> A White House aide told the *Post* that the President "liked the prop....It drove the point home." Bush and his advisors also decided that crack should be seized in Lafayette Park across from the White House or nearby so that the president could say that crack had become so pervasive that men were "selling drugs in front of the White House."[42]

White House and Justice Department operatives, however, found it quite difficult to find any drugs being sold in the vicinity of the White House. As a last resort, they had to entice an 18-year-old to come to the park and sell them the crack. Rather than "seizing" the crack, they bought it from him and sent him on his way. "Seizure" implies that an arrest was made; and if an arrest had been made, the White House might have had to answer some sticky questions about entrapment and the whole setup would have been brought more readily to the public's attention.

The "bag of crack speech" provides a good example of how the public was being manipulated throughout the drug scare years. While reporting about the drug "epidemic" was skyrocketing, actual drug use was not. Reports of the "epidemic" rarely, if ever, referred to objective data. Surveys showed that drug use was actually going down at the time of the scare. These surveys did not distinguish between different types of cocaine use, but they did show that cocaine use, in general, was dropping.[43] While the networks were reporting that crack was "flooding America" and that it had become "America's drug of choice," in 1986, report Reinerman and Levine, *there were no prevalence statistics at all on crack.*"[44]

> The first official measures of the prevalence of crack began with [the] National Institute on Drug Abuse's 1986 high school survey. It found that 4.1 percent of high school seniors reported having tried crack (at least once) in the previous year. This figure dropped to 3.9 percent in 1987, and to 3.1 percent in 1988, a 25 percent decline. This means that at the peak of crack use, 96 percent of America's high school seniors had never tried crack, much less gone on to more regular use, abuse, or addiction.[45]

The objective data hardly indicated a plague or crack epidemic; and if those who touted the problem were so concerned about drug use's threat to our health, they might have mentioned that alcohol and tobacco are, by far, the most popular drugs among Americans, including teenagers, and that they account for far more deaths than do powder or crack cocaine.

While drug use was dropping, surveys indicated that the number of Americans who thought drugs to be the most serious problem facing the country went up dramatically. "The percentage reporting that drug abuse was the nation's most important problem," notes Katherine Beckett, "jumped from 3 percent in 1986 to 64 percent in 1987."[46] Since this dramatic change in the popular perception of drugs was not due to actual increases in drug use, it must have been related to the rhetoric of politicians and/or the intensified media coverage. According to Beckett as well as Reinerman and Levine, the drug scare was largely the result of a political initiative.[47]

As with the serial homicide scare, the drug problem resonated with the conservative ideology that was very popular at the time. Liberal ideology had fallen from grace, and social welfare programs were being defunded. Society's problems were seen, not in terms of inequality and social structural arrangements, but as indicative of a moral breakdown. The solution, according to First Lady Nancy Reagan's antidrug crusade, was learning to "just say no." To the extent that it was recognized that crack was used disproportionately by poor, inner-city minorities, poverty was considered the effect, not the cause, of drug abuse. Reinerman and Levine write,

Drug problems fit neatly onto this ideological agenda and allowed conservatives to engage in what might be called sociological denial—to scapegoat drugs for many social and economic problems. For Reagan-style conservatives, people did not so much abuse drugs because they were jobless, homeless, poor, depressed, or alienated; they were jobless, homeless, poor, depressed, or alienated because they were weak, immoral, or foolish enough to use illicit drugs.[48]

Meanwhile, in Congress, this conservative ideology had become so popular that both Republicans and Democrats were jostling to demonstrate who could be tougher on crime. A "feeding frenzy" ensued, resulting in more and more media coverage of the issue and tougher and tougher legislation aimed at drug abuse. Lengthier and mandatory sentences were imposed, and rather than just focusing on sellers, the casual user became the target of stronger law enforcement measures. In the 1980s, the U.S. incarceration rate more than doubled, becoming one of the highest, if not the highest, in the world. This expansion was due in large part to the "war on drugs" and the legacy of this war is still seen today in the vast numbers of people and resources going into our prisons.

From the perspective of critical constructionism, all of these crime scares diverted the public's attention away from other problems whose remedies might threaten elite interests.

STREET CRIME

Although the media, politicians, and various activists may succeed in exaggerating the amount of crime, there is no denying that the United States has high rates of street crime, especially violent crime and, even more so, lethal violence. In the words of Steven Messner and Richard Rosenfeld, "When it comes to lethal violence, America remains the undisputed leader in the modern world."[49] Using data from the World Health Organization and comparing the United States with 15 other industrialized nations, they note that the United States has a homicide rate more than three times our nearest competitor, Finland, while it is almost nine times higher than Japan's. Regarding nonlethal violence, they examine data on robbery (defined as "threats accompanied by force or the threat of force") from the International Police Organization. Again, comparing the United States to the same 15 industrialized nations, they found U.S. robbery rates to be more than twice as high as our nearest competitors (Canada and France) and 158 times higher than those in Japan.[50]

The reasons for such a high incidence of violence in the United States are, of course, very complex and subject to debate, but they seem to be deeply rooted in our culture and social structure.

One often-heard explanation for our high rates of violence is the relative lack of gun control in the United States. Americans, both criminal and noncriminal, arm themselves at extraordinarily high rates, whereas in most other industrialized countries in the world, guns are very hard to come by. Japan, for example, with its extraordinarily low rates of violence, notes David Bayley, "has the toughest laws on the ownership of firearms, especially hand-guns, of any democratic country in the world....No handguns are permitted in private hands, even registered, with the exception of people who partici-pate in international shooting competitions."[51] While the availability of guns in the United States almost assuredly contributes to a significant proportion of violence, especially violent fatalities, the evidence indicates that American society would be relatively violent even without firearms. That is, according to Messner and Rosenfeld,

> even if all of the gun-related homicides were eliminated from its homicide rate, the United States would still have a *non-gun* homicide rate that is higher than the total homicide rates of other developed nations.... We simply want to call attention to the...sobering point that even if none of these weapons were ever used in another killing the United States would still have the highest rate of homicide of any advanced industrialized nation.[52]

It appears that violence in the United States is also not due to some fleeting or sudden changes in the culture, such as a breakdown in morality. While there have been surges in violent crime, namely in the 1920s and 1970s, dur-ing this century, even our lowest homicide rates exceed the highest rates in other industrialized countries.[53] In other words, it would appear that there are some enduring features of American culture and/or social structure that explain its violent nature.

Robert Merton and the American Dream

In perhaps the single most important theoretical formulation in the American sociology of crime and deviance, Robert Merton identified the "American Dream" as the feature of American culture that explains much of its crime problem.[54] All cultures define values for their members. One culture might be distinctive in the emphasis it places on the value of having a tight-knit family. Another culture might be distinctive in the value it places on military service. The United States is distinctive in the value it places on monetary success. A well-socialized American (i.e., most of us) is one who is directed to the goal of financial success. This goal is so strong in the United States that we have even named it after our country, "the American Dream," and the value placed on it exceeds all other cultural values. While we may pay lip service to the preeminence of the values of family and/or education, most Americans judge themselves to be successful based on their ability to achieve the American Dream. Cultures specify not only the goals for which their members are to strive but also the means to attain them. The culture directs us to strive for monetary success, and we are told to follow legitimate means to this success. That is, we are supposed to be ambitious, work hard, innovate, and follow the rules. Unfortunately, the goal of success receives far more emphasis than do the means to achieve it. (Thus, it is far more important whether "you win or lose" than "how you play the game.") Consequently, people are tempted to resort to illegitimate means in order to attain the all-important goal of success.

The emphasis that our society places on the American Dream can be seen as beneficial in that it serves as the driving force of our capitalist economy and provides motivation to better oneself through hard work and innovation. However, it can also be problematic in that the social structure limits the ability of many, especially those in the lower class, to achieve success. Unlike the preeminent values defined by some societies, the goal of monetary success is not achievable by all. Though the American Dream is a virtually universal goal in our culture, the capitalist economy simply is not designed to provide monetary success to all members of society.

The American Dream presupposes equality of opportunity. Almost all Americans are brought up to believe that it is available to them. This belief suffuses our culture, pervading our political, economic, media, educational, and religious institutions. Yet, as mentioned in Chapter 2, it is much easier to stay rich in the United States if you are born rich than it is to get rich if you are born poor. Those born rich are quite likely to stay rich; those born poor are quite likely to stay poor. While individual motivation, hard work, and innovation are not irrelevant, the poor need far more of these qualities to achieve monetary success than do the rich. Consequently, there is not equality of opportunity in the United States.

To summarize Merton's theory, there is so much crime in the United States because of our culture's emphasis on the goal of monetary success. The emphasis on success is so great that it becomes the yardstick by which we measure our self-worth and the worth of others. The emphasis on success is so great that any emphasis on legitimate means of achieving it pales in comparison. The goal of success propels and strains all of us, but people in the lower class are under considerably more strain because they have fewer avenues for attaining monetary success. They, therefore, experience greater temptation to pursue illegitimate means to achieve success, such as violence, prostitution, drug dealing and such.

At first glance, Merton's theory perhaps explains property crime as well as or better than it explains violent crime. Property crime can be more easily seen as an illegitimate means of achieving the culturally defined value of monetary success. However, most violent crime is concentrated in the lower class, and Merton's theory helps us understand the frustration of living in the lower class in a capitalist society, especially in the United States. Remember that when a society places so much emphasis on a goal for its members, the ability to achieve that goal becomes the yardstick by which people measure their self-worth and the worth of others. Those who have little regard for their own lives, as measured by this yardstick, will likely have little regard for the lives of others. Thus, the violence that is endemic to the American lower class—both that which is oriented toward monetary gain and that which is not—should not be unexpected.

Other American Values and Their Contributions to Crime

There are several important principles from the sociology of values that will help us understand the contribution of American values to the American crime problem. First, the more important values that define and are defined by a culture tend to permeate that culture, its social structure, and its institutions. For example, as mentioned above, the American Dream can be found in and is reinforced by many of society's institutions. The theme of the American Dream is reiterated by governmental leaders, religious leaders, industrial leaders, classroom teachers, athletic coaches, popular culture idols, and numerous other representatives of society's institutions. A second theme relative to our analysis represents one of Karl Marx's more important contributions to the sociology of values. Marx asserted that the dominant institution in any society is its economic institution and that the dominant values will support the prevailing economic arrangements in that society. Hence, as mentioned above, the American Dream is a critical component of American capitalism, providing us with the motivation to work hard and innovate—also providing us, inevitably, with winners and losers. A final principle from the sociology of values is that the more important values in a society tend to be interrelated and to reinforce one another. Two such important and interrelated values often identified with the American "character" are individualism and competition.

Few would argue with the contention that the United States is among the most capitalist countries in the world. Adam Smith enunciated the guiding principles of capitalism: namely, that if everybody pursues his or her own *individual* self-interests in a market of free *competition,* then the best-quality products will be made available at the lowest possible prices and the society will thrive. Individualism and competition are the foundation of our economic structure, and they are integral components of our value structure. (Americans are so fiercely individualistic that it is likely more difficult to teach sociology in the United States than in most other countries. That is, Americans are inclined to think of their destinies solely in terms of their individual efforts; in contrast, sociology emphasizes that so much of our life chances depend upon group influences and one's position in the social structure.) More so than people of other countries, Americans view life as a competition between individuals, with winners and losers, and losers have only themselves to blame. Again, this belief presumes the preexistence of equal opportunity, which can be easily refuted. However, the tenacity with which so many Americans hold this view speaks volumes about the nature and importance of these values.

These values help to explain the problem of poverty in the United States, and the connection between street crime and poverty is inescapable.

American individualism, combined with the premium that we place on competition, results in a form of *Social Darwinism,* or a "survival of the fittest" mentality. As seen in Chapter 2, in the United States, more than in most other countries, the poor are blamed for their own poverty, for their lack of individual initiative. Rather than sympathy, contempt for the poor is not unusual. Consequently, the poor get very little help in the form of governmental assistance. And, as we have seen, the United States provides less in the way of welfare assistance than most other advanced industrialized countries in the world. While it is true that poverty itself does not cause crime (i.e., all poor people do not commit crime), it could hardly be refuted as a source of crime. The vast majority of people who commit the vast majority of street crimes—both violent and nonviolent—are poor.

Independently of their contribution to poverty, the values of individualism, competition, and financial success provide powerful motivation to succeed by any means necessary. Criminologist Edwin Schur writes,

> It is difficult not to conclude that American society has embraced an ideology of what might be termed capitalism with a vengeance—a reverence for the values of individualism, competition, and profit of such intensity as to provide incentives to crime that go well beyond a level that must be considered inevitable in a modern complex society, even a basically capitalist one.[55]

The American Dream is a powerful motivator, not just for those who strive for success in legal employment. Ethnographer Philippe Bourgois describes inner-city drug dealers as "ambitious, energetic inner-city youth [who] are attracted to the underground economy precisely because they believe in the rags-to-riches American Dream. . . . In fact, they follow the traditional model for upward mobility: aggressively setting themselves up as private entrepreneurs."[56] Motivated by the same values that motivate us all, the drug dealer, the pimp, the burglar, and the robber are all entrepreneurs in neighborhoods that provide few opportunities for legitimate entrepreneurship. As Merton would argue, they are innovators in a country whose claim to fame is innovation.

Race and Street Crime

Referring to the disproportionate representation of minorities in prison, journalist Alan Elsner writes,

> African Americans make up only 2 percent of the population in Iowa but 20 percent of the prison population. In Florida they make up about 15 percent of the population and 48 percent of inmates; in Alabama, 26 percent of the population and 62 percent of those in state prisons.
>
> What does this mean in practice? It means according to Department of Justice statisticians, that almost one in every three black men (28.5 percent) . . . can expect to spend time in prison during his lifetime; that young black men in

California are five times as likely to go to prison as to a state university; that in 1999 in the middle of the greatest economic boom in U.S. history, the state of Illinois had 10,000 more African Americans in prison than in college. For every four African Americans in college in Illinois, 10 were in prison or on parole...[57]

A critical question that is difficult to answer conclusively is whether African Americans are disproportionately represented because they commit more crimes or because of biases operating in our criminal justice system. As with most difficult questions, the answer is most likely both.

There is certainly no dearth of evidence demonstrating racial bias in the criminal justice system. The highly publicized case in which Rodney King was severely beaten by Los Angeles police officers triggered riots in Los Angeles and brought racial bias to the forefront of the American consciousness, at least temporarily, in 1992. Probably most Americans would agree that this beating (accompanied by racial epithets) would have been far less likely to have occurred had Rodney King been white. However, bias in the criminal justice system is usually far more subtle, and it has the potential to occur at any stage in the criminal justice process, from arrest to prosecution to conviction to sentencing.

One method of determining bias is by examining the ratio of African American males who are arrested versus the ratio incarcerated. Though this method neglects any bias that may lead to arrest, it does provide an indicator of subsequent bias in the criminal justice system. That is, if there were no bias operating, then we would expect the ratio of African Americans incarcerated to be nearly the same as the ratio of African Americans arrested. Relative to their proportion of the population, African Americans are five times more likely to be arrested than whites for serious crimes such as murder, rape, and aggravated assault and three times more likely to be arrested for less serious crimes. However, rather than being incarcerated at a rate of three to five times greater than whites, African Americans are seven times more likely to be incarcerated.[58] In short, African Americans who are arrested are more likely to be incarcerated than whites who are arrested. It is difficult to say exactly where and when this bias comes into play because it does so at different stages in different cases. For some, it may be in the charging process; in other cases, it may be in the plea bargaining; in yet others, it may be in the provision of services by a court-appointed attorney; sometimes there could be a racist jury; other times there may be bias on the part of the presiding judge; of course, in many cases, the process may be completely fair and unbiased. However, the disparity between arrest ratios and incarceration ratios suggests a cumulative racial bias at work in our criminal justice system.

As mentioned, an examination of the difference between arrest ratios and incarceration ratios does not take into account biases that affect the decision to arrest in the first place, which may have an even greater impact than subsequent biases. Reviewing the literature, sociologists Becky Pettit and Bruce Western write, "Although crime rates may explain as much as 80 percent of the disparity in imprisonment,...a significant residual suggests that blacks are punitively policed, prosecuted, and sentenced. Sociologists of punishment link this differential treatment to official perceptions of blacks as threatening or troublesome."[59] In our criminal justice system, in which a person is presumed innocent until proven guilty, the data suggest that African Americans are likely presumed less innocent from their very first contact with the system.

While African Americans are arrested at rates three to five times greater than whites relative to their representation in the population, given the biases evident in the criminal justice system, it is difficult to determine what proportion of street crime they do indeed commit. However, it is not likely that the differences in arrest rates are due solely to biases in the criminal justice system. As mentioned earlier, homicide rates are probably the most accurate crime statistics. Virtually all homicides are reported, and given the seriousness of the crime, the police are likely to use less discretion in making an arrest; that is, racial bias is less likely to come into play. Proportional to their representation in the population, African Americans are arrested six times more frequently for homicide than whites.[60] "This over-representation by African Americans in arrests for murder," writes criminologist Jay Livingston, "cannot be a mere by-product of police racism."[61] Victimization surveys also indicate that blacks are nearly seven times more likely to be identified as offenders in robberies than whites.[62] The disproportionate involvement of African Americans in street crime needs to be explained.

There are those who believe that crime is the result of moral deficiency. When attempting to explain why one socio-demographic group commits more crime than another, this explanation is antisociological. When attempting to explain why African Americans commit more street crime than whites, this explanation smacks of racism because, essentially, it asserts that blacks are less moral than whites. Is this because of their biological makeup (an explicitly racist assumption), or is it because of their position in the social structure and the prejudice, discrimination, and poverty that are likely to go along with it? If the latter, then it is not moral deficiency but the social structure that requires examination.

One of the principal explanations for African American street crime is poverty. As we have seen, African Americans are far more likely to experience poverty than whites. Again, poverty does not itself cause crime; but the connection between poverty and crime can hardly be thought a coincidence. Rates of street crime are especially high among African Americans in poor inner-city neighborhoods. As noted earlier, in the 1970s, job opportunities rushed out of these areas into the suburbs and, more importantly, into countries of the South, where labor is cheaper. As job opportunities rapidly disappeared and the unemployment rate, especially among young African American men, climbed to new heights, these young men became less "marriageable" and less able to support a family, thus contributing to the rise of the single-parent, female-headed household in the black community.[63] In addition to these forces, the inner-city African American community was further destabilized by the exodus of successful African Americans from the inner cities to the suburbs. Before desegregation, successful African Americans were more or less forced to live in the ghettos with their poor neighbors. As housing became less segregated, those who could afford to moved out. They took their jobs, their money, and their more affluent lifestyles with them, further contributing to the dilapidation of the ghettos. More importantly, their presence had provided successful role models for their young, poor neighbors. When they left, according to William Julius Wilson, the role models left.[64] Poor, young African American males were almost exclusively surrounded by those who had failed to achieve the American Dream.

Being surrounded by "failure" does not temper one's desire to achieve the material comforts promised by the American Dream. The values propagated by the American Dream are nearly universal in our culture. These values became even more exaggerated since Merton first made the connection between crime and the American Dream. Notes Elliott Currie, a "hypermaterialist culture" has emerged that has been "fueled by the massive growth of consumer advertising and marketing and celebrated on television, on movie screens, and in popular music."[65]

Probably the most influential medium has been television. Writes Carl Nightingale,

> Television's capacity to reach into the privacy of all households, regardless of class and race boundaries, and the medium's consolidation of image, sound, movement, and color have firmly and inalterably established an intimate familiarity with mass-market America among the poor. Indeed, it appears that poor households and poor teenagers have been significantly more attached to TV than have more affluent kids.[66]

In the first several decades of television, almost all commercials depicted the lifestyle of upper-middle-class whites, with all of its material accouterments. The contrast of this lifestyle with that of most African American viewers must have been frustrating, degrading, and cumulative. Today's television commercials are more or less the same, except that now there are more ads actually targeting poor, inner-city African American youth. Their inclusion on commercial television represents a double-edged sword. On the one hand, it symbolizes a form of acceptance of African Americans into the culture of the American mass market. On the other hand, it increases material expectations and the frustration and humiliation of not having. Charles Derber writes, "Mired in third world conditions of poverty while video-bombarded with first world dreams, rarely has a population suffered a greater gap between socially cultivated appetites and socially available opportunities."[67]

Young African American males experience another form of degradation in our society, with which few others can relate. That is, young African

American maleness has come to symbolize a threat to the physical well-being of other Americans. Everywhere we turn, we are constantly being exposed to the image of the criminally violent African American male, especially on television: on local news, on television documentaries, and on reality-based crime shows. "[W]hen a violent crime occurs," writes Donziger, "the perpetrator who comes immediately to mind to white Americans tends to be a person of color."[68] The stereotype is pervasive, and there needs to be more research on how it affects the behavior and psyche of the young African American male. What we do know about stereotypes, however, is that they tend to be self-fulfilling. According to Nightingale, fulfilling the stereotype can serve as a means of dealing with pain and resentment.

> The unequal burden of proof the African American kids have to shoulder in their dealings with the white world is both a source of humiliation and resentment. But there is another way that kids, and particularly teenage boys, react to the linking of race with violence—or what the rap group Public Enemy has called whites' "fear of a black planet." This is teenage inner-city boys' practice of mixing ridicule of white fear with a glorification of the stereotype of the violent black male to create a self-image that actually helps young black men to compensate for experiences of economic failure and racial insult.[69]

What is the cumulative effect of being eyed with suspicion, of being feared and avoided? According to Gresham Sykes, we all have a basic need to be regarded as trustworthy. When one is regarded with distrust—that is, rejected—by most of society, one defense is to reject one's own rejectors.[70] As a way of fending off the pain of rejection, the rejected come to view their rejectors with disdain and contempt. To the extent that this occurs among poor young African American males, it further drives a wedge between them and white society, alienating them, and thereby contributing to the likelihood of criminal activity. Hence, the stereotype becomes a self-fulfilling prophecy.

THE AMERICAN PUNISHMENT FRENZY

In 1967, the federal courts placed a moratorium on all executions in the United States; the U.S. Supreme Court continued this ban in 1972, and the ban was lifted in 1976. After that, executions were very controversial, with nearly each one accompanied by protests at the prison gates and a good deal of media attention. Today, they have become so routine that, with an occasional exception, they have faded from the public eye. The United States is among a very few industrialized countries in the world that still makes use of the death penalty.

Since the mid-1970s, the United States has escalated its rate of imprisonment at a pace that has seldom, if ever, been matched. According to the Bureau of Justice Statistics, between 1980 and 2009, the number of people incarcerated in the United States rose from 501,886 to 2,284,913, an astonishing increase of nearly 500 percent. The United States went from an incarceration rate of just over 100 in the mid-1970s to over 762 inmates per 100,000 population in 2007, the highest known incarceration rate in the world. In 2009, the number of inmates in state prisons declined by 0.2 percent—a very modest decline, but notable because this was the first decline since 1977. In 2009, there were 7,225,800 people in prison, jail, or correctional supervision, up nearly 400 percent since 1980.[71] The amount of federal, state, and local government expenditures on corrections has risen from approximately $84 billion in 1982 to over $227 billion in 2007. Figure 5.1 shows a breakdown of these numbers by federal, state, and local expenditures (which are by far the largest expenditures).[72] Figure 5.2 displays the incarceration rates for various countries. Box 5.1 puts the American incarceration rate into a different comparative perspective. "So common is the prison experience in America today," writes Hallinan, "that the federal government predicts that one in every eleven men will be imprisoned during his lifetime."[73]

It is frequently argued that prison resources expended on nonviolent offenders represent the biggest waste of prison budgets and that nonviolent offenders could be more effectively dealt with through programs that do not involve institutionalization, such as fines, counseling, victim restitution, and probation. The United States, however, is far more willing to incarcerate nonviolent offenders than most other industrialized nations, and it dispenses longer sentences to these offenders than do other industrialized nations. In 2008, 40 percent of all inmates serving time in state prisons were doing so for nonviolent offenses. In that year, 73 percent of inmates admitted to state prisons were sentenced for nonviolent offenses.[74]

The primary reason U.S. incarceration rates have risen so much over the past few decades is that the criminal justice system has become more

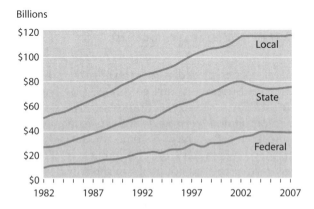

Figure 5.1 Direct Expenditure by Level of Government, 1982–2007

Source: Bureau of Justice Statistics, Office of Justice Programs, U.S. Department of Justice, http://bjs.ojp.esdoj.gov/content/glance/expgov.cfm. Retrieved October 22, 2011.

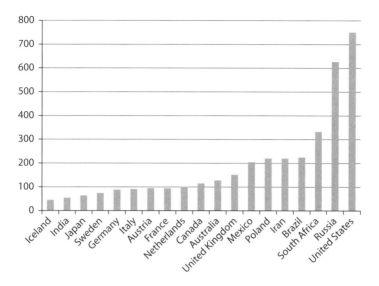

Figure 5.2 Incarceration Rates (Number of Inmates per 100,000 Population) Selected Countries

Source: Using data from Roy Walmsley, "World Prison Population List," 8th ed., International Centre for Prison Studies, King's College London, http://www.kcl.ac.uk/depsta/law/research/icps/downloads/wppl-8th_41.pdf. Retrieved November 1, 2011.

punitive; in particular most states now have mandatory minimum sentences for certain offenses and the length of sentences has been getting longer since the 1980s. This has two effects. First, and most obviously, it signifies a trend in which more convicted offenders are going into prison relative to the numbers that are coming out because they are staying longer than in the past. A less obvious result is that criminal defendants may be more inclined to accept a plea bargain and go to prison even though there may not be enough evidence to convict them if their cases were to go to trial.

The vast majority of convictions, well over 90 percent in federal cases, are the result of plea bargaining, that means that just a 10 percent reduction in plea bargains would nearly double the number of cases going to trial in the already overburdened court system.[75] That is, the system absolutely depends upon very high rates of plea bargaining. Tough sentencing laws and mandatory minimums that were enacted since the 1980s have given prosecutors enormous power to keep this system running smoothly by compelling defendants to plead guilty.

The *New York Times,* for example, recounts the case of *Florida vs. Shane Guthrie.* Guthrie was charged with beating up his girlfriend and threatening her with a knife in 2010. The prosecutor offered him a deal of two years' imprisonment plus probation; or, if he decided to go to trial and were convicted, he would spend a minimum of 50 years in prison. Academics are

---

BOX 5.1   U.S. INCARCERATION RATES IN PERSPECTIVE

738   *Rate in the United States.*

166   *Average rate worldwide.*

135   *Average rate among European Union member states.*

96   *Average rate of Group of Seven: Japan, Germany, United Kingdom, France, Italy, and Canada (U.S. excluded).*

152   *Rate in Rwanda, where nearly 80% (53,000) of the prison inmates are being held for crimes relating to the 1994 genocide.*

133   *Average rate in Iran and Iraq.*

100   *Average rate of incarceration among nations noted by Amnesty International as having some of the most urgent human rights abuse issues (Uzbekistan, Iraq, Myanmar, and Sudan).*

863   *Estimated rate in the feared GULAG of the Soviet Union in 1950.*

Source: Hartney, C. (Nov. 2006) *U.S. Rates of Incarceration: A Global Perspective.* NCCD Focus, Oakland, CA, National Council on Crime and Delinquency. Data obtained from International Centre for Prison Studies, University of London, King's College, *World Prison Brief.* Reprinted with permission from NCCD.

---

calling such deals a "trial penalty," penalizing those who go to trial. Critics charge that when the gap between the plea penalty and the trial penalty is so large, defendants are, in effect, being coerced to plead guilty.[76] In other words, when that gap is so large, it becomes the *rational* decision for an innocent defendant to plead guilty, especially when that defendant cannot afford the best legal representation.

Mandatory minimum sentences, then, have resulted in longer sentences for those who go to trial, and prison sentences for those—innocent or guilty—who plead guilty even though there was not enough evidence to convict them in a trial by jury. Together, along with the war on drugs, these help to explain the high incarceration in the United States.

At some point in the escalation of imprisonment, we must recognize the contradiction between our claim to being the freest society in the world and the fact that we are so prone to incarcerating people who step out of line. "We are rapidly approaching rates of incarceration associated with the likes of Hitler and Stalin," writes Robert McChesney.[77] Jeremy Seabrook writes,

> The U.S. presents a strange paradox of a society which constantly professes its devotion to freedom in an aggressively carceral society: a higher percentage of its people are jailed than in any other country in the world. That these people are, overwhelmingly, poor and black is no secret.[78]

It is difficult to reconcile the United States' claim to being the most democratic society in the world with the fact that 15 percent of the adult black males in the United States are ineligible to vote because of past felony convictions.[79]

Most notably, the escalation in the use of imprisonment in the United States has occurred despite the fact that there has been no corresponding increase in crime. Yet, in spite of incontrovertible cross-cultural evidence to the contrary, popular constructions still hold that our criminal justice system is "soft on crime."

The correctional system grew at such a rapid pace that in recent years criminologists and social commentators have become concerned with the political power of the correctional industry. In 1960, President Dwight D. Eisenhower alerted the public to the presence, or omnipresence, of the "military-industrial complex." He was concerned about the political power of the military and the alliances it had formed with private industry. Of course, the problem with such power and such powerful alliances is that they often serve private interests better than they serve the public interest. Today, we need to be concerned about the "prison-industrial complex." There are a number of interests, other than the public interest, that are served by correctional expansion.[80] For example, prison guards make up one of the more powerful unions in California. The union grew in membership from 4,000 to over 23,000 in one decade,[81] and it contributed more than $100,000 to the committee that pushed through California's punitive "three-strikes" legislation.[82] Norwegian criminologist and prison critic Nils Christie comments, "It is quite a fantastic situation when those who administer the pain-delivery in our society have such a great say. It's as if the hangman's association got together to work for more hanging."[83]

Prison guards are not the only ones to benefit from the incarceration boom of the recent past. Of course, there has also been a great deal of money made in prison construction. Many rural areas with depressed economies and high unemployment rates have benefitted. "Prisons have replaced factories as the economic center-piece of many small towns."[84] In past decades, communities would fight to avoid prison construction in their area. They feared that a criminal population nearby was too great a risk. Today, it is a very different story. For example, Donziger reports that 50 small towns in Texas lobbied for a new prison in their areas. Some even offered incentives, such as country club memberships for the wardens or longhorn cattle for the prison grounds. "A small town in Illinois put together a rap song and bought television time as part of a public relations blitz" to convince legislators to locate a prison in its vicinity.[85] Rural jurisdictions also benefit by the fact that prison populations boost a locality's census population while federal and state funding for social programs are often based on census counts.

Furthermore, both governmental institutions and private corporations reap enormous cost savings from prison labor. Convicts are making such things as clothing, circuit boards, safety goggles, wiring for military aircraft, body armor, road signs, and a host of other products; they are also making phone calls for telemarketing firms and taking phone calls for airline reservations. They might be paid pennies an hour, or if they are employed through the federal Prison Industries Enhancement Program, they might receive up to $1.50 an hour. Christian Parenti writes, "Given all this hard work going on in the big house, it would appear that America's 1.8 million prisoners are becoming a Third World within, a cheap and bountiful labor reservoir already being tapped by big business and Uncle Sam alike."[86]

Joseph Hallinan writes,

> Prisons are tremendous public works projects, throwing off money as a wet dog throws off water. When I began my travels, I had no idea that a single pay phone inside a prison could earn its owner $12,000 a year, or that a warden, if he played his cards right, could make himself a millionaire. But corporate America did. Giant firms like AT&T lined up at prison gates. The inmates on the other side of the fence, AT&T estimated, place $1 *billion* a year in long-distance phone calls. But unlike you or me, inmates don't get to pick their long-distance carrier—the prison does. And so AT&T and its competitors learned that the way to get inmates as customers was to give the prison a legal kick-back: on a one dollar phone call, the prison might make forty or fifty cents. In no time, corrections departments became phone call millionaires.[87]

Compounding the problem, many prisons today are being run by private corporations whose only goal is generating a profit. "The goal of the industry is to keep prisons full. A successful company locks up as many people as possible for as long as possible," says Dr. Jerome Miller of the National Center on Institutions and Alternatives.[88] Electronics corporations have also enjoyed the boom in prison construction. They make a generous profit wiring prisons and developing monitoring systems for prisoners inside the prison and for probationers outside. Food service, medical service, and transportation service companies are among others that profit from the incarceration boom.

Thus, there are various interest groups, whose interests are not necessarily in the public interest, that have formed powerful political constituencies with the goal of continuing the incarceration boom. For these groups, whether or not incarceration is an effective method of crime control is a distant concern. If the American public ever were to come to the conclusion that U.S. incarceration policies were counterproductive or that having so many people behind bars—mostly poor minorities—is not compatible with American democratic values, it would be very difficult to reverse course. Jeremy Travis, senior fellow at the Urban Institute, writes, "[T]he prison network is now deeply intertwined with American life, deeply integrated into the physical and economic infrastructure of a large number of American counties."[89]

Some might argue that the decline in violent crime in the United States in the late 1990s and continuing into 2011 was the result of the increasing use of incarceration. However, this decline did not occur until *20 years after* the United States began its "imprisonment binge." Further, the suggestion that the solution to the U.S. crime problem is to lock up a large portion of the young black male population ignores the reasons why violent crime is disproportionately high among this population; it ignores the cross-cultural comparisons of crime rates and incarceration rates; it is quite possibly motivated by racism; and it is unconscionable. Given the disproportionately high rates of crime still being committed by young African American males, wholesale imprisonment appears to be having little deterrent effect. In fact, there is very little evidence indicating that imprisonment has any impact on crime rates. According to Joseph Dillon Davey, "despite extensive research on the subject, a direct link between increased incarceration and lower crime rates has never been empirically established."[90] Interestingly enough, many of the states with the highest incarceration rates also have the highest crime rates (e.g., Florida), and many of those with the lowest incarceration rates have the lowest crime rates (e.g., Minnesota). If incarceration were an effective and necessary deterrent, we would not expect to find such patterns.

The research on the relationship between incarceration rates and crime rates appears to be irrelevant, however, because prison expansion seems impervious to logic. If crime rates are down, people say that proves the success of prisons and therefore we need more; if crime rates are up, they argue we are going too easy on criminals and, therefore, we need more prisons. Philosopher Ernest Boyer writes,

> Like the military-industrial complex, the *prison-industry complex* has an implacable internal logic that allows it to expand regardless of whether its stated objectives succeed or fail. If crime rates rise, we need more prisons; if crime is down, we need to build more prisons so it stays down. And money is then siphoned away from education, the best crime-prevention measure.[91]

Some believe that incarceration acts as a general deterrent; that is, it serves as an example of what happens to wrongdoers and deters would-be criminals. Others argue that it serves as a specific deterrent; that is, as long as a felon is incarcerated, he or she is deterred from committing further criminal acts. However, in an often-cited study, Isaac Erlich concluded that a 50 percent reduction in incarceration rates would result in only a 5 percent increase in crime rates. Conversely, Peter Greenwood and Allan Abrahamse found that increasing the prison population by 50 percent would lead to only a 4 percent drop in the crime rate.[92] Taken together, these two studies indicate that, as a general deterrent, incarceration has a very negligible effect and, to say the least, is not very cost-effective. In terms of specific deterrence, there is no denying that the felon is not committing street crime while he or she is incarcerated; however, the vast majority of felons will eventually be released. Davey writes,

> [T]he truth is that almost all convicted criminals will be back on the streets just a few years after their convictions. And it is very likely that their experiences in prison will not succeed in improving their behavior. If we were to increase our prison budget by, say, 25 percent overnight, that would be enough

to hold the average inmate for only a little while longer, but the costs would be staggering.[93]

Thus, to achieve effective levels of specific deterrence, we would have to continue on our present course of prison escalation and basically "lock them up forever"—despite the fact that we already lock "them" up at higher rates and for longer sentences than almost every other country in the world. Yet, most of those countries have lower rates of violent crime. In other words, contrary to popular belief, the causes of crime in the United States have less to do with the mollycoddling of criminals (because we do not mollycoddle criminals in the United States) and more to do with the other features of our culture and social structure.

The growth of in-state correctional budgets means that money is being diverted from other—perhaps more worthy—state endeavors. If you are reading this book, you are most likely doing so as part of a college course and you know how expensive a college education has become. In many states, three or four decades ago, most in-state students paid only several hundred, perhaps a thousand dollars, per semester in tuition and fees to go to a state university. Such low fees were made possible because the states subsidized the preponderance of the costs of a college education for its residents. Today, in a rapidly increasing number of states, the vast majority of these costs are being paid by students and their families. Meanwhile, as the shares of the states' expenditures on higher education have been dwindling, the shares of expenditures on prisons have been increasing. Figure 5.3 shows how states' spending on corrections has far outpaced spending on higher

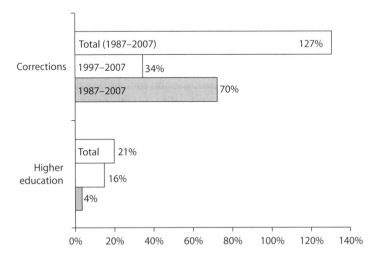

Figure 5.3 Growth in State Spending on Corrections and Higher Education
Source: National Association of State Budget Officers, "State Expenditure Reports," 1989, 1998, 2006. Liana Fox, "Burgeoning Prison Populations Strain State Budgets," Economic Snapshot, March 12, 2008, Economic Policy Institute, www.epinet.org.

education. As of 2007, at least five states were spending more of corrections than on higher education.[94]

A primary emphasis of critical constructionism is on the relative priority assigned to a given social problem vis-à-vis another social problem on the public agenda, in this case: corrections versus the cost of a college education. Given that the relationship between incarceration rates and crime rates is unsubstantiated, that U.S. incarceration rates are four times the world average, that the disproportionately high incarceration rate for African Americans is morally unsustainable, and that the job opportunities that tend to follow educational opportunities might be more effective in reducing crime—the critical constructionist is likely to argue that more state revenues should be diverted from corrections back into education.

Societies More Punitive Than the United States

While people may tend to think of crime and deviance as being inherently wrong, it is, in fact, culture that defines such things as wrong; and this is demonstrated by the cultural relativity of crime and deviance. Likewise, while people may tend to think that punishment is inherently right, it is, in fact, culture that defines such things as right. This is demonstrated by the cultural relativity of punishment. While the American public tends to believe that we coddle criminals (based on their belief in the inherent right-fulness of punishment), a cross-cultural analysis indicates otherwise. It is worthwhile to note that, generally speaking, the countries that do impose more severe punishments than the United States are those that Americans would least like to emulate in all other political respects. There is an interesting contradiction regarding the American "get-tough" approach to crime. That is, freedom and democracy are two of the most powerful ideals in the American value system. Yet, as the United States gets tougher on crime, its criminal justice system—a very important symbol of whether a country is free and democratic—begins to resemble the criminal justice systems of regimes that most Americans recognize to be repressive and authoritarian. As I have written in another volume,

> While the death penalty has been and continues to be associated with repressive regimes, the United States is using it more and more. While other nations that are making the transition from military or communist governments to democratic societies often immediately abolish capital punishment, the U.S. legislatures devise more and more crimes to which it should be applied.[95]

American criminology and criminal justice professors are often confronted by students who are upset about the mollycoddling of criminals in the United States and say something to the effect, "Why don't we just cut off their hands like they do in Iran?!" It is true, some crimes in Iran are punishable by amputation. Some prisons are equipped with amputation devices. They also have the death penalty and sometimes order violators to be stoned to death.[96] However, how many Americans would like to live in a society like Iran's? Most Americans would find Iran intolerably repressive, and its criminal justice system is a stark reflection of its repressiveness. If we look through history, those societies that inflict the worst punishments on their deviants and criminals are generally the most repressive in other political respects. Classical criminologist Cesare Beccaria made this point over 200 years ago, and it still holds today.[97]

Get-tough proponents in the United States are concerned that criminals—or the accused—have too many rights and that prison life is too comfortable; and they would like to see more executions. If they got what they wanted, how closely would the American criminal justice system resemble that in the People's Republic of China? There, the few rights enjoyed by the accused are easily abrogated by special "administrative sanctions," prison conditions are often miserable, and wholesale executions are common, perhaps as many as 20,000 per year. (A report from the Lawyers Committee for Human Rights notes, "[T]he official number of death sentences is considered a 'state secret' and is not made public."[98])

Get-tough proponents in the United States would argue that the People's Republic of China has gone too far in its get-tough policies, that they do not wish for anything quite so draconian in the United States. How do we in the United States know when we have gone too far? The answer to this question is a matter of opinion; but an informed opinion would, again, be aware of practices in other countries.

Societies Less Punitive Than the United States

When a great many Americans trace their heritage, they refer with pride to Western Europe. Interestingly, it is in Western European countries that we find perhaps the greatest tolerance of criminal wrongdoing and leniency in the treatment of criminal offenders. Among these, the Netherlands is probably the most famous among penologists and criminologists worldwide for its progressive criminal justice system. In democratic societies, such as the Netherlands or the United States, the treatment of criminal wrongdoers, whether lenient or harsh, depends largely on the public's attitudes toward them. In the Netherlands, public attitudes are far more forgiving, and, criminologist David Downes reports, there is an "active fostering of community tolerance and media support for broadly rehabilitative rather than punitive policies."[99] This stands in stark contrast to the situation in the United States.

As with many other American beliefs and attitudes, American-style perceptions of crime and criminality are starting to spread into many countries around the world. Dutch incarceration rates doubled between the mid-1980s and mid-1990s. Nevertheless, despite this doubling, the Dutch incarceration rate is roughly only one-seventh the rate in the United States. Dutch prisons are still considered among the most humane in the world. They are relatively small, housing only 80–120 inmates. Each inmate has his or her own cell.

In contrast to the United States, Dutch prison administrators are allowed to accept new inmates only if they have a cell available.[100] There appears to be mutual respect between prisoners and their guards, and there is an elaborate grievance procedure that takes prisoners' complaints seriously. An Australian prison administrator who studied Dutch prison management comments,

> In the wings, the workshops and recreational and communal areas, there was a notable lack of tension. A number of social and physical factors contributed to this impression; the fact that prisoners and detainees wore ordinary clothing and subdued styling of the officers' "uniform," the use of standard fittings and furnishings in buildings that in Australia would bristle with locks, bars, and hardened glass, the intermingling of staff and inmates were some of the factors involved. Even more telling was the naturalness of the interactions observed between members of the staff as well as between staff and inmates. To say that the prisoners appeared "natural" in their relations with staff is not to imply that their interactions were always cordial. Prisoners expressed annoyance in our presence but their feelings were focused on specific grievances and the response they received from staff conveyed not a hint of questioning their right to be angry. It should, however, be said that the social environment was generally friendly, robust and, as far as I could judge, devoid of the point-scoring that tends to characterize staff/inmate relations in Australian prisons.[101]

The Dutch are not alone in their humane treatment of criminal offenders. In Germany, for example, there is a women's prison called the *Mutter-Kind-Heim*, which allows its inmates to keep their young children with them. The prison is specially designed so that the children do not see bars and gates. The women live with their children in little apartments. The children spend the days with staff members, who are responsible for their education and recreation. They may leave the prison to go to a museum or the zoo. Meanwhile, their mothers work either in the prison or at jobs outside of the prison. In the evening, mother and child reunite in the apartment, where she cooks their dinner. Marie Douglas describes this as a very successful program with a 0 percent recidivism rate (i.e., none of its inmates reoffend after release). Norway has an island prison with a sauna and sunbed and no cells or armed guards. It claims to be the "world's first self-sustaining 'Ecological Prison'" and prisoners' work on the island may require them to use knives, axes, and even chainsaws. Even though its residents include convicted drug dealers and murderers, the prison boasts one of the lowest recidivism rates in all of Europe.[102]

These are just a few examples of less punitive reactions to crime found in European societies. There are other examples: the Scandinavian countries, in particular, are renowned for their progressive treatment of criminal offenders. Also, it should be noted that there are progressive, humane programs being tried in the United States. The decentralized nature of the U.S. criminal justice system allows for more flexibility and permits the testing of various treatment programs that may be difficult in the nationalized systems of most European countries. In spite of this flexibility and the alternatives available, the United States continues its imprisonment binge—regardless of its costliness and the lack of evidence demonstrating its effectiveness. Nonetheless, in spite of their relative lack of punitiveness, most European countries experience less violent street crime, especially homicide, than the United States. This, again, suggests that the explanation for crime in the United States lies in the culture and the social structure rather than in our "lenient" handling of criminal offenders.

THE MEDICALIZATION OF DEVIANCE

The 7 million people in prison, jail, on probation or on parole are under the control of the criminal justice system. According to those concerned about the "medicalization of deviance," there are likely many more millions under the control of the medical profession, psychiatry in particular. All societies have ways of ensuring that their people follow the norms. Sociologists call the means societies have for keeping people in line "social control mechanisms." These include informal mechanisms, such as rumor, gossip or ostracism, and formal mechanisms, such as after-school detention or prison. Agencies of social control include the police and the church. According to Thomas Szasz, as societies have secularized and religion has played a diminishing role in keeping people in line, psychiatry has risen to take up the slack.[103]

The problem, says Szasz, is that unlike other branches of medicine that base their diagnosis on objective observation of *structure*, psychiatry bases its diagnosis on *behavior* that can only be subjectively observed. Millions of Americans taking psychiatric medications have been and are being told that their afflictions are biologically based when, in fact, no biological defect has been detected in them. "Thus," he writes, "whereas in modern medicine new diseases were discovered, in modern psychiatry they were invented. Paresis was proved to be a disease, hysteria was declared to be one."[104] Modern psychiatry, he says, has progressed very little from the days when escaped slaves were diagnosed with the disease "drapetomania," which causes an overwhelming desire to runaway, and from the late nineteenth century when women with a variety of symptoms, including a tendency to cause trouble, were diagnosed with hysteria or a "wandering womb."

In the 1960s, hundreds of thousands, perhaps millions, of American children were diagnosed with MBD, "minimal brain damage," and prescribed methylphenidate, brand name Ritalin, which is chemically quite similar to cocaine.[105] The diagnosis was based, not on objective observation of biological defect, but on behavior that deviated from the norm. Unable to identify a biological etiology, the diagnosis eventually became "minimal brain dysfunction," and then "hyperkinesis," or "hyperactivity," and now "attention deficit disorder." While it is almost 50 years later and the drug regimen has changed slightly, there are still no biological tests involved in the diagnosis of this "medical" disorder. The same can be said for schizophrenia, bipolar disorder, depression, and virtually all other psychiatric "diseases."

The social control implications of the medicalization of deviance are profound. In the 1970s, blacks, women, and poor people who went to the doctor complaining of anxiety were more likely to be prescribed antianxiety medications than whites, men, and middle-class patients who complained of anxiety.[106] What blacks, women, and poor patients had in common, of course, is that they may well have had good reasons for feeling anxious and the source of their anxiety may have had something to do with how their status in society affected their life chances. Treating the individual with chemicals diverts attention away from the societal sources of stress. Change the individual, maintain the status quo. And, if a child has an "attention deficit disorder," maybe what he or she needs is more attention. Instead, with the medicalization of deviance, rather than society investing more time and money in that child, he or she is likely to be given amphetamines.

It is said that "necessity is the mother of invention." Perhaps anxiety is the true mother of invention. If the status quo induces stress in someone, perhaps they will be motivated to change it. Perhaps society today would be different if millions of African Americans, women, and poor people were not having their stress levels chemically reduced in the 1970s.

The critical constructionist does not deny the anguish and suffering of many of those diagnosed (labeled) mentally ill. But the scientific understanding of the source of their suffering is not there. Most of these patients are told by their physicians that they suffer from a chemical imbalance in their brain, but there are no chemical tests preceding their diagnosis. Nor have medical professionals specified what the proper balance of chemicals should be in the brain.

But whatever the etiology of their "disorder," these patients' suffering is exacerbated by the fact that our society marginalizes people who are different and capitalist societies, in particular, marginalize those who are not productive, who cannot or do not pull their weight in society. Paradoxically, the prognosis for schizophrenia in many poor countries of the South is much better than it is in the United States, with its advanced medical technology, where per capita spending on health care is the highest in the world. That is, people displaying the symptoms of schizophrenia in some countries of the South are frequently more likely to recover from their condition than those displaying the same symptoms in the United States. Richard Warner notes the sizeable amount of money spent on the treatment of schizophrenia in the United States and writes,

> Such a substantial investment should surely have yielded Americans significantly better rates of recovery than in less affluent parts of the world. By contrast, psychiatric care is very low on the list of priorities in developing

countries. Despite this fact, the evidence points overwhelmingly to much better outcome from schizophrenia in the Third World.[107]

In some countries of the South, people displaying the symptoms of schizophrenia are less likely to be receiving psychiatric medications; but more importantly, they are more likely to be embraced by their families and communities—often seeing them as possessed by spirits or touched by the gods—and less likely to be shunned or pressured to engage in productive activities.

So insistent are we that people occupy themselves productively that, in the past, medical professionals would administer various forms of shock "therapies," or lobotomize those who were unproductive. These were dramatic treatments, but if they had any chance of transforming the patient into productive members of society, doctors and their patients' families were willing to take the risk. If they did not work—and often they failed miserably—the patients were often locked away in frequently inhumane conditions. The very potent psychoactive drugs that are administered to patients today seem much more benign than treatments of the past and so the thresholds for mental illness have been lowered and millions more people are being diagnosed and treated for mental disorders.

The more traditional means of social control through the criminal justice system may be described as the "coercive model" of social control, whereas the medicalization of deviance offers an alternative model, the "treatment model." The coercive model says "we are going to *force* you to fit in;" the treatment model says "we're going to *help* you to fit in." The treatment model may be more effective because people like to be helped and they do not like to be forced. They even volunteer themselves for the help offered by the medical profession. The treatment model may also be more cost-effective because people (or their insurance companies) will even pay for the help. But, the critical constructionist warns, the treatment model is also more insidious because people do not recognize it as a form of social control and it is, therefore, more difficult to limit its application. So for the critical constructionist, not only are the constructions of crime and deviance at issue, but so too are the constructions of punishment and treatment.

Street Violence versus Corporate Violence

The critical constructionist is also concerned with how society constructs the seriousness of crime depending on the class and status of the offender. While American levels of street violence are quite high, while street violence and exotic crimes occupy the public imagination and fire its rage, and while public officials and law enforcement agencies expend a great deal of time and energy on these crimes, many sociologists who specialize in crime argue that corporate violence does more harm to society and deserves far more attention than it gets.

Ronald Kramer defines *corporate violence* as

corporate behavior which produces an unreasonable risk of physical harm to employees, the general public, and consumers, which is the result of deliberate decision-making by persons who occupy positions as corporate managers or executives, which is organizationally based, and which is intended to benefit the corporation itself.[108]

Arguably, corporate violence injures and/or kills more people than street crime. Its victims include people whose lives and homes are wrecked by pollution, whose children are born with birth defects due to pollution, who are exposed to hazardous chemicals at work and develop cancers years later, who buy dangerous products and are consequently injured or killed, who work on farms in countries of the South and are exposed to exported pesticides that have been banned in the United States, and the list goes on. Depending on the estimates used, the number of victims ranges between hundreds of thousands and millions who are injured or killed every year. Many would argue that when corporate officials knowingly risk the life or health of the public, consumers, or their employees, they should be held criminally liable, prosecuted, and punished as much as or more than any street criminal would be punished. Yet, when such officials are held accountable for injuries they have caused, their cases are frequently heard in civil or regulatory courts rather than criminal courts.

An often-cited example of alleged corporate violence surfaced with the uncovering of the so-called Pinto papers. The Pinto papers were internal memoranda at Ford Motor Company that allegedly demonstrated that officials at Ford knew the Pinto automobile was dangerous; the papers indicated that they knew it tended to explode on rear-end collision and that they estimated that about 180 people would die of burns incurred in such collisions and another 180 serious burn injuries could be expected. They also knew this problem in the Pinto could be fixed for about $11 per vehicle if they issued a recall. According to journalist Mark Dowie, to determine whether a recall was cost-effective, they proceeded to estimate the "cost" of a human life—that is, how much they could expect to settle with each victim's survivors—which came to just over $200,000. Using that figure, Dowie alleged that Ford officials determined that a recall would cost more than settling these cases and decided not to issue a recall for the Pinto. Dowie quotes a critic of Ford as saying, "One wonders how long Ford Motor Company would continue to market lethal cars were Henry Ford II and Lee Iacocca [the top Ford officials at the time] serving twenty-year terms in Leavenworth for consumer homicide."[109] (A very similar internal memorandum from General Motors, with allegedly very similar calculations pertaining to burn deaths, surfaced in 1999.[110] Consistent with their procorporate bias, this memo received very little coverage on the networks' evening news broadcasts.)

As with the Pinto, corporate officials are sometimes in a position to make decisions that can result in large numbers of deaths or injuries. Sociologist Stuart Hills notes,

> The following examples are the result of such decision-making: the decision to continue to sell the deadly Ford Pinto and defective Firestone 500 radial tires; the midnight dumping of poisonous wastes; the cover-ups by Johns-Manville officials and company doctors of the hazards of working with asbestos, thereby subjecting thousands of workers to slow and painful deaths by cancer; the Three Mile Island nuclear disaster; the horribly deformed thalidomide babies; the manufacturing of defective airplanes and cutbacks in airline maintenance; and other hazards to life and limb brought on in large measure by corporate negligence, the quest for profits, and deliberate violations of health, safety, and environmental laws.[111]

Such examples of corporate disregard for human life and suffering abound. The tobacco industry has been embroiled in legal battles all over the United States. Tobacco has been linked to lung and heart disease, which are linked to hundreds of thousands of deaths every year in the United States alone. Beyond these harmful physical effects of tobacco, most experts would agree that the nicotine it contains is addictive. For decades, however, tobacco companies had denied the connections between tobacco and lung cancer and heart disease and that nicotine is addictive. However, internal memoranda and testimony from former employees cast serious doubt about what corporate officials had actually known for many years and about what they had been hiding. In other words, there is a strong case to be made that tobacco officials have been selling products they have long known to be deadly and that they have been covering up evidence of its deadliness. If this is indeed true, then there is a substantial argument to be made that the acts of corporate officials in the tobacco industry *alone* cause more deaths and other physical and financial harm to society each year than street crime.

Why does street crime receive so much more attention relative to corporate violence? That is, why is street crime considered much more of a social problem than corporate violence? Many would argue that street crime receives more attention because it is more threatening than corporate violence. People choose to smoke cigarettes, knowing—whether tobacco companies admitted it or not—that it may be hazardous to their health. People, however, do not choose to be robbed while walking down the street. Besides that, tobacco companies and their officials contribute to society by stimulating the economy and providing thousands of jobs to company employees and tobacco farmers. Their economic activity cannot be compared to that of a robber. The critical constructionist holds that corporate hegemony has trained us to think like that.

The Great Recession, which has caused millions to lose their jobs and many more to suffer other serious financial losses, was triggered by the connivances of major players in the financial industry. They made loans and issued mortgages to people they knew could not pay, then bundled these securities and circulated them and recirculated them at ever-increasing prices. They knew a system such as this could not go on indefinitely, but this did not stop them from reaping in the profits while they could. Recently, Citibank has settled with the government for hundreds of millions of dollars because it is alleged that they sold such securities and, at the same time, invested in derivatives, or "placed bets" in the derivatives market, essentially betting that the securities they sold were overvalued. No one went to jail in this case. Very few individuals have been prosecuted in similar cases. In fact, if the media are correct, few, if any, laws were broken in the slew of financial maneuverings that brought on the Great Recession. The critical constructionist is concerned with the vast array of powerful interest groups that influence our legislators and that explain why these activities were not covered by criminal law.

The critical constructionist argues that the problem of crime is socially constructed. We have been trained to see crime as being a problem largely of lower-class individuals wreaking havoc on each other and on the rest of society. The majority of the times we hear about crime, our attention is drawn to the violent behavior of lower-class individuals. However, politicians and the media, who are training us to view crime in this manner, largely represent the interests of the corporate elite. The politicians depend upon contributions from corporations for their campaigns, and the media are themselves corporations that depend upon other corporations for their advertising dollars. Their interests and the interests of the corporate world are one and the same. They do not want to focus our attention on problems created by the corporate world, by the tobacco industry, or by the financial industry; instead, they focus our attention on the problems created by certain lower-class individuals. The problem, they maintain, is not in the social and economic structure but in the moral breakdown of society and in certain pathological individuals. Critical constructionism does not hold that there is a conspiracy among political, media, and corporate officials to divert attention away from their questionable activities but that, due to their unity of interests, things work out as if there were a conspiracy.

APPLICATION: TERRORISM

The hijackings and attacks on the World Trade Center and the Pentagon on September 11, 2001, were, first and foremost, horrific crimes; and if ever there were an act of terrorism, those attacks would qualify as prime examples. However, the use of the word *terrorism* is quite problematic to the critical constructionist. The word has little or no social scientific value, and like so many other phenomena discussed in this book, it is socially constructed. It has different meanings to different audiences in different contexts. The term describes a class of phenomena of which we do not approve, but it does not distinguish the objective reality of such phenomena from very similar phenomena of which we do approve. The word *terrorism* is a politically loaded one. It usually, but not always, is used in reference to violence; but if a group happens to approve of the violence in question, then it is not likely to be considered "terrorism." Palestinian suicide bombers are often seen as martyrs by many Palestinians and people from some other Muslim groups who support the Palestinian goal of independence, whereas they are considered "terrorists" by most Israelis and by most Americans, who are less sympathetic to their goals. Hence, as the expression goes "one man's terrorist is another man's freedom fighter"; or, as an article that appeared in the *Economist* reads,

> Who is or is not a terrorist? The suicide bomber, the rebel guerrilla, the liberation front, the armed forces of the state? In practice, what act or person earns the label depends on who wants to apply it. To Ulster loyalists all IRA violence is terrorism; to Sinn Fein it is part of a legitimate war. To many Israelis, everyone from the suicide bombers in Jerusalem or Ashkelon to the Hizb ollah [*sic*] grenade-thrower in South Lebanon is a terrorist; to many Arabs during the 1982 Lebanon war, the worst terrorists in the Middle East were the—entirely legitimate, uniformed—Israel Defense Force.[112]

A commonly accepted definition of terrorism refers to violence perpetrated against innocent civilians to achieve a political objective. Very often, the term *terrorist* is used by powerful entities (i.e., representatives of powerful groups or countries) to refer to the violence perpetrated by entities with far less power. When a group (e.g., a racial, ethnic, or religious group) or a country has a grievance against a government that has far more political, economic, or military resources at its disposal, it may be quite rational and sometimes quite effective for that group to turn to violence. It may also be quite rational for the less powerful group to target innocent civilians because the group with which it has a grievance may have a tremendous military advantage; targeting only their military resources would lead to certain defeat. "Terrorism is the way that non-soldiers engage in war,"[113] and its victims are usually nonsoliders as well. At what point does a group's grievance justify war? And if their grievance does justify war, what do they do if they are at a severe military disadvantage? Acts that we consider "terrorism" may well be a reasonable and effective solution to the problem.

While political leaders inevitably claim that terrorism is a desperate and futile strategy that is doomed to failure, history has proven it to be a sometimes effective strategy. In 1948, for example, Zionists blew up the King David Hotel, the British headquarters in Palestine; this was a key event in forcing the British to leave and paving the way for the establishment of Israel. Subsequently, attacks on civilians by the Palestinian Liberation Organization undoubtedly drew the world's attention to the plight of Palestinian refugees. While political leaders frequently state they will never negotiate with terrorists, they do indeed frequently negotiate with them. Gerry Adams and

Yasser Arafat were leaders of alleged terrorist organizations, and both became prominent players in peace negotiations. Now deceased, Arafat, is regarded by millions in the Middle East as a historical leader in international politics and a hero.

The critical constructionist perspective does not legitimate such violence, but it does put it on par with violence perpetrated by military forces. During war, each side has grievances with the other and turns to violence as a means of addressing such grievances. While military resources may be targeted, civilians are often killed and often killed knowingly. Eighty-four percent of those killed during the Korean War and 90 percent of those killed during the Vietnam War were civilians.[114] Of the 7 million people who have been killed in wars between 1989 and 2003, 75 percent have been civilians.[115]

Those who support the definition of terrorism given above would emphasize that acts of violence during wartime are distinguished from terrorist violence because the latter actually targets civilians, whereas in war civilians are incidental casualties ("collateral damage"). This distinction constructs an inflated difference between *intentionally* killing civilians and *knowingly* killing civilians. There are many shades of gray between the two, if they are not indeed two sides of the same coin. What about the hundreds of thousands of people killed in Hiroshima, Nagasaki, and Dresden during World War II? Were these acts of "terrorism?" (Would our "military" objectives have been accomplished so effectively if so many civilians had not been killed?) In 1989, the United States aggressively bombed a well-populated, poor neighborhood in Panama in its effort to oust President Manuel Noriega, killing hundreds of civilians (some estimates go into the thousands). Was this an act of terrorism?

Your answer to these questions likely depends on whether you think these military actions were legitimate and whether you think the goals (grievances) being addressed by these actions were legitimate. Such a judgment is based upon your values and not upon the objective nature of these actions. The BBC has a policy of not using the word *terrorist* in its news broadcasts because to do so would imply that it is taking sides in a political conflict. This policy reflects a critical constructionist argument which holds that the word terrorist is principally a term used by one side in a political conflict (usually the more powerful side) to demonize the enemy and delegitimate its tactics. The use of the word terrorist is an indicator of which side you are on in a political conflict.

In the days of American slavery, most Southerners thought of the abolitionists Nat Turner and John Brown in terms similar to those we use with regard to contemporary terrorists. Today, we think of Turner and Brown in a different light because we have more sympathy for their cause. The city of Charleston, South Carolina, recently erected a monument in honor of Denmark Vesey. Vesey was executed in 1822 for plotting to free the slaves of Charleston by burning down the city.[116] No doubt, he was seen as the equivalent of a terrorist by the white population of his day; but today he is honored for his courage and conviction because a substantial part of Charleston's population has strong sympathy for his grievance against slavery.

Professor of law Paul Butler writes,

> The uncertainty about how to evaluate the morality of some terrorists (one might also think about the original American rebels) has two possible explanations: (1) we have a double standard about terrorism and morality depending on our sympathy for the terrorists' cause or (2) there may be some extreme cases in which the taking of innocent lives in pursuit of an urgent objective is warranted. If we accept the former explanation, the appropriate moral solution probably requires absolute condemnation in every case. If we endorse the second explanation however, there may be exceptions to the general rule that terrorism is immoral. These exceptions must be carefully delineated and then rigorously scrutinized to make sure they are not self-serving.[117]

Both of the explanations provided by Butler employ values and, therefore, relativity. Values determine our sympathy for the "terrorists' " cause and values determine whether we consider an objective as an urgent one that warrants the killing of civilians. While terrorism is spoken of in popular rhetoric in absolutist terms, though it might be distasteful to some during the "war on terrorism," it is difficult to refute the critical constructionist argument that it is indeed a relative term that poorly reflects any objective reality. The use of the term in popular political discourse, at least, has corrupted its potential for any meaningful use in the social sciences.

SUMMARY

Crime and deviance are universal and unavoidable. Their presence in a society does not mean there is something wrong with that society. Crime and deviance are not only universal, occurring in all societies, but also relative to time and culture; that is, different societies define crime and deviance differently. Since definitions of crime and deviance vary, depending upon time and culture, this means that their definition depends upon things external to the behavior itself. That is, definitions of crime and deviance depend upon characteristics of social structure and culture, not upon the actual harm caused by the crime or deviance. Thus, for example, homosexuality was once defined as more deviant than it is currently. Changes in the deviant status of homosexuality were the result of (1) changes in the culture (changes in attitudes and beliefs about inequality, prejudice, and discrimination and changes in values attributed to new sexual freedoms) and (2) changes in the social structure (different institutions acknowledging and giving way to the demands of oppressed minorities).

Since reactions to crime and deviance depend upon features external to the behavior, there is not a one-to-one correspondence between levels of public fear and the actual threat posed by a particular type of crime or deviance. The media, a critical institution affecting social problem construction, help to define which types of crime and criminal are most threatening; and they tend to distort the real world of crime based upon their considerations of which types of image and story will "sell." Consequently, they opt for graphic depictions of violent street crimes because they are easy and inexpensive to cover; they appeal to the audience on a visceral level, their images are captivating even in the absence of a thoughtful explanation, and their perpetrators are most likely poor and in no position to fend off media coverage. The "reality-based" crime shows also have to consider their need for cooperation from law enforcement authorities. To ensure this cooperation, they have to depict law enforcement in a positive light.

"Crime scares" are another example of the way externalities affect the public's definition of criminal threats. The problems of missing children, serial murder, and drugs serve as examples of how particular types of crime and deviance can be exaggerated by the media, public officials, and various interest groups and how these exaggerations can affect the public's perception of a threat. Again, factors external to the actual threat are critical to understanding when and why a particular type of crime or deviance comes to be recognized as problematic.

In general, the type of crime the American public views as most problematic is street crime, especially violent street crime. The United States does indeed have high levels of street violence relative to other industrialized countries in the world. This is sometimes blamed on the availability of guns; however, even without access to guns, research indicates there would still be a disproportionately high incidence of violent crime in the United States. Also, the high incidence of violence does not appear to be due to any recent changes in the American "moral fiber" because we have consistently had disproportionately high rates of violence throughout the past century. The high incidence of violence in the United States must then be due to enduring features of the American culture and social structure. The most important feature of the American social structure that helps to explain street crime is its extremely capitalist economy; the most important features of its culture are the values placed on financial success (the American Dream), individualism, and competition. All of these combine to encourage a degree of ruthlessness among both winners and losers in the battle for success.

Political ideology is an important external factor that helps to define why certain social problems are defined as more threatening than others. Conservative ideologues, in particular, like to focus on crimes and especially on the individuals who commit them. Conservatives are more likely to view social problems as problems of moral breakdown or individual pathology, not as problems of the economy or social structure. Hence, in conservative times, the prescription for crime is not to change the social structure, the economy, and the poverty that it engenders but to get increasingly punitive. The American punishment binge, however, does not appear to be a success. As measured by the implementation of the death penalty and by incarceration rates, the United States is already one of the most punitive societies in the industrialized world, yet compared to most other industrialized countries it has relatively high rates of violent crime, especially homicide. The cause of the high rates of street crime in the United States, therefore, must be in the social structure and in the culture, not in the criminal justice system's leniency. The solutions, then, must address changes in the social structure and/or the culture.

Street crime does not necessarily pose a more serious threat to society than crimes that receive less public attention. It is arguable that if the degree of public concern were to approximate the degree of threat to the public, more attention should be paid to corporate violence, which affects millions of Americans each year, either directly or indirectly, yet receives very little attention relative to street crime. Again, a critical constructionist analysis shows that factors external to the degree of threat explain not only the high levels of concern for street crime but also the relatively low levels of concern for corporate violence.

Presently, "terrorism" looms large in the popular imagination as one of the most serious crimes threatening the United States. Ambiguities in the definition of the phenomenon are frequently used to the advantage of powerful entities in delegitimating the tactics of their enemies. It is difficult to argue that the problem referred to as "terrorism" is overexaggerated because another serious attack is always possible; yet, it is also difficult to dispute the fact that certain powerful interest groups stand to gain by exaggerating this threat. As with crime scares, the critical constructionist remains circumspect when references to the threat of terrorism appear continuously in popular discourse, especially when such references can be used to consolidate the power of certain interest groups, to the detriment of the public interest.

Discussion Questions

1. Imagine you are a high-level government (state or federal) official. You have a substantial sum of money to use to deal with the problem of crime. Are you going to use the bulk of that money to deal with street crime or with corporate crime? Would it matter whether you were an elected or an appointed official? Explain your reasoning.

2. Imagine you are writing an article for your college newspaper about the "war on drugs." What position would you take? What evidence would you use to support your position?

6

Problems of the Environment

TECHNOLOGY AND THE ENVIRONMENT

I t is technology that gives humans the ability to destroy virtually all life on earth. It is technology that gives our species so much control over the natural environment. And it is technology that has impacted the environment so much over the past century that environmental issues have become of such concern to people throughout the world today. Technology allows us to extract and consume the earth's resources at ever-increasing rates, and extraction and consumption almost invariably produce waste. Technology threatens the environmental health of the planet, and many of us are planning to go on extracting and consuming at present rates, hoping that future technologies will restore the planet's health.

Technology has long been constructed in the Western mindset, especially the American mindset, as the solution to all problems vis-à-vis the environment. While there seems to be increasing recognition that the earth's resources are finite, historically we have tended to rely on technology as though it could stretch them forever. Technology, of course, has played a pivotal role in American history. Columbus's ships were the product of technology. Technology helped the settlers to wrest the land from the Native Americans. Technology made it possible for the United States to become first an agricultural leader, then an industrial leader, and now a leader in the post-industrial world. Our affinity for technology perhaps reached its zenith in what has been called the "soaring '60s." In 1962, a committee of the National Academy of Sciences advised President Kennedy that science and technology would provide a future of abundance and that if natural resources, such as iron ore and petroleum, were depleted, better and cheaper substitutes could be developed. The committee predicted "dramatic increases" in food and energy and recommended a "shift away from a philosophy of conserving scarce resources," which had been recommended by the Paley Commission during the Truman administration. Then, in 1969, technology had its greatest public relations triumph with the lunar landing. President Nixon called it "the greatest week since the creation of the earth!"[1] Later, in 1973, referring to American technology's role in making the atomic bomb as well as the lunar landing, Nixon launched Project Independence, the goal of which was to "free the United States from dependence on foreign oil" by 1980.[2]

This kind of optimism—expecting technology to free us from the limits of the earth's resources—while it may have been justified to some extent by past technological successes, has failed to play itself out as anticipated. In fact, the belief that technology has provided us with so many benefits in the past is itself, in part, a social construction. An alternative construction is that the past availability of natural resources accounted for technology's successes. The automobile and highway systems that have changed our lives and "solved" so many of our problems are important technological achievements, but they would not have had such powerful impacts on our society if it were not for the availability of petroleum. Likewise, many hail technological advances in agriculture and improvements brought about by mechanization, irrigation, and hi-tech pesticides, fertilizers, and herbicides; but once again, the availability of petroleum has made many of these advances possible by powering farm machines, providing electricity for irrigation pumps, and serving as an essential ingredient in many of the pesticides, fertilizers, and herbicides. In many ways such as this, *technology has not freed us from the limits of the earth's resources, but it has increased our dependence on these resources*; the greater our dependence, the more is at stake. In the words of former Secretary of the Interior Stewart Udall, "America has preened itself for three decades on the wizardry of its technologists. All the evidence suggests that we have consistently exaggerated the contributions of technological genius and underestimated the contributions of natural resources."[3]

SCIENTIFIC UNCERTAINTY

The role of the sociologist in the environmental debate is less than obvious at first glance. On the one hand, many of the issues that are part of the public discourse about the environment would not seem to fall within the domain of sociological inquiry. Is global warming taking place? How many people can the earth sustain? Is the ozone hole indeed expanding? These are questions for the natural sciences. However, these changes definitely can and do have profound effects on society, and society's responses to these problems (or potential problems) are of considerable sociological import. Sociology can help to clarify some of the issues in the environmental debate.

The essential questions in the debate are, How serious is the damage being done by humans to the planet? How much do we know about this impact? Can we go on with business as usual? Unfortunately, the debate is riddled with uncertainty; but that uncertainty varies with the type of human impact under discussion. Generally speaking, we are more certain about some of the *local* effects of human impact than we are about the *global* effects. For example, it is quite certain that human sewage in the water supply can produce a local outbreak of cholera and other diseases. It is quite certain that the thousands of people who died in Bhopal, India, after a gas leakage in the Union Carbide plant in 1984 died because of that leakage. It is almost certain that sharp increases in thyroid cancer among people living in the area of Chernobyl were in large part attributable to the accident at the nuclear power plant in 1986. However, local effects are not always that certain. If a factory is leaking toxic chemicals into a lake and the residents living in the area develop unusually high rates of leukemia, it may be quite likely that the toxins are linked to the leukemia, but it may also be difficult to prove and, therefore, less than certain.

For most of the history of environmental concern, most of the attention has been focused on local impacts. Then, in the 1970s, attention was drawn to the fact that emissions from factories and automobiles were carrying acid across national borders and damaging crops and forests in other countries. "Acid rain" became one of the first environmental issues of international, though not global, concern. Scientists and government leaders were certain enough of the impacts of acid rain to hold international talks on the matter in Berlin in 1985. International agreements and regulations soon followed. In the 1980s, ozone depletion was among the first environmental issues to raise global concern. The ozone layer in the atmosphere serves to protect the earth from the more damaging effects of the sun's ultraviolet rays. Its depletion, caused by human-made pollutants (namely, chlorofluorocarbons, or CFCs), could possibly lead to increased rates of skin cancer, damage to marine life, and lower crop yields. In 1985, an ozone "hole" was discovered over Antarctica. Awareness of the problem culminated in international treaties to phase out CFC production and use. The issue of ozone depletion was quickly followed by the issue of global warming. Gas pollutants, mostly from automobiles and factory emissions, are accumulating in the atmosphere and allowing the sun's heat to warm the earth but preventing that heat from escaping the atmosphere, producing a "greenhouse" effect. Thus, the more greenhouse gases that accumulate, the warmer the earth's temperature becomes. An average increase of just a few degrees could melt polar ice caps, raise ocean levels, flood coastal plains, change the world's climate and vegetation patterns, and, therefore, alter the conditions of life on earth. While the United States agreed to reduce ozone depletion, it has taken the lead in resisting measures to alleviate global warming.[4] This will be discussed later in the chapter.

It is important to note that problems associated with both ozone depletion and global warming are partly theoretical and, therefore, uncertain. The causes and effects of such phenomena continue to be debated by scientists. If nothing were done, the worst effects of either might not be experienced for generations to come. Thus, a question of particular interest to the constructionist is, Why were publics and governments so much more responsive to the issue of ozone depletion than global warming? According to Sheldon Ungar,[5] the imagery of a "hole" in the earth's protective shield is more evocative than any imagery associated with global warming. (There actually is no "hole" in the ozone layer but an area that is considerably thinner than the rest.) During the 1980s, an era of *Star Trek* movies, the Cold War, and Star

Wars technology, the public was receptive to the notion of death rays penetrating faulty force shields. The "C-word"—cancer, which could result from exposure to these rays—had been a particularly powerful motivator as well. The issue of global climate change, on the other hand, without that kind of imagery, has failed to overcome the debate about scientific uncertainty that has surrounded it from the beginning.

In 1992, the Royal Society of London broke an official 300-year silence on public issues to join the U.S. National Academy of Sciences to issue a statement about population and climate change, warning that "if current predictions of population growth prove accurate and patterns of human activity on the planet remain unchanged, science and technology may not be able to prevent either irreversible degradation of the environment or continued poverty for much of the world."[6] The Intergovernmental Panel on Climate Change (IPCC), established by the United Nations and the World Meteorological Organization in 1988 and made up of 2,500 scientists and other experts from around the world, concluded in 1995 that human activity is indeed having an impact on the earth's climate and that there is urgent need to cut back on greenhouse gas emissions. Further data analysis prompted the IPCC to reiterate these findings in its 2001 report. And in 2007, the IPCC reported, "Warming of the climate system is unequivocal, as is now evident from observations of increases in global average air and ocean temperatures, widespread melting of snow and ice and rising global average sea level."[7]

Even though the vast majority of climatologists who have weighed in on the issue agree that global warming is a threat,[8] skeptics continue to exploit what little scientific uncertainty remains. The sequencing of their arguments could have been predicted by anyone who understood that many or most of them received financial backing from corporate interests whose mission, from the beginning, was to stave off any mandatory limits on greenhouse gas emissions. First they argued that there was no evidence of any global warming trends. Then, in the face of overwhelming evidence to the contrary, they argued the global warming was not due to human activity. Then, as evidence to the contrary accumulated, they argued that, though there is global warming due to human activity, the consequences of such will not be so severe as to warrant corporations, nations, and people to change their behavior. Some see the latter argument as a concession and have stuck to denying the contribution of human activity as a cause of climate change while others still stick vociferously to the denial of climate change.

Meanwhile, in 2010, the National Oceanic and Atmospheric Administration, an arm of the U.S. Department of Commerce, issued a report announcing,

The 2009 *State of the Climate* report released today draws on data for 10 key climate indicators that all point to the same finding: the scientific evidence that our world is warming is unmistakable. More than 300 scientists from 160 research groups in 48 countries contributed to the report, which confirms that the past decade was the warmest on record and that the Earth has been growing warmer over the last 50 years.[9]

A 2007 article in *Newsweek* reports, "…the length of heat waves in Europe has doubled, and their frequency nearly tripled, in the past century. The frequency of Atlantic hurricanes has already doubled in the last century. Snowpack whose water is crucial to both cities and farms is diminishing."[10] The year 2003 saw a heat wave in Europe that killed tens of thousands of people; 2005 saw Hurricane Katrina devastate the Louisiana and Mississippi coastal regions (which, if it was not caused by global warming, could well be a sign of things to come). Insect-born diseases are becoming endemic in more northerly regions where they never appeared before. You can go on YouTube and watch glaciers calving into the seas at rates far exceeding those in recorded history. The government of the island nation of the Maldives is considering a plan to buy land in India so that its natives can relocate should the island continue to be swamped by rising sea levels. And the vast majority of climatologists say we are only just beginning to see the effects of global warming.

In previous chapters, critical constructionism has shown us how often subtle elite interests have influenced the public debate concerning various social problems. With regard to climate change and other environmental issues, elite corporate interests are far less than subtle. Environmentalists claim that significant cutbacks in greenhouse emissions and other industrial pollutants would require substantial investments in environmental technology and/or substantial cutbacks in industrial production—either of which could present serious threats to corporate profits. In previous chapters, the case has been made that the resources that corporate interests can bring to bear in public debate often overwhelm the voice of social scientists who have studied the issues systematically. In the case of social problems dealing with the environment, the voices of both social and natural scientists who have weighed in on the debate have been frequently overwhelmed by an array of persuasive devices employed by corporate interests.

CORPORATE SUASION

Environmentalists generally seek government regulation, and corporations, preferring to operate in the so-called free market, are almost always opposed to regulation. In the 1970s, the environmental movement was at its peak, enjoying a great deal of public and political support throughout North America and Western Europe. In the United States, by the mid-1970s, "5.5 million people contributed financially to nineteen leading national organizations, and perhaps another 20 million to over 40,000 local groups. Environmentalism," write Daniel Faber and James O'Connor, "had arrived as a mass-based movement."[11] Environmentalists were winning significant political victories, and the corporate world was rocked by the passage of legislation such as the Clean Air Act, the Clean Water Act, and the establishment of the Environmental Protection Agency. In their "near-hysterical determination" to "put the environmental lobby out of business," according to Sharon Beder, corporations formed coalitions and alliances, established "public affairs" departments or increased the status of existing departments, and diverted increasing resources to lobbying Congress. In 1971, there were 175 firms represented by lobbyists in Washington; by 1982, the number had climbed to 2,445.[12] Since college graduates were among those most supportive of the environmental movement, many corporations and conservative foundations pumped millions of dollars each year into establishing endowed chairs of "free enterprise"; establishing the Institute of Educational Affairs, "which was conceived," writes Beder, "...to coordinate the flow of money from corporations into the production of conservative ideas"; and funding scholars "whose views were compatible with the corporate view."[13] According to Beder, in her book *Global Spin: The Corporate Assault on Environmentalism,*

> In the late 1970s U.S. business was spending a billion dollars each year on propaganda of various sorts "aimed at persuading the American public that their interests were the same as business's interests." The result of all this expenditure showed in the polls when the percentage of people who thought there was too much regulation soared from twenty-two percent in 1975 to sixty percent in 1980.[14]

The corporate world succeeded throughout most of the 1980s in its battle against the environmentalists, and many environmental regulations were repealed or went unenforced during the Reagan administration. Ozone depletion, climate change, and other environmental concerns attracted a great deal of public attention in the mid- to late 1980s; but this time the corporate world was ready for battle with the techniques they had learned earlier.

Exploiting Uncertainty

One of the corporate world's principal weapons in the battle against scientific findings that are unfavorable to its interests is to exploit the presence of scientific uncertainty. According to environmental sociologists Frederick Buttell and Peter Taylor, "Scientific uncertainty can be an enormously powerful tool and it is one that is often wielded against environmentalists with particular effectiveness."[15] As long as there is a shred of scientific uncertainty (and there almost always is), it can be exploited by skeptics. Many of us are familiar with this tactic as it was used by the tobacco companies. Despite the endless number of scientific studies linking cancer and cigarette smoking, the tobacco companies could always claim that it had not been proven that smoking causes cancer. Theoretically, they had a point; the link between smoking and cancer, after all, could be due to the possibility that people who are prone to cancer are more likely to smoke rather than smokers being more likely to contract cancer. Virtually the only scientific study that could determine which is the cause and which is the effect would require taking a random sample of newborn babies, randomly dividing them into two groups, later forcing one group to smoke incessantly, never allowing the other group near a cigarette, and then later examining which group developed higher rates of lung cancer. Obviously, for ethical reasons, such a study could never take place. The problem then with this type of research is one of methodology, and all scientific research encounters some sort of methodological difficulty. Few of us today, however, doubt there is a causative link between smoking and cancer.

One of the principal tactics for exploiting uncertainty is for industry and its defenders to claim that more research is needed (often, while, at the same time, they are covering up research findings that are detrimental to their interests). Gerald Markowitz and David Rosner, authors of *Deceit and Denial: The Deadly Politics of Industrial Pollution,* write of the "political value of scientific ambiguity."

> The call for more scientific evidence is often a stalling tactic. The inability of science in the 1920s to prove that lead in gasoline, for example, was dangerous resulted in severe damage to children a half a century later. The inability of science to agree about whether or not there is a problem with the use and disposal of plastics and the willingness of industries to use new chemicals before they are proved safe may also have terrible consequences for society.[16]

While calling for more research into these matters, industry is fully aware that government and private foundations have limited resources and often cannot afford to conduct costly scientific research. More often than not, such research is conducted or funded by the industries themselves. Just as much of the research that once found tobacco to be a harmless substance was funded by tobacco companies themselves, much of the research that fails to find a link between various pollutants and environmental harm is funded by corporations. The corporation, of course, has an interest in producing findings that minimize the harm caused by its product or its emissions; therefore, it is reasonable to suspect that corporate-funded research is significantly biased. As with the tobacco companies, beyond using methodologies that are likely to produce desirable findings, corporations have been discovered on a number of occasions to have covered up findings that may lead to an increase in their production costs or a reduction in their profits.

Defenders of industry say that we should trust industry to look after the public interest and that, when there is uncertainty about a product's safety, government regulation is rarely in the public interest. History has shown this stance to be very problematic. The tobacco industry did all that it could to cover up the dangers of tobacco; the asbestos industry did all that it could to cover up the dangers of asbestos; and the lead industry did all that it could to cover up the dangers of lead. Just these three products alone have been responsible for the deaths of millions of people and for the impairments of millions more.

Environmental law requires that chemical companies have to turn over any research findings that indicate a substance may be harmful to people's health or to the environment. In 1991 and 1992, the Environmental Protection Agency offered an amnesty, allowing corporations who had not yet done so (who had been covering up) to turn such scientific documents over with impunity. Chemical manufacturers produced documents from over 10,000 studies indicating that their products produced substantial risks. "Until the amnesty was offered, until it was clear that they wouldn't be sanctioned, the manufacturers simply kept those studies to themselves, even though they were obligated by law to turn over the information."[17] In the name of profit, they had kept these documents secret, breaking the law, violating the ethical tenets of scientific discovery, and putting the environment and the public at risk. It is likely many damaging documents were not turned over because the products were still turning profits.

Public Relations

Corporations have also been very successful at fending off regulation by hiring public relations (PR) firms to fight their battles against environmentalists. "Rather than substantially change business practices so as to earn a better reputation," writes Beder, "many firms are turning to PR professionals to create one for them. After all 'It is easier and less costly to change the way people think about reality than it is to change reality.'"[18]

Of course, one of the tactics employed by PR firms to protect their clients is to exploit the uncertainty surrounding so many environmental issues. For instance, when CFCs were implicated in ozone depletion, the $3 billion aerosol industry engaged the services of PR firms. The PR firms issued press releases emphasizing that the CFC link was theoretical, and they produced a handbook for their clients instructing them how to testify in hearings and respond to news journalists. When asked if aerosols should be banned, for example, the handbook suggested an appropriate response might be "There is slight risk that thousands of different products could be modifying the atmosphere to one degree or another. I do not think it is reasonable or proper to ban products at random to eliminate a threat that many qualified people doubt even exists."[19] U.S. Gypsum, which was being sued for installing asbestos in public buildings, was reportedly advised by its PR firm that by

> enlisting "independent experts," the issue of asbestos, instead of being a public health problem, could be redefined as "a side issue that is being seized on by special interests and those out to further their own causes...." The media and other audiences important to US Gypsum should ideally say, "Why is all this furor being raised about this product? We have a non-story here."[20]

The best PR is that which is not recognized as such. In fact, a good deal of PR output today passes as "news." To put it another way, much of today's newspaper and television news is generated by PR firms. It is estimated that "40 percent of all 'news' flows virtually unedited from public relations offices."[21] A former editor of the *Wall Street Journal* admitted that approximately half of their news stories were generated by press releases but added, "In every case we try to go beyond the press release." The *Columbia Journalism Review*, however, upon examining the *Wall Street Journal*, found that more than half of its news stories were "based solely on press releases" often "almost verbatim or in paraphrase" even though those articles usually carried the byline "By a *Wall Street Journal* Staff Reporter."[22] As mentioned above, the PR campaign for the aerosol industry involved sending out press releases emphasizing "knowledge gaps" rather than ozone holes, and its releases were often reprinted as news.[23]

A sophisticated and attractive alternative to the press release is the production and distribution of the video news release (VNR). PR firms are now producing video segments that are indistinguishable from—often more professional than—the segments produced in-house by television news staffs. Martin Lee and Norman Solomon, authors of the book *Unreliable Sources: A Guide to Detecting Bias in News Media*, report, "Every week, hundreds of local TV stations, beset by budget and staff cutbacks, air these free, ready-made news releases, which look increasingly realistic. Even veteran media observers often fail to distinguish between video PR spots and station-produced news."[24] One survey found that "eighty percent of U.S. news directors use VNRs a few times each month."[25] Together, the traditional press release and the VNR "ensure that much of the news people read or watch on television is manufactured by PR firms rather than discovered by journalists."[26] Thus, corporations, in addition to those actually owning the news agencies, are involved in the business of news production and it has become increasingly difficult to distinguish the news from corporate advertising.

Another tactic used by PR firms is to advise their corporate clients to establish or work through what are sometimes called "front groups." Front groups are organizations that are supported by corporate interests and are made up of citizens or "experts," which are mobilized to achieve particular political ends. Corporations that are often accused of environmental destruction frequently fund, what many consider, antienvironmental organizations such as the Wise Use Movement. If an organization that suits its cause does not already exist, the corporation can hire a PR firm to organize one. Lawyers for electric companies opposed to the Endangered Species Act reportedly advised their clients to "[i]ncorporate as a nonprofit, develop easy-to-read information packets for Congress and the news media and woo members from virtually all walks of life. Members should include Native American entities, county and local governments, universities, school boards...."[27] According to an article in *Consumer Reports*, PR firms organizing such groups often recruit with financial incentives, paying as much as $500 "for every citizen they mobilize for a corporate client's cause."[28]

Referring to the deceptive nature of industry front groups, the same article in *Consumer Reports,* entitled "Public Interest Pretenders," observes,

> There was a time when one usually could tell what an advocacy group stood for—and who stood behind it—simply by its name. Today, "councils," "coalitions," "alliances," and groups with "citizens" and "consumers" in their names could as likely be fronts for corporations and trade associations as representatives of "citizens" or "consumers."...[Many industry front groups] use names that make them sound as if they represent the public interest, not a business interest....Someone looking at the logo of the National Wetlands Coalition, which features a duck flying over a marsh, would have no clue that the coalition is made up mainly of oil drillers, developers, and natural gas companies that want national policy on wetlands use and development shaped for their industries' benefit.[29]

One might think the Global Climate Coalition (GCC) was an organization concerned with the prevention of global warming; instead, it was a coalition of "fifty U.S. trade associations and private companies representing oil, gas, coal, automobile, and chemical interests" whose aims were likely altogether different.[30] As the GCC was increasingly exposed as a front group for industry intent on obstructing measures to prevent climate change, many of its prominent corporate members began withdrawing from the group (including DuPont, British Petroleum, Texaco, and General Motors).[31] Consumers for Responsible Solutions was a front group allegedly funded by Philip Morris to defeat antismoking statutes in Florida. The group was disbanded when its connection to Philip Morris became public.[32]

PR firms have developed a vast array of tactics in addition to press releases, VNRs, and front groups. In the 1990s, the PR firm representing the California raisin industry reportedly undertook a campaign to discredit David Steinman's book *Diet for a Poisoned Planet* even before it was published. In his book, Steinman recommended that people eat no fruits and vegetables other than those grown without pesticides. Ketchum, one of the largest PR firms in the country, specializes in "crisis management"; and apparently it was perceived that the publication of the Steinman book would precipitate a crisis for their clients. John Stauber and Sheldon Rampton detail Ketchum's campaign against the book in their exposé of the PR industry, entitled *Toxic Sludge Is Good for You.* The campaign was carried out in the utmost secrecy. According to Stauber and Rampton, a memo from a senior vice president at Ketchum warned, "All documents...are confidential....Make sure that everything—even notes to yourself—are so stamped....Remember that we all have a shredder.... All conversations are confidential, too. Please be careful talking in the halls, in elevators, in restaurants, etc...."[33] Using an informant at Steinman's publishing company, Ketchum managed to get an itinerary of his publicity tour, according to the vice president's memo, "so that we can 'shadow' Steinman's appearances; best scenario: we will have our spokesman in town prior to or in conjunction with Steinman's appearances."[34]

Then, according to Stauber and Rampton, Ketchum employees contacted newspapers and television shows, describing Steinman as an "off-the-wall extremist without credibility" or demanding equal time to present opposing arguments.

The vice president's memo also mentioned other "external ambassadors" who might be recruited in their campaign against the book. One such apparent "ambassador" was Elizabeth M. Whelan, a "prominent antienvironmentalist" and head of the American Council on Science and Health (ACSH). ACSH is funded largely by the chemical industry and happened also to have been a client at Ketchum. Stauber and Rampton report that Whelan sent a letter to John Sununu, chief of staff at the White House, warning that Steinman and others "specialize in terrifying consumers" and "were threatening the U.S. standard of living and, indeed, may pose a future threat to national security."[35] The introduction to Steinman's book had been written by Dr. William Marcus, senior science advisor to the U.S. Environmental Protection Agency. According to Stauber and Rampton, Marcus was pressured to have his introduction removed; he refused and was later fired. Since then, government policy was changed to prohibit officials from writing book forewords.

Stauber and Rampton also detail PR firms sabotaging other environmental books. In one case, the PR firm "hired an infiltrator to pose as a volunteer"[36] in the author's office. After they obtained a copy of his publicity tour itinerary, the producers of the radio and television shows on which the author was to appear received phone calls from a woman falsely claiming to be the author's publicist and canceling his appearances.

While some of the techniques employed by PR firms are certainly legal and ethical, others might be legal and unethical, and others are certainly illegal. Further, there is no denying that environmental groups have sometimes resorted to similar tactics, some legal and some illegal. However, the financial resources that industry can use to sway popular constructions far outweigh those that are available to environmental groups. The PR firms might claim that they are just trying to expose the public to the truth or even to the uncertainty of environmental issues, and they are reasonable in their claim that both sides to an issue should be presented. Yet, we should keep in mind that the PR firm is merely representing a paying client and has little or no interest in getting at the truth regarding their client's product or emissions that may cause harm. By using sometimes underhanded methods and by exploiting the uncertainty involved, PR firms are often very effective at preventing environmentalists' messages from ever reaching the public. Stauber and Rampton write,

Neither Ketchum Public Relations nor the White House has any right to interfere with your access to good food or good reading materials.... You have never voted for a politician who campaigned on a pledge that he would work to limit your access to information about the food you eat. You have never voted for Ketchum PR, and, if you are like most people, you've never even *heard* of them. You never gave consent for them to be involved in your life, and in return, they have never bothered to ask for your consent. After all, they're not working for *you*. They are working for the California Raisin Board.[37]

SLAPPs

Another weapon in the corporate arsenal is the lawsuit. Oftentimes environmentalists and other activists are sued for defamation, nuisance, interference with contract, or a similar charge by the industry that feels threatened. The party initiating such a suit often has no intention of winning but is instead attempting to tie the issue up in court, drain the financial resources of the activists, and intimidate others who might be thinking of publicly criticizing their operations. Such lawsuits are called *SLAPPs*, or "strategic lawsuits against public participation." There have been thousands of such cases filed in the courts, with the plaintiffs often seeking millions of dollars in damages. One woman in Texas, for example, was sued for $5 million for simply calling a landfill a "dump." The case dragged on for 3 years, costing the defendant thousands of dollars in legal fees. Finally, the case was dropped; and following an investigation, the Environmental Protection Agency ordered that the site be cleaned up.[38]

Critics, of course, argue that SLAPPs are a threat to activists' freedom of speech. Beder writes,

> Multi-million dollar lawsuits are being filed against individual citizens and groups for circulating petitions, writing to public officials, speaking at, or even just attending, public meetings, organizing a boycott and engaging in peaceful demonstrations. Such activities are supposed to be protected by the First Amendment of the U.S. Constitution, but this has not stopped powerful organizations who want to silence their opponents.[39]

University of Denver professors George Pring and Penelope Canan were among the first to study this phenomenon, and they were the ones who coined the term *SLAPP*. They found in their research that two-thirds of SLAPPs are dismissed before trial and, of those that are decided in favor of the plaintiff, most are overturned or dismissed on appeal.[40] Nonetheless, SLAPPs can be a traumatic ordeal for defendants, and they can be very effective at chilling the speech of those who might otherwise engage in protest. Pring and Canan write, "[T]ens of thousands have been SLAPPed, and still more have been muted or silenced by the threat."[41]

The Media

As discussed in earlier chapters, the media play a critical role in shaping popular constructions of social problems. The media are themselves run by corporations, and they are dependent upon the advertising revenue of other corporations. Consequently, corporate interests are highly influential in shaping the content of what we read in newspapers and see on television. In the early days of network television, presenting the news was seen largely as a public service and news programs were not expected to bring in big profits. Small newspapers might be considered a success by their owners if they could simply produce enough revenue to pay the costs of overhead and salaries. Today, however, more and more media are being bought out by huge corporations. Media ownership is in a constant state of flux, but at various points in recent history, ABC belonged to Disney, CNN belonged to Time Warner, and NBC belonged to General Electric. These are all multibillion-dollar, transnational corporations that are heavily invested in a number of other businesses and industries. Meanwhile, both large and small newspapers are being bought up in a frenzy of corporate media acquisitions. "Gone is the owner-editor who purchased a press because, for better or worse, he had something to say."[42] Like their television counterparts, newspaper owners have one overriding goal—the same goal of almost all other corporate executives—profit. Relates Calvin Exoo, author of *The Politics of the Mass Media,*

> Indeed, when GE took over NBC and installed one of its corporate lawyers as its president, he firmly declared that the network's overriding responsibility was to "shareholders." At that point, a member of the news division asked whether the network had another responsibility, whether the news was a "public trust." "It isn't a public trust," replied the boss. "I can't understand that concept."[43]

Americans cherish the notion of a "free press" and loathe the notion of "censorship." The press, as it is popularly construed today, is considered to be free of censorship; but this construction considers only government censorship. Indeed, there is relatively little government censorship of U.S. media. *Corporate censorship,* on the other hand, guides so much of media content that it is hardly recognized as such. Beder writes, "Commercial television and radio [and newspapers] receive most if not all of their income from advertisers. Tens of billions of dollars are spent every year just on television advertising, and the media does its best to create a product that suits those advertisers."[44] The goal of both a news program and an entertainment program is to hold the audience's attention long enough to get them to the commercial, to "deliver the audience to the commercial." It is overwhelmingly in the media's best interest to present a procorporate bias in its program content. To do otherwise would compromise their ability to maximize their profits.

A survey of news editors found that 33 percent admitted they would not "feel free" to air a program that might harm the interests of their parent company.[45] (That is only the proportion who admitted that they might violate the ethics of news journalism in favor of corporate interests.) In the 1970s, *New York Times* editors were reportedly instructed to downplay the role of the auto industry in air pollution because the auto industry was one of the paper's major advertisers.[46] Lee and Solomon write,

> These days, no commercial TV executive in his right mind would produce a program without considering whether it will fly with the sponsors. Prospective

shows are often discussed with major advertisers, who review script treatments and suggest changes when necessary....Procter and Gamble, which spends over a billion dollars a year on advertising, once decreed in a memo on broadcast policy "There will be no material that will give offense, either directly or indirectly to any commercial organization of any sort." Ditto for Prudential Insurance: "A positive image of business and finance is important to sustain on the air."[47]

Lee and Solomon discuss in some detail a documentary aired by NBC about nuclear power plants in France, which "could have passed for an hour-long nuclear power commercial." The correspondent stated, "Looking at a foreign country where nuclear power is a fact of life may restore some reason to the discussion at home....In most countries, especially the U.S., emotions drive the nuclear debate and that makes rational dialogue very difficult." The implication is that opposition to nuclear power in the United States is emotional, not rational. No mention was made that NBC's parent company, General Electric, was a major supplier of nuclear power, with 39 nuclear reactors in the United States. Nor was there mention of contentious debate among the French about nuclear power. Nor did NBC later report the accidents injuring seven people in French nuclear power plants only one month after the airing of the special, accidents that received a good deal of coverage in the French media and some coverage in U.S. newspapers.[48]

When the major media outlets are owned by transnational corporations and dependent upon advertising revenue from corporations, they do not constitute a "free press." In the strictest sense, there probably is no such thing as a free press. Government-controlled media are, of course, not free either. Both government-controlled media and commercially controlled media are inherently inclined to bias. However, of interest to the critical constructionist is the popular perception of corporate control as representing the opposite of government control and, therefore, representing the "free" alternative. This construction enables corporate interests to have immeasurable influence on social problem construction. According to David Edwards,

> [T]he mass media system is not a medium for the "free" discussion of ideas and viewpoints, but is deeply embedded in, and dependent on, the wider corporate status quo, and on the related capacity of corporate communications to boost facts, ideas, and political choices that are conducive to profit maximization, and to stifle those that are not.[49]

Irrespective of their ties to the corporate world, the status quo receives further nourishment from news journalists by their ostensible obsession with "impartiality." Though, as described above, their interests are aligned with corporate interests, news journalists are very careful not to appear to be taking sides. News journalists frequently boast about their objectivity, to be "fair and balanced" claiming to be impartial in obsessively covering "both" sides of the issues—even when there might be more than two sides to an issue or when one of the two sides to an issue happens to represent a minority opinion or the lunatic fringe. The British tend to take the issue of climate change much more seriously than do Americans. Fiona Harvey, environment correspondent for the *Financial Times,* explains, "In the United States, you have lots of news stories that, in the name of balance, give equal credence to the skeptics. We don't do that here—not because we're not balanced—but because we think it's unbalanced to give equal validity to a fringe few with no science behind them."[50]

In the realm of politics, one can be either for maintaining the status quo or for change. If one is not in favor of change, then, in effect, one supports the status quo. In striving to maintain the appearance of objectivity, in failing to take sides, news journalists are thus supporting the status quo by default. Those advocating change face an uphill battle trying to influence problem construction when the media can always be expected to give the opposing side "equal time." Environmental sociologist John Hannigan writes,

> [R]eporters may turn to the "equal time" technique whereby both environmental claims-makers and their opponents are quoted with no attempt to resolve who is right. In this case it becomes difficult for environmentalists to convince the public that an "issue" is in fact a "problem."[51]

The principle of impartiality in news journalism makes it very easy for corporations (and often their paid skeptics) to exploit the scientific uncertainty surrounding climate change. According to Paul Rauber,

> In the pursuit of "impartiality" the U.S. news media reflexively seek out the Two Sides to Every Question....It happens more so when the topic is the least bit technical; most reporters don't know much about science, and are unable to distinguish legitimate scientific dispute from bogus posturing. Which is why there is still a "debate" about global warming.[52]

Though it is likely that many of the scientists who are skeptical of global warming are sincere and not just "posturing," the skeptics do make up a very small minority in the scientific community, and the tendency of news journalism to present both sides "equally" obscures their minority status, thereby weakening the argument of the majority. The public is left with the impression that "nobody knows what they are talking about" and, therefore, there is no need for more regulations on industry.

Since James Hansen, director of NASA's Institute for Space Studies, alerted the public to the potential devastation of global warming in 1988—even if U.S. policymakers took up the mantle today—the denial, obstructionism, and foot-dragging that has taken place over the past 20 years is not likely to have been without consequence. Mark Hertsgaard writes in a 2006 *Vanity Fair* article,

> But if the deniers appear to have lost the scientific argument, they prolonged the policy battle, delaying actions to reduce emissions when such cuts mattered

the most. "For 25 years people have been warning that we have a window of opportunity to take action, and if we waited until the effects were obvious it would be too late to avoid major consequences," says Oppenheimer [a professor of geosciences and international affairs at Princeton]. Had some individual countries, especially the United States, begun to act in the early to mid-1990s, we might have made it. But we didn't, and now the impacts are here."[53]

CONSUMERISM

To survive in a capitalist, free market economy, it is generally assumed, business competitors have to expand. Indeed, political commentators have argued that for capitalism to survive political challenges, it must provide for an ever-expanding economy. By its very nature, capitalism engenders inequality and, at least, relative poverty, if not absolute poverty. In order to quell those in poverty, rather than slicing up the pie differently, the poor are assured that the whole pie will expand and their lives will improve. "[C]apitalism's need for growth," writes journalist Mark Hertsgaard, "coincides with a broader political imperative: it keeps the peace. Without growth, the only way to satisfy the demands of the poor majority for a better life would be to share existing resources more equitably. Privileged classes throughout history have been less than keen on that idea...."[54] In a similar vein, sociologist Juliet Schor writes,

> Since the Second World War, growth has been the foundation of political consensus and stability in the North.... The postwar regime was premised on steady increases in income and consumption, in that the Keynesian alliance between business, labor and government was essentially an agreement to avoid conflict over shares by ensuring higher absolute levels for all.[55]

Thus, economically, capitalism requires individual competitors to grow to ensure their own survival and, politically, it requires growth to ensure its own survival.

"Growth," in this context, is generally dependent on increasing the sale of commodities to a consuming public. Unfortunately, such growth is responsible for a great deal of the environmental deterioration of the planet. The production of commodities is commonly connected with polluting emissions, and the consumption of commodities contributes to resource depletion and the generation of waste. In today's economy, growth depends upon consumption and consumption commonly results in environmental deterioration. Retailing analyst Victor Lebow summed up the relationship between growth and consumption:

> Our enormously productive economy...demands that we make consumption our way of life, that we convert the buying and use of goods into rituals, that we seek our spiritual satisfaction, or ego satisfaction, in consumption.... We

need things consumed, burned up, worn out, replaced and discarded at an ever increasing rate.[56]

In this sense, capitalism and conservation may well be antithetical. Mary Mellor writes,

> Private ownership and profit-oriented economies within a system of nation-states are not conducive to seeing the natural heritage of the planet as a common resource for all humanity....The commodified market economy quickly turns natural resources into cash. The seas are stripped of their fish, the hillsides of their trees, the rivers of their fresh water, and the land of its fertility. Under the logic of self-interest and survivalism, nothing will stop the fisher fishing the last fish, the logging company taking the last tree, or the dam withholding the last drop of water.[57]

As consumers, of course, we all play a pivotal role in resource depletion and waste production. In the United States, one's quality of life is, to a large extent, judged by one's capacity to consume. Consumption has become the principal measure of success, and most of us spend a great deal of our lives striving for it. "To go malling," comments Ynestra King, "has become a verb in American English—shopping has become our national pastime, as...U.S. consumers seek to scratch an itch that can never be satisfied by consumers."[58] We are spending increasingly long hours making money, which enables us to spend more time shopping and consuming more plastics, lumber, petroleum, and electricity. These activities take their toll on the environment. "The United States alone," writes Hertsgaard, "contains 5 percent of the world's population but accounts for 22 percent of fossil fuel consumption, 24 percent of carbon dioxide emissions, and 33 percent of paper and plastic use."[59]

Of course, our consumption is encouraged by a constant onslaught of corporate advertising. Americans are "being bombarded by up to 3,000 marketing messages a day"..."by highly sophisticated and carefully targeted commercial messages."[60] Notes James Twitchell, author of *Adcult USA*, "Almost every physical object now carries advertising, almost every human environment is suffused with advertising, almost every moment of time is calibrated by advertising."[61] Sociologist Douglas Goodman writes,

> Not only are ads plastered on billboards, shown between breaks on TV shows, popped up on our computer screens, and placed beside text in our newspapers, but they are also beamed into classrooms, played in elevators, featured as props in movies, placed above the urinal in men's bathrooms, made part of athletes' uniforms, and displayed in every place and in every manner that human ingenuity can devise.[62]

Ironically, though all of us think we are too sophisticated to be manipulated by advertising, corporations are spending hundreds of billions of dollars year after year believing otherwise; and their marketing research confirms that money spent on advertising is money well spent. Goodman continues, "We seem to be currently engaged in a grand experiment to see just how much of our society can be given over to the economic system, and perhaps the riskiest part stems from the constant exposure of people—from cradle to grave, from waking to sleeping—to advertising."[63]

Among the most insidious forms of advertising are those ads shown on Channel One, broadcast in classrooms, introducing children to the value of consumption. Gary Ruskin and Robert Weissman address the issue,

> The best example of coercive techniques is Channel One, which uses compulsory school attendance laws to make eight million schoolchildren watch two minutes of ads in 12,000 schools each day. Channel One lends television and video equipment to schools in exchange for a guarantee that students will watch, every day, a 12-minute "news" show that includes two minutes of ads.[64]

Outside of class, children are watching more TV, to the point that they are watching approximately 40,000 TV commercials annually.[65] (The CEO of Prism Communications notes, "They aren't children so much as what I like to call 'evolving consumers.'"[66]) The overall impact is likely to be an increasingly consumerist culture. Ruskin and Weissman write, "[T]he overriding message of advertising is not to encourage people to buy particular products. Rather, the primary effect is to promote the ideology of buying: wants are good, and more possessions bring happiness, contentedness, love and fulfillment."[67]

To make matters worse, the U.S. appetite for consumption is being carefully propagated throughout the world by the "global integration" of capitalism and by corporate advertising. The first item on the "wants list" of so many people in countries of the South is a television. Once they have a television, they want so many of the other commodities they can see Americans consuming on the tube. (Their desire to have what Americans have is more than understandable, but this aspect of global integration poses serious ethical problems that will be discussed later in this chapter.) Global integration is helping to put a television in millions of homes in the South, and television is helping to facilitate global integration. For this reason, corporations in the North have an interest in propagating American television programs depicting lifestyles and habits of consumption in the North. Also, many countries in the South are modeling their economies after American capitalism in the hopes of achieving American lifestyles. "Most, if not all, less developed countries," writes Alain Lipietz, "have no other dream than to imitate the model of development that precisely led to the global crisis."[68] If Americans go on consuming at present rates, and if countries in the South are successful in their economic plans, then the burden on the planet will be unbearable.

China, for example, is enjoying rapid economic expansion. Patrick Tyler describes China's economic successes after its move to a free market economy in a *New York Times* article: "There is not an adjective that soars high enough or detonates with enough force to describe China's economic explosion or the promise of its future....The Chinese are buying, building and consuming as if there were no tomorrow."[69] In the meantime, China is becoming one of the most polluted nations on earth. Farmland, increasingly critical for the expanding population, is being paved for roads and developed for housing. "Instead of conserving its resources," writes Tyler, "it is exhausting them with a vengeance...[continuing] to squander farmland and water resources in its quest to catch up with consumption levels in the West...."[70] Chinese leaders are reluctant to enact new environmental regulations or enforce existing regulations because that might slow economic development, create a restive public, and threaten their regime.[71] China is already one of the biggest polluters in the world, with only 9 cars per thousand eligible drivers, compared to 1,148 for every 1,000 Americans.[72] What happens to local and global pollution levels when and if this figure increases 50-fold? In 2008 *Business Week* reported that the Chinese auto market was second only to the American market and projected 9.5 million vehicles would be sold the next year.[73] In their first meeting in 1995, Bill Clinton reportedly told China's president, Jiang Zemin, that China's greatest security threat to the United States was not a nuclear, military, or trade threat but an environmental threat. "Specifically, Clinton feared that China would copy America's bad example while developing its economy and end up causing terrible pollution and global warming."[74]

The Automobile

Easily, one of the most environmentally threatening consumables is the automobile. The United States ranks number one in the world for per capita car ownership. Automobiles account for half of the carbon dioxide emissions associated with global warming[75] and half of the world's oil consumption, and automobile exhaust is the principal cause of air pollution in many cities throughout the world.[76] A study by a team of Harvard University researchers found that 30,000 Americans die each year of respiratory illnesses related to automobile exhaust and another 120,000 lives are shortened due to such exhaust.[77]

Car ownership is necessary for millions of Americans because they live in the suburbs and must commute to work. Owning a car is necessary for millions of other Americans because public transportation in most cities is inadequate. These conditions—urban sprawl and poor public transportation—do not exist to such a degree in European countries, and it is not accidental that they came to exist in the United States. Once again, corporate interests are implicated.

Until the 1930s, railways and trolleys were the principal form of transport in the United States, and they posed a major stumbling block to their competitors in the auto and oil industries. Then in 1932, General Motors

(GM), Firestone Tire, Standard Oil (later to become Exxon), and a number of other corporations secretly joined together to form a front company. In the name of National City Lines, they bought railways and trolleys throughout the country, dismantled them and replaced them with gas-powered buses. The buses proved far less profitable and most of the companies were soon shut down. They bought up and eventually shut down almost 100 public transportation systems in 45 cities.[78] Between 1936 and 1955, the number of trolley cars operating in the United States declined from 40,000 to 5,000.[79] Eventually, GM and its co-conspirators were tried for violation of antitrust laws. When found guilty of what Hertsgaard calls one of "the great corporate crimes of the century," GM was fined a mere $5,000; the GM executive who plotted the crime was fined $1.[80]

In the meantime, tax revenues were being diverted from public transport to road systems. Los Angeles, for example, which once boasted one of the finest public transit systems in the country, began building its freeway system. As public transportation began to decline, private transportation became more appealing. As public transportation began to decline, cities became less appealing. A costly highway system, paid for by public taxes, made it possible for people to escape the cities and move to the suburbs. People became auto-dependent, and the auto manufacturers and oil companies enjoyed tremendous profits. (Today, automobile manufacturing and oil are among the biggest industries in the world.[81])

Constructing the "Good Life"

If scientists are correct, people may not feel the full impact of the harm caused by climate change and the thinning of the ozone layer for generations to come. The only way to prevent the decline in the living standards of future generations caused by climate change, ozone thinning, and other forms of environmental deterioration may be to make substantial changes in our patterns of consumption today. While the well-being of future generations resonates strongly in political and social discourse, what sacrifices are people willing to make to protect future generations from harm, especially given that the extent of the potential harm is uncertain? Even if it could be proven that our descendants living 50 or 100 years from now will experience marked increases in poverty and disease because of our lifestyles today, what proportion of the public would be willing to cut automobile and electricity usage, garbage output, and shopping in half if that is what it would take to ensure the livelihoods of our distant descendants? The answer to that question depends in large part upon popular constructions of the "good life." One of the main messages in constructionism is that there are alternative ways of constructing perceptions, and perceptions of the "good life" can be and have been constructed so as not to center around consumption.

Of the people and interest groups that do not perceive environmental problems to be a threat to future generations, there are those who are not convinced by the majority of scientific opinions and those who are depending on the development of future technologies to thwart the threat. However, relying on future technological solutions is risky business, especially when technology has had and continues to have so many negative impacts on the environment. Nor can we rely on political solutions (regulations) to work by themselves. If consumption is indeed a large part of the problem, then social solutions—lifestyle change—must be part of the equation. Finnish sociologist Markku Wilenius writes, "Prevailing ideas of how we ought to manage the global environment still largely refer to the Western notion of control over the environment, rather than the intelligent limitation of human action, and this bias may lead us to emphasize technological and political solutions rather than social solutions aimed at redirecting our ways of life."[82]

"Redirecting our ways of life" away from consumption does not necessarily mean lowering our standard of living. It means, literally, changing our standard. Constructions of economic growth, for example, rely on the gross domestic product (GDP) as a standard of measurement. The GDP is a measure of the total amount of economic activity in a country. It is generally understood that the higher the GDP, the healthier the economy. That standard could be changed, and it should be changed, according to many critics. As mentioned in Chapter 2, the GDP does not distinguish between good and bad economic activity. When money changes hands, the GDP goes up. Thus, as noted earlier, when divorce rates increase, more money is paid to divorce lawyers and the GDP rises. When crime goes up, more people buy security devices, increasing the GDP. An earthquake or an environmental disaster will raise the GDP because of the money spent on funerals and rebuilding. Epidemics and surging rates of cancer can do wonders for the GDP. Write Clifford Cobb and his colleagues,

> Pollution shows up twice as a gain: once when the chemical factory, say, produces it as a by-product, and again when the nation spends billions of dollars to clean up the toxic superfund site that results. Furthermore, the extra costs that come as a consequence of that environmental depletion and degradation—such as medical bills arising from dirty air—also show up as growth in the GDP.[83]

Thus, the GDP can be a misleading indicator of "growth," especially when it is used to measure societal welfare. Though the GDP may bear a relationship to people's incomes, societal welfare, argue Paul Ekins and Michael Jacobs, also includes the "environment, employment, working conditions, leisure, income distribution, and the safety of the future."[84] While environmental regulations and reduced consumption might effect a reduction in GDP, as is often feared, societal welfare would not necessarily be adversely affected. There would be a trade-off: incomes may decline, but the environment would become more livable and "safety of the future" would be better assured.

If people consumed less, industrial production would have to decline and there would be less strain on the environment. The GDP emphasizes production, but a decline in the country's productive output—while anathema to corporate interests and the constructions they propagate—could also enhance societal welfare by increasing the amount of leisure time that people have available to them. Production increases at the cost of harder and longer workweeks. People are spending more time on the "treadmill of consumption,"[85] with less and less leisure time to spend with family. If we compare the annual salaries of American workers to those in Western Europe, we find that the American worker earns 29 percent more than his or her European counterpart.[86] However, the European worker has *4–10 weeks more leisure time* than his or her American counterpart.[87]

Even though those long hours at work may have enabled Americans to buy more, they are not necessarily happier. Annie Leonard, who became somewhat of a YouTube sensation with her animated documentary *The Story of Stuff*, writes,

> After a certain point, economic growth (more money and more Stuff) ceases to make us happier. I mean, if everyone were having fun and enjoying leisure, laughter and well-being, we might decide that the pursuit of growth was worth the trashing of the planet. But the majority of us are not having fun; instead we are reporting high levels of stress, depression, anxiety, and unhappiness.[88]

Social scientists who have studied the issue have found very little evidence of a link between wealth (buying power) and happiness. In surveys, the percentage of Americans who identified themselves as "very happy" peaked in 1957, even though most are able to buy far more today. In 1960, a survey of people in 14 countries found people were happiest in Cuba, Egypt, and the United States, 3 countries where the people had exceedingly different buying power.[89] In his classic essay "The Original Affluent Society," anthropologist Marshall Sahlins argues that hunter-gatherer societies may be the most satisfied of all, even though they have very little in terms of material possessions. "Wants may be 'easily satisfied' either by producing much or desiring little.... [Taking] the Zen road to affluence...a people can enjoy an unparalleled, material plenty—with a low standard of living."[90] The hunter-gatherer desires little, spends only a small part of his or her day working, eats well, and has a great deal of leisure time. Modern peoples, on the other hand, spend an enormous part of their lifetimes producing (i.e., working).

Schor describes "the work and spend cycle" that typifies modern life:

> Employers set schedules and workers conform to them. When productivity rises, employers pass the gains along in the form of higher wages, rather than reduced worktime. Workers take the extra income and spend it. They become accustomed or habituated to the new level of spending and develop an aversion to their previous, lower level of spending. Preferences adapt such that workers are unwilling to reduce current incomes in order to get more leisure.[91]

Schor, however, sees signs that the work and spend cycle can be broken. One sign is the growth of an anticonsumerist undercurrent in the United States, often going by the name of the "voluntary simplicity" or the "frugality" movement. The movement is made up of people "motivated by concern for the environment, a desire to be liberated from oppressive and meaningless work, and a traditional frugal attitude to money,"[92] who often leave high-paying, high-stress jobs to accept lower-paid, lower-stress, often part-time jobs. There is also a growing number of "downshifters," who spend less time at work so that they can spend more time with their families. While the 1985 Current Population Survey found that only 8 percent of workers indicated they would prefer to work less for less pay, Schor believes the low response had to do with the wording of the question. A 1977 survey, for example, asked instead, "Would you like to spend less time working so that you could spend more time with your (husband/wife) and (children), even if it meant less money?" This survey found that 38 percent of fathers and 53 percent of mothers indicated they would want to work less. A 1991 survey asked if respondents would prefer to take one extra day off per week for one day's less pay; 70 percent of those earning $30,000 or more indicated they would and 48 percent earning $20,000 or less said they would.[93]

Increasing awareness of environmental problems may itself increase people's willingness to accept fewer work hours and consume less. In one survey, 77 percent of respondents either "strongly" agreed or "somewhat" agreed with the statement "Americans' overuse of resources is a major global environmental problem that needs to be changed."[94] If the standard for "the good life" were to change, environmental problems might be averted and increased leisure time would be a bonus. "Difficult as it may be to tame northern appetites," writes Schor, "there may be no other choice if the planet is to escape environmental crisis."[95]

INEQUALITY AND THE ENVIRONMENT

> Environmental externalities are not simply inflicted by identical agents upon each other; they are often what the rich and powerful do to the weak and hungry. They are what Union Carbide did to the people of Bhopal, what the Soviet State did to the people around Chernobyl, and what greenhouse gas emissions in the U.S. will do to the people of Bangladesh.
>
> *(V. Bhaskar and Andrew Glyn)*[96]

Environmental Injustice

Soon after problems in the environment were recognized, the environmental justice movement began to emerge. Representing a fusion of civil rights and environmental activism, the movement is concerned with the fact that environmental problems frequently have a greater impact upon minorities and the poor. The origin of the movement has been traced to an incident in

1967, when an 8-year-old girl drowned at a garbage dump in Houston, Texas. Students at a nearby, mostly black college questioned why a garbage dump had been located in the middle of a mostly black neighborhood. Similar questions have arisen ever since with regard to disproportionate exposure of minorities to environmental toxins. "They question," Carita Shanklin writes, "why communities of color and the poor breathe dirtier air, have higher blood lead levels, and host undesirable land uses such as landfills and incinerators."[97] In fact, from the 1920s until the late 1970s, all of Houston's municipal landfills and six out of eight of its incinerators were located in neighborhoods that were mostly African American.[98]

Environmental justice activists are often critical of mainstream environmentalists for only attending to issues that are fairly abstract or that will not become serious matters for generations to come. The issue of wetlands preservation, for example, should not take attention away from the more pressing environmental concerns facing the minorities and the poor. Martin Lewis notes, "[E]nvironmentalism was often regarded with suspicion by civil rights activists, some of whom denounced it as little more than an elitist movement concerned primarily with preserving the amenities of prosperous suburbanites."[99] One major problem addressed by the environmental justice movement is the lack of minority representation in the upper echelons of state and local regulatory boards, in environmental organizations (e.g., the Audubon Society and the Sierra Club), and in the management of corporations that pollute.[100] For example, better minority representation might have prevented the National Institute for Environmental Sciences and the National Cancer Institute from excluding Hispanics from their 10-year epidemiological study of the effects of pesticides on farmers and their families, "even though demographic data on farmworkers reveal that 70 percent of seasonal workers and 91 percent of migrant farmworkers are Hispanic."[101]

In spite of the attention attracted by the environmental justice movement, minorities continue to suffer the brunt of pollution. The National Wildlife Federation reviewed 64 studies that examined whether or not environmental discrimination was an issue; all but one "found environmental disparities either by race or income...."[102] Similarly, a study of the location of hazardous-waste dumps in the southeast conducted by the U.S. Government Accounting Office found that three out of four facilities were located among majority African American populations.[103] "Garbage dumps," writes environmental sociologist Robert Bullard, "are not randomly scattered across the landscape. These facilities are often located in communities that have high percentages of poor, elderly, young, and minority residents."[104]

Exposure to lead poisoning at an early age is associated with poor mental development and lowered IQ, and such effects are permanent and can reduce a person's life chances. When the dangers of lead were confirmed, it was banned from house paint and gasoline. Today, children who are exposed to lead are likely to come into contact with it through the dust in their homes. House dust (which can be brought in from outside of the house) may contain the remnants of old, deteriorated lead-based paint;[105] hence, children living in neighborhoods with deteriorating housing are more susceptible to exposure. While some argue that the location of hazardous sites is an issue of socioeconomic status and not race, according to findings of research conducted by the federal Agency for Toxic Substances Disease Registry, lead poisoning disproportionately affects African American children, irrespective of social class. Writes Bullard,

> Even when income is held constant, African American children are two to three times more likely than their white counterparts to suffer from lead poisoning....The ability of an individual to escape a health-threatening physical environment usually correlates with income. However, racial barriers complicate this process for millions of African Americans.[106]

Poor and minority children, especially, are at risk of environmental hazards. According to the *Journal of Environmental Health*, "Because children breathe more air, drink more water, and consume more food relative to their body weight than do adults, they receive higher doses of contaminants present in air, food, and water."[107] Children breathe twice as much air, relative to their body weight, than adults, and the air they breathe is closer to the ground, where there are higher concentrations of dust.[108] Children are further at risk because their organs and immune systems are in early stages of development. The *Journal of Environmental Health* notes,

> As a group, children of color are at greatest risk from environmental threats. More African-American and Hispanic children than white children have unacceptable levels of lead in their blood. More African-American and Hispanic children suffer from asthma and are therefore especially vulnerable to the effects of air pollution. Children of farm workers are more likely to be exposed to pesticides because they may accompany their parents to work in the fields and live in housing exposed to pesticide drift from nearby fields.[109]

Historically, Native Americans have been subjected to some of the worst forms of environmental discrimination. It began with the confiscation and clearing of their land for white settlers and continues today with the disposal of nuclear and toxic wastes. "The United States," writes King, "has detonated all of its nuclear weapons in the lands of indigenous people; over six hundred of those tests within property belonging to the Shoshone nation."[110] With a large proportion of North America's natural resources under their land, Native Americans will likely continue to suffer environmental discrimination.

Efforts to resist hazardous sites are often fought in the courts and because corporations usually have extensive financial and legal resources, undertaking such a fight can be very expensive. Minorities and the poor have few resources to resist the location of hazardous sites in their neighborhoods. "These are the people," write Tam Hunt and Kevin Lunde, "who have least access to the legal tools to protect their rights and fend off would-be pol-luters."[111] They lack economic as well as political resources. State and local boards that issue the permits for industrial sites are likely to give less weight to the concerns of these communities. "Since capital always seeks to pollute in ways that encounter the least political resistance," Faber and O'Connor note, "peoples and communities that have the least political power or social resources to defend themselves are the most vulnerable."[112]

In 1994, President Clinton signed Executive Order 12898, titled "Federal Actions to Address Environmental Justice in Minority Populations and Low-Income Populations." It instructed all federal agencies to "make achieving environmental justice part of its mission by identifying and addressing, as appropriate, disproportionately high and adverse health or environmental effects of its programs, policies, and activities on minority and low-income populations in the United States."[113] This was not a new law, "but it stress[ed] compliance with existing federal laws and regulations."[114] The impact of the executive order was muted because it did not address two problems. First, it did not provide for the correction of past environmental discrimination, which has left minorities and the poor with a disproportionate burden of pollution, perhaps for generations to come. Second, it did not consider what might be considered *de facto* discrimination, referring to the fact that while a hazardous facility might be located in a racially and economically mixed neighborhood, those who can afford it will likely move away, leaving behind a neighborhood that is disproportionately minority and poor to suffer the effects.

Environmental justice is not only relevant to chemical wastes and other man-made pollutants, but also to so-called natural disasters. In August 2005, Hurricane Katrina hit New Orleans, leaving in its wake over $70 billion in damage and 1,836 dead.[115] New Orleans has long been known to be vulner-able to potentially disastrous hurricanes. "In 2001, FEMA experts ranked a hurricane striking New Orleans, a terrorist attack on New York City, and strong earthquake in San Francisco as the top three catastrophic disasters most likely to occur in the country."[116] The hurricane was forecast well in advance and the mayor issued the first ever mandatory evacuation in New Orleans' long history. Unfortunately, the evacuation plans did not sufficiently account for residents who did not own cars. Writes Bullard,

> Hurricane Katrina demonstrated to the world the race and class disparities that mark who can escape a disaster by car. Emergency plans were particu-larly insufficient with regard to the evacuation of the car-less and "special needs" populations—individuals who cannot simply jump into their cars and drive away....At least 100,000 New Orleans residents—and more than one-third of New Orleans African American residents—did not have cars to evacuate in case of a major storm....New Orleans had only one-quarter the number of buses that would have been needed to evacuate all car-less residents.[117]

FEMA's Guide to Avoiding Disaster
Source: © 2005 Pittsburgh Post-Gazette, Rogers.

The question that arises, then, is why did federal and local officials not plan better for this disaster? Drawing on his analysis of similar "natural" disasters taking place in the South in the twentieth century, in which blacks and the poor incurred severely disproportionate losses, Bullard concludes that a sort of environmental racism and lack of concern for the poor explains this dereliction in planning for Katrina as well as the inadequate response in the aftermath of the hurricane. So, while in the popular imagination, "natural disasters" are unavoidable, for Bullard, when the consequent deaths and destruction could reasonably have been prevented—as is often the case—the disaster is "unnatural."

GLOBAL INEQUALITY

In 1972, India's prime minister, Indira Gandhi, said at a conference on the environment in Stockholm, "Poverty is the worst form of pollution." Today, few familiar with pollution in countries of the South would take issue with her statement. Though rarely acknowledged in the rhetoric of most American environmentalists, poor people in the South face the worst forms of pollution. Environmental problems faced by them are immediate and certain, not uncertain or potential problems, as is global warming. There are millions of pollution-related deaths in the South every year. "All over the world," Geoffrey Lean writes, "the poor account for the most deaths from pollution, and are by far the greatest victims of the degradation of the natural world."[118] Besides living in more polluted areas, the poor are more vulnerable to various pollutants because of the lower immunity that results from malnutrition. Poor children are the most vulnerable, accounting for as much as two-thirds of preventable diseases associated with environmental conditions.[119]

One of the most serious ecological threats worldwide is the lack of potable water. About a billion people in the world have little or no access to clean water. Throughout most of the countries of the South, water that is available to the poor is likely to be contaminated, especially by human fecal matter; "human feces," according to the World Resources Institute, "remain one of the world's most hazardous pollutants."[120] Oral intake of fecal matter can lead to, among other things, often lethal bouts of diarrhea. Frequently, the water that is available, contaminated or not, has to be carried more than a mile from its source back to the home. In such cases, only limited amounts of water can be used for washing, exacerbating already unsanitary conditions. Inadequate water supplies and the consequent inability to wash may be responsible for even more diarrheal diseases than contaminated water itself.[121] UNICEF reports that 4,500 children die every day because of unsafe water or lack of sanitation facilities and that "[a] child born in Europe or the United States is 520 times less likely to die from diarrheal disease than an infant in sub-Saharan Africa, where only 36 per cent of the population can access hygienic sanitation."[122]

Increasingly, families in the South who are well-off are resorting to buying clean water, often paying 12 times as much as it would cost to build the facilities to pipe in clean water. Water often accounts for as much as 20 percent of household expenses in parts of Nigeria and Haiti.[123] A concerted worldwide effort to ensure access to clean water in countries of the South would be inexpensive, relative to the costs of present conditions. "Americans spend $8 billion a year on cosmetics," writes Noreena Hertz, "while the world cannot find the $9 billion the UN reckons is needed to give all people access to clean drinking water and sanitation."[124]

Airborne contaminants are another form of pollution that exacts a high toll on people of all financial means in the South, especially the poor. Although there have been incidents in which air pollution has been known to kill people, attention did not focus on the dangers of air pollution until almost 4,000 people were killed by smog in London in 1952. A more recent ecological disaster involving air pollution happened in Bhopal in 1984, which was mentioned earlier in this chapter. However, even when localized disasters are not taking place, air pollution is still associated with millions of deaths. Acute respiratory infection (ARI) is one of the leading causes of death among children worldwide.[125] ARI is associated with, but not limited to, environmental pollution. Asthma attacks, for example, often increase when pollution levels are high. Interestingly, indoor air pollution poses a greater risk than outdoor pollution to the poor of the South, who often live in small, poorly ventilated homes and use traditional fuels, such as wood or coal, for heating and cooking. Data collected by the World Health Organization "suggest that many tens of millions of people in developing countries routinely encounter pollution levels reached during the infamous London killer smog of 1952, leading to a huge estimated toll in disease and premature death."[126] As many as 2 or 3 million people die as a result of indoor air pollution every year.[127] The World Bank ranks it among the most serious global environmental problems.

The poor of the South also suffer the most from many other forms of environmental degradation. The lives of numerous tribal peoples throughout the world have been devastated by the clear-cutting of rainforests and by industrial development. These once thriving hunter-gatherers are often forced to live in cities that are already teeming with millions of the poor and unemployed. Displaced and living in an alien environment, they may suddenly find themselves living in absolute destitution.

The poor in countries of the South are those most vulnerable to any kind of ecological disturbance. The Darfur region of the Sudan is struggling to recover from a crisis brought on in large part by drought and the desertification of the region. Hundreds of thousands of people have been displaced and the competition for scarce resources brought on deadly conflict, resulting in mass starvation and widespread government-backed massacres. Experts fear similar events could occur in other parts of Africa and the Middle East.[128]

Poor people are often the most dependent on the fish they catch, the livestock they raise, or the crops they grow. Lacking any kind of financial buffer, their livelihoods are easily devastated by natural and not so natural disasters. Any ecological event or fluctuations in the commodities markets that hinder or reduce global food production could eventually affect us all, but such events affect the poor almost instantaneously. Recent fluctuations in the price of oil have driven the price of food up throughout most of the world. Poor countries are affected first and foremost. Overfishing, desertification, and soil erosion potentially threaten all of us in the future; but they can and do mean malnutrition and hunger for tens of millions of poor people in the South, who live just one step away from epidemics and famine.

Global Imbalance

The potential for global environmental problems together with pollution and poverty in the South pose serious moral and ethical questions for the North. As mentioned in Chapter 2, much of the success of the North has come from the exploitation of the South. "The industrialization and high levels of consumption in the North have depended on access to the whole world's resources. But if the majority of the rest of the world industrializes," note Bhaskar and Glyn, "this shrinks the hinterland whose resources can be exploited for benefit elsewhere."[129] Given that resources are limited, if the South is unable to use its resources for its own development, then that development will be very problematic; if the North is unable to continue exploiting the resources of the South, then economic expansion in the North will become very problematic. The competition for resources between countries of the North and the South—as they all strive for economic expansion—will quite likely lead to conflict. Recent surges in the worldwide price of oil, for example, were brought on in large part by increasing demand from developing countries and conflict over oil supplies could well be on the horizon.

As mentioned earlier in this chapter, many peoples of the South and their political leaders are aspiring to Northern standards of living; but environmentalists who examine the global situation are generally in agreement that the economies of the North and the South cannot both expand without future environmental disaster, which will devastate the earth's natural resources and produce intolerable levels of pollution. So how should development in both the North and the South proceed?

The answer frequently heard in environmental circles is "sustainable development"; that is, if development is to proceed, it must be in a manner that can be sustained into future generations. Sustainable development emphasizes that the earth's resources are finite and that "we all share one world, and thus a common future."[130] Proponents frequently argue that development needs to be coordinated on a global basis and that there must be negotiations and a certain give-and-take between countries. All parties will have to make sacrifices. Frank Amalric expresses the essence of sustainable development:

> Since we all share the same world, we all have to make some efforts to save it, and thus, implicitly, we all have to make some sacrifices for it. This world we share is a world of limited natural resources, of limited global commons. In other words, what we share is a common problem, the global environmental crisis, because it may affect the lives of us all. Furthermore, through this crisis, we all become supposedly interdependent: each person's behavior and well-being is connected to other people's behaviors through the global biospheric system.[131]

Of course, when negotiations, give-and-take, and sacrifices are involved, the issue of fairness always comes into play. Representatives from countries of the North say they already have enough environmental regulation and that the South needs to do more to control environmental degradation because, in their haste to industrialize, they have implemented impossibly weak controls over waste disposal, clear-cutting rainforests, and industrial and automotive emissions. Indeed, they have a point. On the other hand, representatives from countries of the South say that the North was able to achieve its level of industrial development without concern for environmental regulation and that it is now so far ahead in industrialization and material comfort that it has no moral right to ask the South to slow down its economic growth by way of environmental regulation. If anybody is going to make sacrifices, it is frequently heard, the North should take the lead by cutting down on consumption.

Seventy-five percent of the world's carbon dioxide emissions are produced by industrialized countries. The average American produces 2.5 times more carbon dioxide emissions than the average European and 10 times more than the average African, South American, or Asian.[132] Notes Martin Khor Kok Peng, "[T]he North with 20 percent of the world's population uses 80 percent of the world's resources and has an average per capita income fifteen times higher than the South."[133] Given the extent of absolute poverty in the South and with the average American producing waste and consuming resources at rates 15–35 times greater than the average resident of the South, it may be argued that the South's emissions are largely a matter of survival. Further, at least from the Southern perspective, the emissions of the North are largely a matter of maintaining luxury.[134] Thus, the North's call for developing countries to implement costly environmental regulations often tends to ring hollow. "It is easy for outsiders to warn against the long-term costs of damming Africa's rivers, ruining its scenery, or destroying its woodlands," says Hertsgaard, "but it is akin to a glutton admonishing a beggar to watch his carbohydrates."[135] Also, while greenhouse emissions in the South are increasing by leaps and bounds, their "per capita emissions" are only a tiny fraction of the per capita emissions in the North. If the world is to be viewed as a "global commons," some argue, then perhaps the countries with the larger populations should be permitted to create more pollution.

Since the issue of fairness often includes historical events, the South is not oblivious to the fact that so much of the material comfort of the North was achieved and continues to be achieved at the expense of the South. Mellor writes, "The eco-economic chasm between rich and poor is created by a global market system that allows the over-consuming rich, white North, now joined by Japan, to scoop out the raw materials of the South, exploit its people as cheap labor, and use it as a dump for toxic waste."[136] It is not so difficult to understand the South's disdain for the North's call for them to cut back on economic growth in favor of environmental regulation. "This," states Anil Agarwal, director of the Centre for Science and Environment in India, "is a very status quo approach in which the rich and powerful keep creating problems, and then the rest of the world, once those problems are created, must get together and try to solve them."[137]

APPLICATION: OVERPOPULATION

Many demographers argue that population growth is among the most, if not the most, critical strain on the environment today. People, of course, need to expend resources in order to survive; and population growth has strained the earth's capacity to provide enough resources. A joint statement issued by the national science academies of 58 countries asserted that the more serious social, economic, and environmental problems of the world could not be successfully addressed without a stable global population.[138] Billions of dollars, for example, have been spent on improving the problems of water supplies to the poor countries of the South that were discussed earlier in this chapter. However, many of these improvements have been overwhelmed or negated by the strains of population growth.

Despite declines in birth rates throughout most of the world, the human population is growing by approximately 80 million people a year, just about the population of Germany. Today, both China and India have populations of over one billion. To make matters worse, the vast majority of the almost quarter of a million people born tomorrow will be born in the poorest countries, those least able to afford them. Throughout most of history and most of the world, birth rates have been highest among the poor. The poor are often dependent upon large numbers of children to help in producing more food for the family. In agricultural societies, for example, the more offspring a couple has, the more help there is in the field. Higher child and infant mortality rates among the poor also tend to push up their birth rates in that parents have to produce more children to compensate for those who can be expected to die at an early age. Further, lacking any kind of security for old age, additional children help to provide for their elder parents. Value systems develop around these essential needs until high reproduction rates become part of the culture—sometimes even when the population becomes urbanized and large families become dysfunctional.

At the encouragement of the North, and often with its financial assistance, many countries of the South are tackling the problem with aggressive population control programs. "[A]bout 61 percent of the people in the world live under a government that incites them to have fewer children," writes Amalric.[139] Such family planning programs bribe or entice women to use contraception. Birth control pills may be issued, intrauterine devices (IUDs) inserted, or Jadelle implanted. (Jadelle, formerly known as "Norplant," is a time-released birth control device implanted underneath the skin on the arm that can be effective for up to 5 years.) In the 1970s, the Dalkon Shield was removed from the market in the United States as it posed risk of serious infection, but more than a million of them continued to be distributed in the South.[140] Women issued these and other forms of birth control were frequently not told of possible side effects, nor were they provided with the opportunity to have these devices and implants removed if complications developed.

As another means of birth control, governments in the South and their family planning agencies often encourage men and women—especially women—to undergo sterilization procedures; 15 percent of contraceptive use in the North involves sterilization, whereas almost half (45 percent) of contraceptive use in the South involves sterilization, with reported rates as high as 86 percent in Nepal, 70 percent in India, and 66 percent in the

Dominican Republic.[141] Although male sterilization is a simpler procedure, female sterilization is more common. According to a 2009 study, the most common form of birth control worldwide is female sterilization.[142] In the North, women are twice as likely to be sterilized than men; and in the South, they are almost three times more likely to be sterilized.[143] Reportedly, China, India, Bangladesh, and Indonesia have forced some women to be sterilized.[144] More often, however, governments in the South have offered women financial incentives or disincentives; but when financial incentives are offered to someone living on the brink of destitution, there is, of course, some question as to whether consent has been given voluntarily. Asoka Bandarage writes, "[C]oercion does not pertain simply to the outright use of force. More subtle forms of coercion arise when individual reproductive decisions are tied to sources of survival like the availability of food, shelter, employment, education, health care, and so on."[145]

A critical constructionist analysis recognizes that population growth strains the environment and that contraceptives should be made available to those who want them; however, such an analysis emphasizes, first, that in terms of per capita impact on the environment, populations in countries of the North do far more harm than populations in the South. The average per capita consumption of energy in the United States is more than 37 times greater than that in India and more than 55 times that in Nigeria.[146] Over the course of his or her lifetime, the average American has 13 times more impact on the environment than the average Brazilian and 35 times that of the average Indian.[147] Although poverty in countries of the South is often blamed on the fact that they are "overpopulated," they frequently have population densities considerably lower than their wealthy counterparts, such as Hong Kong and the Netherlands. Thus, *the problem of population growth could be reconstructed as one relating to the distribution of resources between and within countries.* The North, which consumes disproportionate amounts of resources and produces more than its share of waste, is rarely considered "overpopulated" because it can afford to consume and waste at present rates. In this sense, the problem of overpopulation boils down to the problem of poverty, and to blame poverty on overpopulation amounts to circular reasoning. The plight of the poor in the South is not so much due to overpopulation as it is to poverty itself. There is little doubt that if they had more money, they would have more food.

There is also little doubt that if they had more land, they would have more food. Much of the problem of poverty in the South stems from the inequitable distribution of land. This is especially the case in the former European colonies. When the Europeans took over these countries, they took the best lands for themselves; but when they gave their former colonies their freedom to become independent countries, they did not redistribute the land to the natives. Instead, much of the best land has remained in the hands of descendants of the European colonists or descendants of those who collaborated with their European oppressors. In Guatemala, for example, until relatively recently 80 percent of agricultural land was owned by 2.1 percent of the landowners. Prior to land reform in El Salvador in 1980, less than 2 percent of the population owned almost all of the cultivable land. In Nicaragua, before the Sandinista revolution, 23 percent of the arable land was owned by one family.[148] Many of these countries do indeed have the land resources to adequately feed their populations, but wealthy landowners, instead, use their lands to grow crops that can be exported to the North, such as coffee and bananas. Many of these countries, writes Bill Weinberg, "are producing massive quantities of luxury cash crops, such as coffee, for export. The beef from the livestock is not consumed domestically, but exported. It is not food to feed 'their expanding populations.' "[149]

Given that the problem of overpopulation is as much or more one of resource distribution, critics often charge that the North's involvement in birth control programs in the South amounts to little more than eugenics, with the mostly Caucasian North demanding that the mostly non-Caucasian South limit its reproduction. Some critics also see it as a form of "population imperialism." Fearing that the teeming hordes of poor throughout the world will become a political threat to both regional and global stability, the elite have mounted a campaign to reduce their numbers. Uruguayan leftist Eduardo Galeano expressed these concerns in his classic book *Open Veins of Latin America*:

> In the eye of this hurricane 120 million children are stirring. Latin America's population grows as does no other; it has more than tripled in half a century. One child dies of disease or hunger every minute, but in the year 2000 there will be 650 million Latin Americans, half of whom will be under fifteen: a time bomb.... The United States is more concerned than any other country with spreading and imposing family planning in the farthest outposts.... [They] have nightmares about millions of children advancing like locusts over the horizon from the Third World.... [I]n our day this global offensive plays a well-defined role. Its aim is to justify the very unequal income distribution between countries and social classes, to convince the poor that poverty is the result of the children they don't avoid having, and to dam the rebellious advance of the masses. While intrauterine devices compete with bombs and machine-gun salvos to arrest the growth of the Vietnamese population, in Latin America it is more hygienic and effective to kill guerrilleros in the womb than in the mountains or the streets.... Most Latin American countries have no real surplus of people; on the contrary, they have too few. Brazil has thirty-eight times fewer inhabitants per square mile than Belgium, Paraguay has forty-nine times fewer than England.... Haiti and El Salvador, the human ant-heaps of Latin America, have lower population densities than Italy. The pretexts invoked are an insult to the intelligence; the real intentions anger us.... [150]

Blaming poverty in the South on overpopulation is, arguably, a form of "blaming the victim" and thereby serves as a means of diverting attention away from the problem of resource distribution. Countries of the North are able to deny any complicity and, thereby, any need to alter the status quo. Elites in the South have a similar motivation to subscribe to the theory of overpopulation and embrace sterilization and other contraceptive programs. Blaming the poor can be one of many means they have of preserving their privileged status.

Again, the critical constructionist does not deny that overpopulation may be a problem but exposes alternative constructions and the possible interests of the elite who favor popular constructions. If overpopulation is indeed a problem, family planning/contraception is only one way of constructing a solution. It is a solution that does not threaten the vested interests of the elite.

Another solution to the problem of overpopulation is the empowerment of women, which, of course, threatens vested interests in patriarchal societies. Patriarchal arrangements, especially in poor countries, force women into a role in which they are valued primarily for childbearing. Poor women of the South are often forced by their husbands to produce large numbers of children, and they are provided few meaningful roles other than that of childbearer. Often, they are not allowed to have a formal education and are kept from jobs outside of the home. Frequently, it is they who seek contraception, often without their husbands' knowledge. The United Nations now recognizes the empowerment of women to be a major step in improving the economies of countries in the South and has made it a top priority in its Millennium Project, the goal of which is to "to reverse the grinding poverty, hunger and disease affecting billions of people."[151]

The first step in the empowerment of women is education. Educating women may impact population growth because an educated woman is better at independent thinking and, therefore, better able to challenge notions about traditional gender roles. An educated woman is better able to get a job outside of the home and, spending her day outside of the home, more likely to be exposed to a variety of ideas about gender roles. Working outside of the home, she becomes less financially dependent on her husband and is able to speak her own mind. Simply put, an educated woman is likely to have more options, other than childbearing, than a woman without an education. A study by the United Nations found that women who completed 7 years of education were likely to have three fewer children than women with no education. The World Bank estimates that if the education of men and women had been equalized 30 years ago, population growth today would be nearly stable.[152] Writes Bandarage, "Economic and social empowerment of women is the key to breaking the cycle connecting women, population, and global crisis."[153] Unlike many of the contraception programs being foisted on poor women of the South, efforts to educate and empower women will, says Reed Boland, be "promoting human rights rather than compromising them."[154]

SUMMARY

Environmental problems can have both local and global impacts. Until fairly recently, only local impacts had been given much attention because they are more easily observed and understood. However, with the issues of ozone depletion and global warming, global environmental issues are receiving a good deal more attention today. Global environmental issues tend to be very complicated in terms of both their causes and their effects. Global warming, if it continues at its present rate, is predicted to have disastrous effects on human society in coming generations. Such a prediction, while it is held by a large majority of climatologists, is hypothetical and cannot be definitively proven. Scientists say that climate change is due in large part to industrial and automotive emissions. Preventing it will require cutting back on such emissions. Corporations that are responsible for a great deal of environmental pollution thus have an interest in delegitimating climate change theory, and they have a number of tools for doing so. First, with the help of hired scientists and PR firms, they do their best to highlight the uncertainty of climate change theory. Corporations, often through their PR firms, will clandestinely finance environmental front groups to fight their battles so that the corporation's true interests remain concealed. PR firms have also been known to use less than legitimate tactics to prevent environmentalists from getting their message to the public—for instance, figuratively "burning books," even before they are published. Another method for squelching environmental activists is to "SLAPP" them with a lawsuit when they complain about a particular corporation's contribution to the pollution problem. Such lawsuits are rarely successful in the courts, but they may succeed in intimidating activists and would-be activists because of the time as well as legal and financial resources required to respond to them.

If we are looking for an honest discussion of environmental issues, there is little sense in turning to the media. The media are, for the most part, owned by huge transnational corporations; and they are dependent upon other corporations for their advertising revenues. Their profits are dependent upon presenting the news with a corporate bias. Yet, news journalists almost always claim to be objective and impartial. They offer as proof of their impartiality the fact that they always give equal time to both sides of an issue. Such a "balanced" approach does not favor change, and if it does not favor change, then, by default, it must favor the status quo, a status quo that favors corporate interests.

Irrespective of climate change theory, most agree that the earth's resources are finite. Per capita, countries in the North consume resources and produce wastes at far greater rates than the more populous countries of the South. If the South comes close to achieving its goal of catching up with the North, then resource depletion and waste production would reach levels that the earth probably could not sustain. One tentative solution to this problem would be for the North to cut down on its rates of consumption.

This would require altering constructions of "the good life" and devaluing consumption. Lowering consumption could be both the cause and the effect of a shorter workweek. People might have less money to spend on commodities, but they would have a healthier environment, more leisure, and more time to spend with their family.

Like so many other resources discussed in previous chapters, healthy environments are not distributed equally, either within countries or between countries. Within the United States, minority and poor populations are more likely to be located near hazardous-waste sites. Minority and poor children are more likely to be exposed to lead poisoning and are more vulnerable to other forms of pollution. These injustices gave rise to the environmental justice movement and, later, to a presidential executive order that outlawed environmental discrimination by federal agencies. The effectiveness of this executive order remains questionable. Inequalities in the distribution of healthy environments are even more stark when we examine the differences between countries. Countries of the South face far greater levels of pollution, and millions die as a result. Water pollution is perhaps the most serious environmental problem in the South, leading to millions of deaths from diarrheal diseases, especially among children. Air pollution levels in many areas of the South are also inordinately high; indoor air pollution, especially, is a very serious threat to poor residents of the South. Poor people of the South are more vulnerable to these and almost all other forms of pollution because of their poor diet and lowered immunity. Both global and regional environmental disasters almost invariably affect them first.

Aware that the earth could not sustain 7 billion people living Northern lifestyles, it is generally recognized, at least among environmentalists, that industrial development cannot proceed uncontrolled. Sacrifices will have to be made. However, the North wants to see the South make sacrifices in terms of tougher environmental regulations. The South responds that it cannot afford tougher environmental regulation, but the North could better afford to reduce its levels of consumption. Indeed, the average resident of the North places many times more stress on the environment and enjoys a material lifestyle far greater than the average resident of the South. So when the countries of the North ask the countries of the South to slow down development with environmental regulation, they may be seen as lacking a certain moral authority.

Concern about strains on the environment often focuses on overpopulation. The poverty of the poor in the South and their unhealthy environments are often blamed on overpopulation. However, the critical constructionist notes that there are enough resources to feed, clothe, and shelter everyone in the world. Many rich countries that place more strain on the environment than their poor counterparts are rarely, if ever, considered "overpopulated." Many poor countries have population densities that are lower than some of their wealthier counterparts. Many poor countries that allegedly do not have enough resources to feed their own people are, nonetheless, able to grow luxury crops for export to the North. The real problem of overpopulation, then, could easily be constructed as a problem of poverty and of resource distribution.

Yet, rather than question a global economic system that leaves billions of people on the brink of disaster, the problem of overpopulation in poor countries is addressed with aggressive birth control programs that frequently compromise the rights of the people. If we indeed accept that overpopulation is a problem that needs to be addressed, an alternatively constructed solution could be the empowerment of women in the South. In these often fiercely patriarchal societies, women are left with few options other than bearing children throughout their fertile years. Education and the empowerment of women would provide them with more alternatives, and there is evidence that such an approach would reduce birth rates.

Like the other problems discussed in this book, many of those associated with the environment and overpopulation can be alternatively constructed as problems of inequality and can be addressed by examining the distribution of resources. In the case of poor women in the South, the resources that need to be redistributed include education, access to employment, and political power. And like so many other problems discussed in this book, if these kinds of resources were more equitably distributed, a multitude of other—often seemingly unrelated—problems might be alleviated.

Discussion Questions

1. Farmers throughout much of the North receive billions of dollars worth of government subsidies to defray their costs, reduce their losses in times of market fluctuation, encourage them to grow certain crops, and discourage them from growing others. Critics of these subsidies say that they undermine the economies of poorer countries and help to perpetuate poverty in the South. Do a little research on the Internet and discuss the connection between farm subsidies in the North and poverty in the South.

2. With China likely to add 10 million cars per year to their roads, with India not that far behind, and with a limited supply of oil in the world, do you think we are headed toward global "resource wars"? What trends or events might lessen the potential for such a future?

Conclusions

Though it is not the purpose of this book to provide solutions to all of the problems that are discussed in the preceding chapters, critical constuctionism, with its roots in conflict theory, does lend itself to certain policies that would alleviate many of them. Sociologist Douglas Kellner describes one of the most fundamental problems addressed in this book, that of corporate power:

> [T]he most powerful corporate forces have tightened their control of both the state and the media in the interests of aggressively promoting a pro-business agenda at the expense of other groups. The consequences of neoliberalism and its program of deregulation, tax breaks for the wealthy, military buildup, cutback of social programs, and the widening class divisions are increasingly evident in the new millennium. As the new century unfolds, globalized societies confront the specter of ever-increasing corporate and military power, worsening social conditions for the vast majority, and sporadic mixtures of massive apathy and explosive conflict.[1]

In keeping with Kellner's assertion, we need to recognize the power of corporate interests in shaping social and economic policy as well as our perceptions of what is right and what is wrong with our society.

In 2008 the subprime mortgage crisis triggered an economic decline that has left millions more Americans unemployed than "usual" and threatened the economic security of almost everyone else. The crisis was a tragic illustration of how corporate elite can influence government to the detriment of the lower and middle classes and of the democratic principles on which the country is based. Banks and financial institutions lobbied Congress and made enormous campaign contributions while Congress looked the other way and failed to pass minimal commonsense legislation to regulate an industry run amok. The result: massive foreclosures, a surge in homelessness, the devastation of whole neighborhoods, the ravaging of the property tax base of cities throughout the country, and severe cutbacks at the federal, state, and local levels. In response, the government rushed in to bail out the financial institutions with hundreds of billions of dollars of taxpayer money, thus, protecting corporate investors from losing their shirts while the less advantaged were losing their homes and jobs. The government bailout lent credence to economist John Kenneth Galbraith's famous dictum, "In America, the only respectable form of socialism is socialism for the rich." With government assistance, the corporate elite have managed to shift much of the risk of business and entrepreneurship off of themselves and onto the middle and lower classes. The risks of the bad investments of others, of paying for catastrophic illness, and of financially surviving retirement are far greater today for the average working family and far lesser for corporate enterprises than they have been for the past half century.

Before long-term solutions to the problems discussed in this book can be addressed, we must first address the influence the corporate elite have over government. Political campaigns have become prohibitively expensive, often costing tens of millions of dollars (or, in the case of presidential campaigns, hundreds of millions). Candidates and politicians have become beholden to corporations and powerful interests for campaign contributions. If their campaign platforms or their legislative voting records do not suit the interests of their corporate contributors and potential contributors, they run the risk of not being elected or reelected.

Both the Democratic and Republican Parties are beholden to corporations for campaign contributions. While the more conservative Republican Party attracts more corporate donors, the Democratic Party struggles to keep up. As *Economist* writers John Micklethwait and Adrian Wooldridge put it, "The Democrats are marginally less addicted to corporate largesse than the K Street conservatives at the helm of the Republican Party, but only in the way that a cokehead is in less trouble than a heroin junkie."[2] In various campaigns, a number of corporate entities—including Verizon, AT&T, AIG, Pfizer, Bristol-Myers Squibb, IBM, and Microsoft[3]—have given large sums to *both* parties. While they may explain that they "merely want to support the democratic process," it seems obvious that they want the winner from whichever party to be in their debt. "Without an effective presidential public financing system," writes Craig Aaron, "there's no hope of ever having a presidential contender who isn't personally wealthy, beholden to wealthy special interests or both."[4]

Supreme Court decisions of recent decades have been guided by the principle that "money is speech," and that restrictions on campaign contributions are the equivalent of restrictions on free speech. The problem with the money-is-speech doctrine is that it means that "free speech" is far from free and the elite are entitled to more speech than everybody else. The money-is-speech doctrine results in a somewhat less than democratic election system when, according to Ellis Jones and his associates, "One-quarter of 1% of the US population gives 80% of all of the private money in our elections."[5]

In 2010, recent efforts at campaign finance reform were reversed by the U.S. Supreme Court's decision *Citizens United v. Federal Elections Commission*. This case lifted past restrictions and allows corporations and unions to spend unlimited amounts of money on campaign advertising as long as the ads are not actually coordinated by the candidates or their campaigns. The ramifications of this case are highly significant because the main reason why campaigns are so expensive is the exorbitant cost of running ads on television and any candidate who can draw upon the enormous cash reserves of the corporate world has a huge advantage over his or her opponents. Even the threat of having corporate money fund an opposing candidate could well be enough to make incumbent politicians shy away from legislation imposing regulations on large corporations.

Since corporate executives are more likely to oppose taxes and regulations and favor the Republican Party, and since unions are more likely to support regulations protecting workers and favor the Democratic Party, some say the *Citizens United* case will result in a "wash," with corporate spending on campaign ads and union spending balancing each other out. But corporations have a lot more money at their disposal and they have managed to keep billions in reserve during the Great Recession, while unions have taken a huge blow during the recession with millions of layoffs in both the public and private sectors. Even before the Great Recession and *Citizens United*, in 2004, for example, Jones and his colleagues note, "PACs linked to corporations spent four times as much as PACs linked to labor unions."[6]

Legislation should be passed limiting the costs of advertising. Most of the public does not know that the airwaves belong to the public—through federal licensing agreements, the government has signed their use over to multibillion-dollar corporations that use them to make more billions. In return for the use of those airwaves, the networks should be required to offer free prime-time spots to candidates who meet certain conditions (to be determined) for their campaign ads.

Keeping in mind the critical role played by the media in problem construction, for the use of those airwaves that earn them billions, the networks should also be required to provide us with an hour of prime-time, commercial-free news every night. While the news will still be tainted by the network's corporate interests, it would be less influenced by the advertisers' corporate interests; moreover, the networks might feel less compelled to turn their news shows into "infotainment" if they are not worried about selling commercial airtime during that hour.

Furthermore, the public needs to be more aware of the interests that slant the media's news coverage. If our media functioned as an "arm of the government," the people would be outraged, fearing the specter of totalitarianism. However, the media today function as no less than an "arm of the corporate world," and that specter should be just as frightening.

It is the news that does not get covered, or gets only brief mention, which may well be of greatest concern. For example, the media's coverage of public demonstrations is either missing, scant, or highly distorted. At the turn of the new millennium, huge demonstrations were taking place throughout the world, protesting globalization, free trade, and the extreme forms of capitalism that benefit elite and corporate interests to the detriment of the billions of the rest of us. It is not in the corporate media's vested interest to fairly cover such demonstrations, and therefore, these protests were either not mentioned or mentioned briefly in passing. When such demonstrations are covered, every effort is made to discredit the protestors either by distorting their motives (diverting attention away from issues that may compromise the media's corporate interests) or by focusing far more extensively on violence perpetrated by the protestors than on violence perpetrated by the authorities.

As this book goes to press, the Occupy Wall Street movement has been under way for several months and most of the media coverage about the protesters concerns their lack of a consistent message. There have been a lot of interviews of individuals in the crowds who express different concerns as the reasons for their participation. But an examination of the alternative press as well as the international press makes it pretty clear that there is a consistent expression of anger directed to the corporate capitalist system where the "top 1 percent" is able to influence public policy to its own benefit and to the detriment of the "99 percent." In fact, one could probably wander through any crowd of protesters throughout history and interview some protestors whose concerns are inconsistent with the concerns of most people in the crowd—as the mainstream media appear to have done in this case. The United States was founded in civil disobedience and public protest; but such coverage, or lack thereof, severely diminishes the voice of the people, which is so critical to a healthy democracy.

This is not to suggest that the people cannot get adequate information or to say that they cannot have a voice in politics today. It is merely to say that we cannot expect the people's interests to be adequately voiced in the mainstream corporate media. There are indeed other sources of information available that are not so heavily influenced by corporate interests. A different kind of news can be found at various sites on the Internet. Some notable sites at the time of this writing include factcheck.org, truthout.org, alternet.org, corpwatch.org, and projectcensored.org (a student-produced site).

There are also ways for the people to gain a voice in politics. First, while our voting behavior is frequently misdirected by the mainstream media, our votes do indeed count. (The low voter turnout that has been typical of the United States—and increasingly so throughout an increasingly capitalist Europe—essentially amounts to a strong vote in favor of the status quo since incumbents usually have an advantage.) Second, the powerful influence of the corporate world cannot be overcome if objectors are not active and organized. In other words, people who want to see change need to get involved and, at the very least, vote.

In a world where corporations have undue influence over both the media and our politicians, a potentially effective means for the average person to be heard is through consumer boycotts. The first such boycott known to most Americans was that following the British Stamp Act, leading up to the American Revolution. Today, an increasing number of people are engaging in such activity. One global survey of over 22,000 consumers worldwide found that roughly 20 percent of the respondents reported that they had taken action within the past year to "punish" corporations that they thought were socially irresponsible.[7] In recent years, numerous boycotts have protested genetically modified foods, contaminated beef, sweatshops, child labor practices, animal abuse, and environmental destruction. A Church of England–approved prayer book exhorts its followers:

> where we shop, how we shop, and what we buy is a living statement of what we believe....Shopping which involves the shopper in making ethical and religious judgments may be nearer to the worship of God than any number of pious prayers in church....If we take our roles as God's stewards seriously, shoppers collectively are a powerful group....[8]

Consumers can indeed be a powerful force. Depending upon the extent and the degree of their organization, such boycotts can be quite effective. As one CEO of a leading brand-name corporation confesses, "What we fear most is not new legislation, but consumer revolt."[9] Readers who are interested in learning more about ethical shopping and consumer boycotts can go online to *ethicalconsumer.org*. Consumers have recently been every effective at organizing boycotts and petition drives online. Readers interested in learning more about these initiatives or organizing their own can go online to *change.org*.

These would be but a few steps in the right direction; but there are more fundamental, global, and sweeping problems that need to be addressed. The world is poised on the verge of a social, political, and economic revolution as profound and tumultuous as the Industrial Revolution. More and more countries are becoming more and more integrated into the global economy. Business and political leaders around the world are telling people that in order to compete in the global economy, they can no longer afford regulations restricting the behavior of corporations. Corporations, we are told, must be completely flexible (free of regulation) if they are to meet the demands of an ever-changing market. Less flexible businesses, we are told, will be beaten out by more flexible businesses; and the countries that host the less flexible businesses will be beaten out by those that host the more flexible ones. However, the regulations that are being sacrificed in the name of flexibility and competitiveness have everything to do with our quality of life. In the name of flexibility, corporate interests can disregard the need for families to have access to stable employment; they can disregard employees' needs for health benefits, time to be with their families, and a minimum standard of living; and they can disregard society's need for an environment that does not put our health at risk. If government regulations force corporations to attend to such concerns, the argument goes, then they will lose their competitive edge and the economy will falter.

Corporations have always shunned government regulations as they have always seen them as impeding their quest for profit. Profit is, after all, their one and only goal, their *raison d'être,* not the welfare of society. In the United States, they have fought tooth and nail against government regulations throughout our history. Eventually, people came to realize that slavery is a bad thing, that child labor is wrong, that workers should not be required to work 60-hour weeks in order to keep their jobs, that workers should be guaranteed a minimum wage, and that they should be allowed to organize to fight for their rights. Workers' rights have come a long way in American history; but now, we are told, in the face of global integration, such concerns are too costly. Corporate leaders have always felt that way, but global integration has become their trump card.

Not only are wages, workers' rights, employee benefits, family stability, and the quality of the environment threatened by global integration, but so too are our democratic freedoms. Free trade agreements have given the World Trade Organization (WTO) the authority to undermine regulations that are the result of the democratic process. Democratically elected legislatures in the United States, Europe, Japan, and elsewhere have enacted policies to ensure workers' rights, employment stability, and national self-sufficiency. Government subsidies to farmers, for example, have been intended to protect agricultural workers and nations from dependence on other countries for their food supply. Today, however, the WTO—made up of people who are not democratically elected—has the authority to sanction countries with such policies and regulations because they inhibit free markets.

Capitalism has always produced change. Production modes that are inefficient or targeting wrong markets must change or be wiped out by the competition. However, the problem with today's global capitalism is that the change it is producing is escalating at a pace that will inevitably produce more and more instability. Instability creates more need for change ("flexibility") and, therefore, more instability. Again, people of nations throughout the world are being told that government efforts to control the pace of change will only make their countries less competitive. Global capitalism is sweeping over the world like a juggernaut, and we are told that it is uncontrollable.

A famous sociological principle is called the "Thomas theorem." Named after W. I. Thomas, it states that things perceived as real are real in their consequences. For example, if everybody thinks the stock market will crash, then there will be a huge sell-off and the stock market will indeed crash. Similarly and certainly, if the people of the world are convinced that global integration is uncontrollable, then it will not be controlled. Global capitalism, however, is a product of human action; and it can be influenced by further human action. Capitalism, unlike Frankenstein's monster, is not beyond the control of its human creators. We must maintain our sense of authorship over this awesome phenomenon.

If we are to control the pace of global capitalism and maintain a modicum of stability in our society and our lives, we must first keep in mind that our efforts do not amount to an all-or-nothing gamble. Critics of regulation would have us believe that any given employee benefit or environmental law could make the U.S. economy noncompetitive. Donald Barlett and James Steele—authors of the book *America: Who Stole the Dream?*—write,

What has complicated the debate about the nation's economic course is that most policy issues are cast in either/or terms. Either you're for free trade, or you're a raving protectionist....Either you want government off of business's back, or you favor shackling American companies with onerous regulations....Because there is no middle ground, the doors have been flung open to products made around the world, often by workers whose wages have been counted in pennies—eliminating American jobs. Because there is no middle ground, the progressive income tax—designed so that the very rich would pay their appropriate share of the cost of government—has been gutted. And because there is no middle ground, the notion that government has a vital role in the economic direction of the country has been shoved aside. Either you believe in unfettered private enterprise or that the government should run the economy.[10]

An overregulated economy, such as that of the former Soviet Union, could certainly affect our lives more disastrously than the unregulated economy for which we are headed; but there is a middle ground.

A middle ground would not eschew the role of government in promoting the health and welfare of its citizenry and this frequently requires government spending, paid for by public taxes. The U.S. government simply needs to pay for stuff. The government needs to pay to keep up the nation's infrastructure—its roads, its bridges, its water supply system, its power grid.

Fewer and fewer of the antibiotics doctors have at their disposal are effective as more diseases become resistant to them. Pharmaceutical companies invest relatively little money in developing antibiotics because patients usually only take them for a short time, whereas the big profits are to be made on drugs for chronic diseases that have to be taken for the rest of the patient's life. The government needs to invest in the research and development of new antibiotics or the nation faces the very real potential of an epidemic that will cripple the nation and its economy.

If the United States is to remain competitive it also needs to invest more in the education of its citizens. Indeed the United States is falling behind other countries whose governments invest proportionally more in the education of their preschoolers and primary and secondary students and college students.

The antitax, free market ideology, which holds such powerful sway over the American political process and which is supposed to make us more competitive is effectively making us less so. In many other affluent countries the government has forged much stronger partnerships with private industry than we are used to seeing in the United States. These governments are often investing in new technologies which have the promise of creating huge markets in the not-too-distant future, especially in energy technologies, with consumption expected to increase 58 percent by 2035 and renewables being the fastest growing source of energy.[11]

Capitalism is a powerful force and it is largely responsible for the vast improvement of our standard of living over the past two centuries. But is has also proven to be a devastating force and, with the pace of global integration accelerating, it portends to become even more devastating, enriching the welfare of the already rich and threatening the livelihoods of the destitute and those of us in between. If the pace of global capitalism is to be controlled, the United States must take the lead. The United States has led the industrialized world in opening markets, deregulating the economy, and failing to provide its citizens with safety nets. It must now take the lead in the opposite direction. It may well be the only country in a position to take that lead because it represents such a valuable block of consumers on the world trade scene. It is the wealthiest country in the world, and its citizens, as we have seen, have a taste for consumption. The economic health of our trading partners depends in large part upon trade with the United States.

If the United States adopted policies that closed its markets to countries with certain labor practices, those countries would seriously have to reconsider their labor practices. In the past, for example, the United States has threatened trade sanctions against countries that employed child labor or prison labor. Countries guilty of such labor practices rarely have to reconsider them seriously because the United States has rarely followed through on these threats. Powerful corporate interests and their lobbyists have persuaded government officials that such sanctions could cause us to lose our competitive edge. However, such actions would be a step in the right direction. Proceeding in that direction, we could restrict access to our markets by countries that allow their female workers to be subject to sexual intimidation and rape. We could restrict access to our markets by countries that do not provide a minimum wage, by those that do not allow their workers to unionize, or by those that do not provide a minimum of environmental regulation and enforcement.

Without such leadership, we will see a continual ratcheting down of global working conditions and environmental standards. As long as capitalism's only goal is profit, it will continue scouring the globe for the least expensive, least restrictive production conditions. Wages in the North, for both blue-collar and white-collar workers, will be competing with wages in the China, India, and the South. The costs of employee benefits in the North will be competing with the costs of employee benefits in the South. The costs of environmental standards in the North will be competing with the costs of environmental standards in the South. Without leadership, the North will be under immense pressure to approximate the conditions of the South. If the United States took the lead, countries in the South would be pressured to adopt standards more akin to standards in the North.

If the United States took the lead in controlling the pace of global capitalism, I doubt it would be alone. Western European countries, Canada, Japan, and others have been dragged kicking and screaming into the new global economy. To compete—mostly with the United States—they are having to ratchet down their ability to provide high wages, generous employee benefits, and job security. In addition, European countries have had to scale back government policies that were in place to ensure low unemployment rates. Further, they have had to give up a good part of their national identities to form the European Union and implement a common currency. Japan, long famous for job security and low unemployment, has had to weaken the policies that made these conditions possible. The programs and policies that are now being scaled back in the face of global competition were highly cherished and are being given up only with a great deal of resistance. Further, these countries have neither historically nor culturally placed as high a value on market freedom as has the United States. Many, if not most, countries would breathe a sigh of relief if the United States took the lead in controlling the fierce competition and instability engendered by global capitalism. Together with the United States they would represent a powerful bloc that could indeed slow down global economic integration to a pace that would continue to assure a reasonable standard of living in the North and improve standards in the South. If, however, we succumb to the dictum that government regulation of the economy can only do us harm, then many of the social problems discussed in this book will only get worse.

In conclusion, critical constructionism contributes insight to an otherwise difficult to fathom phenomenon. How is it that the elite—whose average member possesses wealth hundreds to thousands of times greater than the average member of society—and whose financial interests are, therefore, worlds apart from the average member—can convince the average citizen that both of their interests are one and the same? This phenomenon is not unique to the United States with its extreme version of capitalism, but has occurred in many, if not most, societies throughout history. Critical constructionism directs our attention to the power of ideology and to the ability of those in power to use society's institutions to shape people's perceptions of reality. In our society, we must consider how the media, transnational corporations, private think tanks, educational institutions, and governmental institutions have all played a role in making us think that capitalism and democracy are one and the same. Just as extreme forms of socialism are apt to be accompanied by severe restrictions on freedom so too are extreme forms of capitalism. American's near-obsessive vigilance against the tyranny of government has allowed the tyranny of the marketplace to creep into its place. The tyranny of markets is not the only alternative to the tyranny of government. Other countries have managed to strike a balance between these two extremes and if Americans were able to educate themselves about the subject, mindful of the biases of society's hegemonic institutions, more might see the advantages of such a balance.

Discussion Questions

1. As we have seen in this book, capitalist ideology prescribes that individuals should be free to pursue their self-interests in a market free from

government intervention. Do you think that the United States has struck the right balance between freedom of the market and government intervention? Why or why not?

2. Is there a relationship between capitalism and democracy? If so, what is the nature of that relationship?

GLOSSARY

Affirmative action—a policy of giving women and minorities an advantage in hiring to offset the historical advantage held by the white male majority. The policy is usually meant to be a temporary solution to inequality based on discrimination. It is often controversial, with critics charging that it amounts to no more than reverse discrimination.

American Dream—the commonly held belief that the United States is unique in the vast opportunities it provides, where hard work and innovation will pay off in substantial financial rewards. The belief presupposes the existence of equal opportunity and reinforces the idea that the wealthy deserve to be wealthy and the poor deserve to be poor.

Anomie—a condition in society where the norms are in flux or lose their salience to large segments of the population. These norms are behavioral guidelines and they give meaning to the conditions of social existence; thus during periods when society is highly anomic, crime and/or suicide rates tend to climb.

It can also describe a condition in the individual; when the norms lose meaning to a particular person, the connections between that individual and society become unstable.

Capitalism—an economic system in which the means of production and distribution are privately held and government regulation is minimal. In the more extreme versions of this system, both wealth *and* political power tend to accumulate in the hands of a few; growing inequality and diminishing democracy can be the result.

Comparable worth—the belief or practice that men and women should be paid the same when their work involves the same skills, training, responsibility, and exertion. This is suggested as a response to the situation in which occupations dominated by men usually pay more than occupations dominated by women, even though the work involved is often the same or comparable.

Conflict theory—a theoretical perspective in sociology that focuses on inequality and the use and abuse of power. Originating with Karl Marx, this perspective examines how those with power use their power to influence social relations to their advantage and to the detriment of others.

Corporate censorship—refers to the influence that corporate interests have over the content of news and information provided to the public by the corporate media. As corporate entities, invested in other corporations and dependent upon still other corporations for advertising revenue, the media have a vested interest in presenting the news in some ways and not in others.

Corporate violence—activities or decisions made by corporate executives that put employees, consumers, or the public at risk of physical harm.

Creative destruction—in a capitalist economy, this refers to the process where industries and the people who work for them are made obsolete by newer, more efficient industries who, for example, export cheap labor from countries in the South.

Critical constructionism—a theoretical perspective that synthesizes conflict theory and symbolic interactionism. The critical constructionist examines how those with power in society are able to influence the way people give meaning to reality. In this way, the elite are able to mobilize society's resources to alleviate some "problems" in society and not others.

Dark figure of crime—those crimes that do not come to the attention of the authorities and, therefore, are not included in official crime statistics. Social scientists often put the official crime statistics in perspective by examining victimization surveys that generally indicate that there is far more crime than officially reported, but that crime rates do not fluctuate as radically as is often indicated by the official statistics.

Democratic socialism—an economic system that represents a compromise between socialism and capitalism. Most means of production and distribution are privately held; but the state often owns strategic industries and services. Wealth is allowed to accumulate in private hands, but tax rates are high to support government-provided services such as health care, day care, and higher education. Top government officials are democratically elected, indicating that this form of economy is one supported by the people.

Economy food plan—the cost of a bare minimum diet estimated by the U.S. Department of Agriculture and was originally used in the calculation of the U.S. Census Bureau's poverty thresholds.

Environmental discrimination—corporate and governmental policies that put the poor and minorities at disproportionate risk of exposure to environmental harms.

Escape rate—the proportion of those living in poverty in a given country who are able to move out of poverty within a year.

Glass ceiling—the barrier of discrimination blocking women from reaching executive level positions in most business and industry.

Hegemony—a central concept in the works of Antonio Gramsci. Gramsci argued that the exploitation of workers in capitalist society is derived not only from their relationship to the means of production, but also by the manipulation of their consent through society's cultural institutions. He called this manipulation of consent "hegemony."

Human capital perspective—a perspective that views people, especially children, as worthy of substantial social investment. The more a society invests in its children's health, welfare, and education, the more it will get in future returns. Happier, healthier, and better-educated children will become more productive adults and will be less of a drain on society's resources in terms of welfare provisions and involvement in the criminal justice system.

Medicalization of deviance—when a significant number of people or a number of significant people consider certain forms of deviance as having a biological source that is treatable by the medical profession. Sociologists often see this as a form of social control.

The North—see "author's note" on page 22.

Poverty threshold—the official "poverty line" calculated by the U.S. Census Bureau and used to report the numbers and characteristics of those living in poverty.

Prison-industrial complex—the relationship between the political and corporate interests that benefit from the United States' inordinately heavy reliance on incarceration as a response to crime. Industries that employ cheap prison labor, those that are involved in prison construction, and those that run private prisons have an influence over the decisions of policymakers. Their interests are not necessarily the same as the public interest.

SLAPP—acronym for "Strategic Lawsuit against Public Participation." These are lawsuits brought by corporations usually against environmental activists, often alleging defamation. Critics argue these are not meant to redress an injury or exact justice, but to stifle the free speech of those critical of the corporation. Indeed most of these lawsuits are not won, but still manage to dissuade public criticism.

Social control mechanisms—the methods a society uses for ensuring its members follow the rules or norms.

Social movement organization—a significant group of people or a group of significant people who mobilize to alleviate a social problem. According to critical constructionism, the presence of such a group is the defining feature of a given social problem.

Social Darwinism—a social philosophy applying Darwin's work on evolution to human society. Accordingly, those people who are best adapted to the society have more to contribute and will thrive; those who do not thrive are not well adapted and have little to contribute. Though not popular among the social sciences, it does have a certain appeal among the public and conservative elites in that it rationalizes the existence of inequality.

Social problems perspective—a sociological perspective that holds that social problems are social problems because they are defined as such by powerful groups, not because they are harmful or injurious to society. To understand why a social problem is defined as such, one must understand the interests of the group and its relationship to other groups and institutions in the social structure.

Socialism—an economic system in which the means of production and distribution are owned by the government. In such an economy there is little opportunity for the accumulation of wealth in private hands and there is, therefore, more economic equality than in alternative systems. However, in its more extreme form, to prevent the accumulation of private wealth, the government often employs heavy-handed, autocratic methods and there is, therefore, a great deal of political inequality.

The South—see "author's note" on page 22.

Structural adjustment programs—programs imposed upon poor indebted countries requiring them, as a condition for loan repayment, to open their markets to imports from the North and to adopt austerity measures, such as cutting back on welfare, health care, and educational expenditures. These programs have made the poor people in most of these countries poorer.

Subprime mortgage crisis—an economic downturn in the American economy that started in 2007. Banks and financial institutions had been lending money to poorly qualified home-buyers, usually at adjustable rates, often not requiring proof of income or proof of assets. These institutions then bought and sold these mortgages among each other in bundles, with little regard to the quality of the mortgages or the likelihood of their being repaid. When mortgage default rates escalated, these institutions were left holding bad mortgages. Near-record foreclosure rates and corporate bailouts followed.

Symbolic interactionism—a sociological perspective that examines how people give meaning to and respond to their environment (as well as their selves). Accordingly, we give meaning to things based upon our experiences, our social interactions, in particular.

Trial penalty—when criminal defendants are pressured to plea bargain, facing a large gap between the length of sentence if they plead guilty and the length of sentence if they insist on a trial.

Trickle-down economics—an economic philosophy that holds that if government restrictions on the accumulation of wealth are lifted, the rich will get richer and spend more money. The money they spend will "trickle down" and enrich those beneath them. The objective evidence supporting this philosophy is questionable.

Transnational corporation (TNC)—a corporation headquartered in one country and operating in multiple countries. These corporations are subject to no one country's laws and regulations and can move about wherever more favorable conditions avail themselves. Countries who depend upon the presence of a TNC to employ large numbers of their people often have to compromise their working or environmental standards in order to keep the corporation from moving out. Even still, the corporation could leave at any time for a country where labor is cheaper and where there are fewer protections for the workers and the environment.

Unity of interests—the commonality of interests shared by a given social class. For example, a given social policy that is in the interest of one rich person is more likely to be in the interest of another rich person than it is to be in the interest of a poor person. When powerful individuals pursue their own self-interests, it may give the appearance of a conspiracy even when there has been no collusion.

NOTES

Chapter 1: An Introduction to the Sociology of Social Problems

1. *Sourcebook of Criminal Justice Statistics Online,* http://www.albany.edu/sourcebook/. Retrieved December 9, 2008 and Congressional Research Service, "Guarding America," Library of Congress, Order Code RL32670, November 12, 2004.
2. Emile Durkheim, *The Rules of Sociological Method.* Translated by S. A. Solovay and J. H. Mueller, edited by G. E. G. Catlin. New York: Free Press, 1966.
3. Kai Ericson, *Wayward Puritans.* New York: Macmillan, 1966.
4. Daniel Bell, "Crime as an American Way of Life," *Antioch Review,* vol. 13, 1953, 131–154.
5. Malcolm Spector and John I. Kitsuse, *Constructing Social Problems.* New York: Aldine de Gruyter, 1987, 75.
6. Lloyd de Mause, *The History of Childhood.* New York: Psychohistory Press, 1974.
7. Steven J. Pfohl, "The 'Discovery' of Child Abuse," in D. H. Kelly (ed.), *Deviant Behavior,* 3rd ed. New York: St. Martin's, 1989, 40–51.
8. George Herbert Mead, *Mind, Self, and Society.* Edited by C. W. Morris. Chicago: University of Chicago Press, 1934.
9. Neil McInnes, "Antonio Gramsci," *Encyclopedia of Philosophy,* vol. 3. New York: Macmillan and Free Press, 1967, 376–377.
10. Antonio Gramsci, *Selections from the Prison Notebooks.* Translated and edited by Q. Hoare and G. N. Smith. New York: International, 1971.
11. Brent Cunningham, "Across the Great Divide of Class," *Columbia Journalism Review,* May 21, 2004. Reprint available at http://www.alternet.org/story.html?StoryID518759.
12. Daniel Hallin, "Whatever Happened to the News?" *Media and Values* no. 50, Spring, 1990, 2–4.
13. Calvin Exoo, *The Politics of the Mass Media.* St. Paul, MN: West, 1994.
14. Nicholas Kristof, "Crony Capitalism Comes Home," *New York Times,* October 26, 2011. http://www.nytimes.com/2011/10/27/opinion/kristof-crony-capitalism-comes-homes.html?scp=1&sq=crony%20capitalism%20comes%20home&st=cse. Retrieved November 6, 2011.
15. Ben Bagdikian, *The New Media Monopoly.* Boston: Beacon Press, 2004.
16. Arthur E. Rowse, *Drive-By Journalism: The Assault on Your Need to Know.* Monroe, ME: Common Courage Press, 2000, 22.
17. Charles Derber, *Corporation Nation: How Corporations Are Taking over Our Lives and What We Can Do about It.* New York: St. Martin's Griffin, 1998, 176.
18. Robert W. McChesney, *Rich Media, Poor Democracy: Communication Politics in Dubious Times.* New York: New Press, 1999, xiii, 15.
19. Ethan Watters, *Crazy Like Us: The Globalization of the American Psyche.* New York: Free Press, 2010, 1.

Chapter 2: Inequality and Capitalism

1. Robert Pear, "Recession Officially Over, U.S. Incomes Kept Falling," *New York Times,* October 9, 2011.
2. John Gray, *False Dawn: The Delusions of Global Capitalism.* New York: New Press, 1998, 114.
3. Marc Miringoff and Marque-Luisa Miringoff, *The Social Health of the Nation: How America Is Really Doing.* New York: Oxford University Press, 1999.
4. Gregory Mantsios, "Class in America: Myths and Realities," in T. Ore (ed.), *The Social Construction of Difference and Inequality: Race, Class, Gender, and Sexuality.* Mountain View, CA: Mayfield, 2000, 512–526.
5. Robert H. Frank and Philip J. Cook, *The Winner-Take-All Society.* New York: Free Press, 1995.
6. Monica Lesmerises, "The Middle Class at Risk: A Century Foundation Guide to the Issues." New York: Century Foundation Press, 2007, 21.
7. "Trends in the Distribution of Household Income Between 1979 and 2007," The Congress of the United States. Congressional Budget Office, October 2011.
8. Larry M. Bartels, *Unequal Democracy: The Political Economy of the New Gilded Age.* Princeton, NJ: Princeton University Press, 2008, 11. Jeanne Sahadi, "CEO Pay: Sky High Gets Even Higher," *CNN Money,* August 30, 2005, http://money.cnn.com/2005/08/26/news/economy/ceo_pay. Retrieved April 25, 2012. Ray Williams, "Are CEO Salaries Out of Control?" *Psychology Today,* April 12, 2012, http://www.psychologytoday.com/blog/wired-success/201204/are-ceo-salaries-out-control. Retrieved April 25, 2012.
9. Lesmerises, "The Middle Class at Risk," 6.
10. William Julius Wilson, *The Bridge over the Racial Divide: Rising Inequality and Coalition Policies.* Berkeley: University of California Press, Russell Sage Foundation, 1999, 27.
11. Miringoff and Miringoff, *The Social Health of the Nation,* 108.
12. Gray, *False Dawn,* 2.
13. Harold Kerbo, *Social Stratification and Inequality: Class Conflict in Historical, Comparative, and Global Perspective, 6th ed.* New York: McGraw Hill, 2006.
14. Edward N. Wolff, *Top Heavy: The Increasing Inequality of Wealth in America and What Can Be Done about It.* New York: New Press, 1996, 1–2.
15. James Lardner, "The Rich Get Richer," *U.S. News and World Reports Online,* February 12, 2000. Available at wysiwyg://75/http://www.usnews.com/usnews/issue/000221/rich.htm.
16. Richard Leone's introduction to Wolff, *Top Heavy.*
17. Cited in Kim Clark and Margaret Mannix, "Show Me the Money! Debunking the Myth that Everybody but You Is Rich," *U.S. News and World Reports Online,* May 24, 1999. Available at wysiwyg://119/http://www.usnews.com/usnews/issue/990524/24mill.htm.
18. Edward N. Wolff, *Top Heavy: The Increasing Inequality of Wealth in America and What Can Be Done about It,* 2nd ed. New York: New Press, 2002, 2.
19. Ibid., 31.
20. Quoted in Anthony Platt, "End Game: The Rise and Fall of Affirmative Action in Higher Education. Reconfiguring Power: Challenges for the 21st Century," in A. Aguirre, Jr. and D. Baker (eds.), *Structured Inequality in the United States.* Upper Saddle River, NJ: Prentice Hall, 2000, 320.

21. Kerbo, *Social Stratification and Inequality,* 355.
22. Doug Henwood, *After the New Economy.* New York: New Press, 2003, 80; Lawrence Mishel, Jared Bernstein and Sylvia Allegretto, *The State of Working America, 2007/2007,* The Economic Policy Institute, Ithaca, NY: Cornell University Press, 2007.
23. Mantsios, "Class in America," 523.
24. Holly Sklar and Chuck Collins, "Forbes 400 World Series." *The Nation,* October 20, 1997. http://www.phenomenologycenter.org/course/rich.htm. retrieved March 21, 2012.
25. Jeremy Rivkin, *The European Dream: How Europe's Vision of the Future Is Eclipsing the American Dream.* New York: Jeremy P. Tarcher/Penguin, 2004, 38.
26. Jeff Faux, "You Are Not Alone," in S. B. Greenberg and T. Skocpol (eds.), *The New Majority: Toward a Popular Progressive Politics.* New Haven, CT: Yale University Press, 1997, 24 (emphasis in the original).
27. Lester C. Thurow, "Rise in Women's Earnings Masks Deterioration in Men's Pay: Family Income Stagnates," *Boston Globe,* June 15, 1999.
28. Juliet Schor, *The Overworked American: The Unexpected Decline of Leisure.* New York: Basic Books, 1992.
29. Bureau of Labor Statistics, "International Comparisons of Hourly Compensation Costs in Manufacturing, 2009," News Release, March 8, 2011.
30. Quoted in Wilson, *The Bridge over the Racial Divide,* 30.
31. Quoted in Beth A. Rubin, *Shifts in the Social Contract: Understanding Change in American Society.* Thousand Oaks, CA: Pine Forge, 1996, 61.
32. Louis Uchitelle, "Survey Finds Layoffs Slowed in Last Three Years," *New York Times,* August 20, 1998.
33. Noam Chomsky, "How Free Is the Free Market?" Speech given in London, England, 1994. Available at http://www.oneworld.org/second opinion/chomsky.html.
34. Edward Luttwak, *Turbo-Capitalism: Winners and Losers in the Global Economy.* New York: HarperCollins, 1999, 45.
35. Katherine S. Newman, *Falling from Grace: Downward Mobility in the Age of Affluence.* Berkeley: University of California Press, 1999.
36. Ibid., 35.
37. Peter S. Goodman, "White-Collar Work a Booming U.S. Export," *Washington Post,* April 2, 2003, E01. Available at http://www.washingtonpost.com/ac2/wp-dyn/A6456-2003Apr1?language5printer.
38. National Conference on State Legislatures, "Unemployment Steady at 9.1 Percent in August," September 2, 2011, http://www.ncsl.org/?tabid=13307. Retrieved October 6, 2011.
39. Robert D. Hershey, Jr., "When Downsizing Moves Up the Ladder," *New York Times,* May 14, 1999.
40. Jeff Faux, "Losing Ground," *American Prospect,* May 4, 2004. Available at http://www.prospect.org/web/Page.ww?section5root&name5ViewPrint&articleId57639.
41. Chris Isadore, "The Unemployed Risk a Permanent Pay Cut," CNNMoney, October 8, 2011, http://money.cnn.com/2011/10/06/news/economy/unemployed_income/index.htm. Retrieved October 9, 2011.
42. "Few Recover Totally from Downsizing," *USA Today (Magazine),* vol. 127, no. 2639, August 1998 (online).
43. Rubin, *Shifts in the Social Contract,* 79.

44. Rubin, *Shifts in the Social Contract.*

45. Paul Osterman, "New Rules for the New Economy," *Boston Globe,* September 5, 1999 (online).

46. Steven Greenhouse, "Joe Hill in High Tech: Unions Need Not Apply," *New York Times,* July 26, 1999 (online).

47. Rubin, *Shifts in the Social Contract,* 179.

48. Luttwak, *Turbo-Capitalism,* 60.

49. Newman, *Falling from Grace.*

50. James W. Russell, *Double Standard: Social Policy in Europe and the United States.* Lanham, MD: Rowman and Littlefield, 2006, 95.

51. Ibid., 8.

52. Sarah Ramsay, " 'Downsizing' Takes Its Toll on UK Professionals." *Lancet,* vol. 354, no. 9181, September 4, 1999, 843.

53. Donald Barlett and James B. Steele, *America: Who Stole the Dream?* Kansas City, MO: Andrews and McNeel, 1996, 43.

54. Gray, *False Dawn,* 111.

55. Kerbo, *Social Stratification and Inequality.*

56. Phineas Baxandall, "Jobs vs. Wages: The Phony Trade-Off," in D. S. Eitzen and C. S. Leedham (eds.), *Solutions to Social Problems: Lessons from Other Societies.* Needham Heights, MA: Allyn and Bacon, 1998, 136–140.

57. Ibid.

58. Elliott Currie, *Crime and Punishment in America.* New York: Owl Books, 1998.

59. Newman, *Falling from Grace,* 30.

60. Sylvia Nasar, "Where Joblessness Is a Way of Making a Living," *New York Times,* May 9, 1999 (online).

61. Gray, *False Dawn,* 93.

62. Thomas W. Haines, "French Workers Rally for Additional Time Off: Employers Chafe at 35-Hour Workweek," *Boston Globe,* October 17, 1999, A16. Bruce Crumley, "Why France's 35 Hour Week Won't Die." *Time/World,* January 22, 2009. http://www.time.com/time/world/article/0,8599,1873245,00.html. Retrieved March 19, 2012

63. Kerbo, *Social Stratification and Inequality,* 272.

64. Gray, *False Dawn,* 93.

65. Quoted in Haines, "French Workers Rally" (emphasis added).

66. Luttwak, *Turbo-Capitalism,* 40.

67. See Luttwak, *Turbo-Capitalism*; Gray, *False Dawn*; and Barlett and Steele, *Who Stole the Dream?*

68. Guy Molyneau, "The Core Issue is Living Standards." *Los Angeles Times,* March 3, 1996, http://articles.latimes.com/1996-03-03/opinion/op-42700_1_living-standards/2. Retrieved March 19, 2012.

69. U.S. House Committee on Transportation and Infrastructure, "Transportation Committee Leaders and Civil Engineers Highlight Need to Address Deterioration of Nation's Infrastructure," September 4, 2003. Available at www.house.gov/transportation/press/press 2003/release143.html.

70. Ibid.

71. National Education Association, "School Modernization." May 2003. Available at http://www.nea.org/modernization/.

72. The American Society of Civil Engineers, "Report Card for America's Infrastructure: 2003 Progress Report." Available at http://www.asce.org/reportcard/.

73. Charles Derber, *The Wilding of America: Money, Mayhem, and the New American Dream*. New York: Worth, 2004, 91.
74. John Kenneth Galbraith, *The Affluent Society*, 3rd ed. Boston: Houghton Mifflin, 1969, 190.
75. Harold Kerbo, *Social Stratification and Inequality: Class Conflict in Historical, Comparative, and Global Perspective*, 5th ed. Boston: McGraw-Hill, 2003, 21.
76. "Hunger in America: Key Findings," Feeding America, http://feedingamerica. org/hunger-in-america/hunger-studies/hunger-study-2010/key-findings.aspx. Retrieved October10, 2011.
77. "Hunger and Homelessness Remain Most Pressing Issues for U.S. Cities." City Mayors Society, http://www.citymayors.com/features/uscity_poverty.html. Retrieved October 11, 2011.
78. Kerbo, *Social Stratification and Inequality, Boston: McGraw-Hill,* 2000 and Mark Nord, Margaret Andrews, and Steven Carlson, "Household Food Security in the United States, 2006, USDA," http://www.ers.usda.gov/Publications/ERR49/ ERR49_ReportSummary.pdf. Retrieved June 20, 2008.
79. "Households and Persons Having Problems with Access to Food, 2004–2008 (Table 210)," *Statistical Abstracts of the United States, 2011–2012*. New York: Skyhorse Publishing, 2011.
80. "Income, Poverty, and Health Insurance Coverage in the United States: 2010," U.S. Census Bureau, September 11, 2011.
81. "Access to Affordable and Nutritious Food: Measuring and Understanding Food Deserts and their Consequences," Economic Research Service. U.S. Department of Agriculture, June 2009, http://www.ers.usda.gov/Publications/AP/AP036/ AP036_reportsummary.pdf. Retrieved, October 11, 2011.
82. John E. Schwarz, "The Hidden Side of the Clinton Economy," in T. Ore (ed.), *The Social Construction of Difference and Inequality: Race, Class, Gender, and Sexuality*. Mountain View, CA: Mayfield, 2000, 67–70.
83. Jessie Willis, "How We Measure Poverty: A History and Brief Overview," for the Oregon Center for Public Policy, February 2000. Available at http://www.ocpp. org/poverty/how.htm.
84. Quoted in Louis Uchitelle, "Devising New Math to Define Poverty," *New York Times,* October 18, 1999 (online).
85. Danilo Trisi, Arloc Sherman, and Matt Broaddus, "Poverty Rate Second-Highest in 45 Years; Record Numbers Lacked Health Insurance, Lived in Deep Poverty, Center on Budget and Policy Priorities," September 14, 2011, http://www. cbpp.org/cms/?fa=view&id=3580. Retrieved, October 11, 2011; Kerbo, *Social Stratification and Inequality,* 2003.
86. Joseph Dillon Davey, *The New Social Contract: America's Journey from Welfare State to Police State*. Westport, CT: Praeger, 1995, 41.
87. "Hunger and Homelessness Remain Most Pressing Issues for U.S. Cities." City Mayors Society, http://www.citymayors.com/features/uscity_poverty.html. Retrieved October 11, 2011.
88. "State of Homelessness in America," National Alliance to End Homelessness, January 11, 2011, http://www.endhomelessness.org/content/article/detail/3668. Retrieved October 11, 2011.
89. Ralph Nunez and Cybelle Fox, "A Snapshot of Family Homelessness across America," *Political Science Quarterly,* vol. 114, no. 2, Summer, 1999, 289–307.
90. Kerbo, *Social Stratification and Inequality,* 2000, 281 (emphasis in the original).

91. Quoted in John Pease and Lee Martin, "Want Ads and Jobs for the Poor: A Glaring Mismatch," *Sociological Forum,* vol. 12, no. 4, 1997, 546.
92. Ibid., 545.
93. "U.S. Conference of Mayors—Sodexho Hunger and Homelessness Survey 2003."
94. Kerbo, Social Stratification and Inequality, 6th ed., 2006.
95. Michael Harrington, *The Other America.* New York: Touchstone, 1997, 7.
96. Gregory Mantsios, "Media Magic: Making Class Invisible," in P. Rothenberg (ed.), *Race, Class, and Gender in the United States,* 4th ed. New York: St. Martin's, 1998, 514.
97. Brent Cunningham, "Across the Great Divide of Class," *Columbia Journalism Review,* May 21, 2004. Available at http://www.alternet.org/story.html?Story ID518759.
98. Mantsios, "Media Magic," 511.
99. Donald L. Barlett and James B. Steele, *America: Who Really Pays the Taxes?* New York: Touchstone, 1994, 26.
100. Ibid.
101. David Kocieniewski, "G.E.'s Strategies Let It Avoid Taxes Altogether," *New York Times,* March 24, 2011,
102. Donald L. Barlett and James B. Steele, "Corporate Welfare," *Time,* vol. 152, no. 19, November 9, 1998, 38.
103. Ibid.
104. Ibid.
105. Ibid.
106. Mark Zepezauer and Arthur Naiman, *Take the Rich Off Welfare.* Tucson, AZ: Odonian Press, 1996, 8.
107. Michael Parenti, "Imperialism 101," in Heiner, *Social Problems and Social Solutions,* Needham Heights, MA: Allyn and Bacon, 32.
108. Ibid., 34.
109. Ibid.
110. Ibid.
111. Walden Bello, "Global Economic Counterrevolution: The Dynamics of Impoverishment and Marginalization," in R. Hofrichter (ed.), *Toxic Struggles: The Theory and Practice of Environmental Justice.* Philadelphia: New Society, 1993, 197–208.
112. Derber, *The Wilding of America.*
113. Dennis Pirages, "The Global Environment: Megaproblem or Not?" *The Futurist,* March–April, vol. 31, no. 2, 1997.
114. Paul Lewis, "World Bank Says Poverty Is Increasing," *New York Times,* June 3, 1999 (online).
115. *2007 Human Development Report,* United Nations Development Programme. New York: Palgrave Macmillan, 2007, 25.
116. Hazel Henderson, "The Global Environment: Megaproblem or Not?" *The Futurist,* March–April, vol. 31, no. 2, 1997.
117. Larry Elliott, "The Lost Decade," *Guardian,* July 9, 2003. Available at http://www.guardian.co.uk/international/story/0,3604,994440,00.html.
118. Quoted in Greg Palast, *The Best Democracy Money Can Buy.* London: Pluto Press, 2002, 50.
119. Robert Weissman, "Grotesque Inequality: Corporate Globalization and the Global Gap Between Rich and Poor," *Multinational Monitor,* July–August 2003 (online). Available at http://multinationalmonitor.org/mm2003/03july-aug/july-aug03corp1.html.

120. Ibid.
121. Frederick H. Buttell and Peter J. Taylor, "Environmental Sociology and Global Environmental Change: A Critical Assessment," *Society and Natural Resources,* vol. 5, 1992, 225.
122. Robert Weissman, "Corporate Plundering of the Third World," in Hofrichter, *Toxic Struggles,* 186–196.
123. Ibid.
124. Richard W. Stevenson, "Debt Relief Promised, but Who Pays the Bill?" *New York Times,* September 19, 1999 (online).
125. "Journey to Justice," *New Internationalist,* May 8, 2006, 26.
126. Quoted in William Blum, *Killing Hope: U.S. Military and CIA Interventions Since World War II.* Monroe, MN: Common Courage Press, 2004, 65.
127. Ibid.
128. Ibid., 76.
129. See Michael Parenti, *Inventing Reality: The Politics of the Mass Media,* 2nd ed. New York: St. Martin's Press, 1993.
130. Jonathan Rowe and Judith Silverstein, "The GDP Myth: Why Growth Isn't Always a Good Thing," *Washington Monthly,* March 1999, 17–21.
131. Quoted from Miringoff, Marque-Luisa, and Sandra Opdycke Miringoff, *America's Social Health: Putting Social Issues Back on the Public Agenda.* New York: M. E. Sharpe, 2008, 25.
132. Michael Jacobs and the Real World Coalition, "The Politics of the Real World: Hope, Fear, and the New Century," in Heiner, *Social Problems and Social Solutions,* 24.
133. Quoted in Jacobs, "The Politics of the Real World," 25.

Chapter 3: Inequality of Life Chances in the United States

1. Prince Brown, Jr., "Biology and the Social Construction of the 'Race' Concept," in J. Ferrante and P. Brown (eds.), *The Social Construction of Race and Ethnicity in the United States.* New York: Longman, 1998, 136.
2. *Statistical Abstract of the United States, 2011-2012,* The National Data Book, Table 711, U.S. Department of Commerce. New York: Skyhorse Publishing, 2011.
3. Blaine Friedlander, Jr., "Poverty Touches 91% of African Americans during Adult Years," *Cornell Chronicle,* vol. 30, no. 29, April 8, 1999. Available at http://www.news.cornell.edu/Chronicles/4.8.99/poverty study.html.
4. Martin Marger, *Social Inequality: Patterns and Processes,* 3rd ed. Boston: McGraw-Hill, 2005, 267.
5. Ibid. and *Statistical Abstract of the United States,* 2011. U.S. Census Bureau. http://www.census.gov/compendia/statab/2011/tables/11s0696.pdf. Retrieved September 25, 2011.
6. Quoted in Wilson, *Bridge over the Racial Divide.* Berkeley: University of California Press, 2001, 19.
7. Bureau of Labor Statistics, "Labor Force Statistics from the Current Population Survey, Databases, Tables and Calculators by Subject." Data extracted September 25, 2011.
8. Katherine S. Newman, "Job Availability: Achilles Heel of Welfare Reform," in Heiner, *Social Problems and Social Solutions,* 144.

9. Patrick Wall, "Race Gap Widens: Whites' Net Worth Is 20 Times That of Blacks," *Christian Science Monitor,* http://www.csmonitor.com/USA/2011/0726/Wealth-gap-widens-Whites-net-worth-is-20-times-that-of-blacks, July 26, 2011. Retrieved September 25, 2011.

10. Ibid.

11. Conley, *Being Black and Living in the Red.* Berkeley: University of California Press, 1999.

12. Isabel Wilkerson, "Middle Class Blacks Try to Grip a Ladder While Lending a Hand," in P. S. Rothenberg (ed.), *Race, Class, and Gender in the United States,* 4th ed. New York: St. Martin's, 1998, 226.

13. Conley, *Being Black and Living in the Red,* 6.

14. Anthony Platt, "End Game: The Rise and Fall of Affirmative Action in Higher Education. Reconfiguring Power: Challenges for the 21st Century," in A. Aguirre, Jr. and D. Baker (eds.), *Structured Inequality in the United States.* Upper Saddle River, NJ: Prentice Hall, 2000, 322.

15. Wilson, *Bridge over the Racial Divide,* 23.

16. Deborah L. Rhode, "Affirmative Action," in Heiner, *Social Problems and Social Solutions,* 69.

17. Ibid., 70.

18. Ibid.

19. Douglas A. Blackmon, *Slavery by Another Name: The Reenslavement of Black Americans from the Civil War to World War II.* New York: Doubleday, 2008.

20. "Employed persons by detailed occupation, sex…, 2010," Household data, Annual Averages, Bureau of Labor Statistics, http://www.bls.gov/cps/cpsaat11. pdf. Retrieved July 15, 2011. Stephanie Luce and Mark Brenner, "Women and Class: What Has Happened in 40 years?" *Monthly Review,* July/August, 2006, 80–93. Catherine Rampell, "The Gender Wage Gap around the World," *New York Times,* March 9, 2010.

21. Bernice Lott, Karen Asquith, Theresa Doyon, "Relation of Ethnicity and Age to Women's Responses to Personal Experiences of Sexist Discrimination in the United States," *Journal of Social Psychology,* vol. 141, no. 3, June 2001, 310.

22. Twenty-seven percent figure based on calculations from the BLS report cited in note 20. Interactive tables, *CNNMoney,* http://money.cnn.com/magazines/fortune/fortune500/2011/womenceos/. Retrieved July 20, 2011. Racel Soares, *2010 Catalyst Census: Fortune 500 Women Board Directors,* http://money.cnn.com/magazines/fortune/fortune500/2011/womenceos/. Retrieved July 20, 2011.

23. Nancy Folbre, *The Invisible Heart: Economics and Family Values.* New York: New Press, 2001, 6.

24. Linda Babcock and Sara Laschever, *Women Don't Ask: Negotiation and the Gender Divide.* Princeton, NJ: Princeton University Press, 2003, 12.

25. Corinne A. Moss-Racusin and Laurie A. Rudman, "Disruptions in Women's Self-Promotion: The Backlash Avoidance Model," *Psychology of Women Quarterly,* vol. 34, 2010, 186–202.

26. Babcock and Laschever, *Women Don't Ask,* 89.

27. Luce and Brenner, "Women and Class," 85.

28. Doreen Carvajal, "The Changing Face of Medical Care," *New York Times,* March 7, 2001, http://www.nytimes.com/2011/03/08/world/europe/08iht-ffdocs08.html. Retrieved July 22, 2011.

29. David Leonhardt, "A Labor Market Punishing to Mothers," *New York Times,* August 3, 2010.

30. Philip Cowan and Carolyn Pape Cowan, "New Families: Modern Couples as New Pioneers," in M. A. Mason, A. Skolnick, and S. D. Sugarman (eds.), *All Our Families: New Policies for a New Century.* New York: Oxford University Press, 1998, 169–192, at 172.

31. Arlie Hochschild, with A. Machung, *The Second Shift: Working Parents and the Revolution at Home.* New York: Viking, 1989.

32. Suzanne M. Bianchi, John P. Robinson, Melissa A. Milkie, *Changing Rhythms of American Family Life.* Russell Sage Foundation, 2007; "Modern Marriage: 'I Like Hugs and Kisses. But What I Really Love Is Help with the Dishes." Pew Research Publications, July 18, 2007, http:pewresearch.org/pubs/542.modern-marriage. Retrieved June 30, 2011.

33. "Modern marriage," Pew Research.

34. Ibid.

35. Katrin Bennhold, "Feminism of the Future Relies on Men," *New York Times,* June 22, 2010.

36. Katrin Bennhold, "Working Women Are the Key to Norway's Prosperity," *New York Times,* June 28, 2011.

37. Stephen Castle, "Not Afraid to Fight for Corporate Equality," *New York Times,* January 26, 2011.

38. Erwin Chemerinsky, *The Conservative Assault on the Constitution.* New York: Simon and Schuster, 2010, 36.

39. Alabama Constitution, http://constitutions.vlex.com/vid/establish-maintain-white-colored-children-299208. Retrieved September 7, 2011.

40. Jonathan Kozol, *The Shame of the Nation: The Restoration of Apartheid Schooling in America.* New York: Three Rivers Press, 2005, 44–45.

41. "International Education Rankings Suggest Reform Can Lift U.S.," Ed.gov Blog, December 8, 2010, http://www.ed.gov/blog/2010/12/international-education-rankings-suggest-reform-can-lift-u-s/. Retrieved September 8, 2011.

42. Linda Darling-Hammond, "Restoring Our Schools," *Nation,* vol. 290, no. 23, June 14, 2010, 14. Citing research by Gerald Tirozzi, executive director of the National Association of Secondary School Principals, "PISA Scores, Broken Down by Poverty Rate, Indicate U.S. Is Failing to Educate Low-Income Children," National Access Networks, Teachers College, Columbia University, http://www.school-funding.info/news/policy/2011-01PISA.php3. Retrieved November 8, 2011.

43. John Bellamy Foster, "Education and the Structural Crisis of Capital: The U.S. Case," *Monthly Review,* vol. 63, no. 3, July 2011, 6.

44. Diane Ravitch, "Why I Changed My Mind," *Nation,* vol. 290, no. 23, June 14, 2010. Ravitch was assistant secretary of education for research and author of *The Death and Life of the Great American School System,* New York: Basic Books, 2010.

45. Ibid., 22.

46. Ibid., emphasis added.

47. "10 Reasons Why Private School Vouchers Should Be Rejected," *Church and State,* vol. 64, no. 2, February 2011, 2.

48. Naomi Klein, *Shock Doctrine: The Rise of Disaster Capitalism.* New York: Metropolitan Books, 2007.

49. "Income, Poverty, and Health Insurance Coverage in the United States: 2010," U.S. Census Bureau, Press Release, September 13, 2011, http://www.census.

gov/newsroom/releases/archives/income_wealth/cb11-157.html. Retrieved, September, 24, 2011; "Income, Poverty, and Health Insurance Coverage in the United States: 2009 (full report), P60-238," Issued September 2010.

50. Vernellia Randall, "Institutional Racism Is U.S. Health Care," citing *University of Florida Journal of Law and Public Policy* 45-91 (Fall, 2002), http://academic.udayton. edu/health/07humanrights/racial01c.htm. Retrieved November 7, 2011.

51. "Health Care and the Middle Class: More Costs and Less Coverage," The Kaiser Family Foundation, July 24, 2009, http://www.kff.org/healthreform/7951.cfm. Retrieved September 24, 2011.

52. Elizabeth Warren and Amelia Warren Tyagi, *The Two-Income Trap: Why Middle-Class Mothers and Fathers Are Going Broke.* New York: Basic Books, 2003.

53. Kerbo, *Social Stratification and Inequality,* Boston: McGraw-Hill, 2000.

54. Gregory Mantsios, "Class in America: Myths and Realities," in T. Ore (ed.), *The Social Construction of Difference and Inequality: Race, Class, Gender, and Sexuality.* Mountain View, CA: Mayfield, 2000, 512–526.

55. Gregory Weiss and Lynne E. Lonnquist, *The Sociology of Health, Healing, and Illness,* 3rd ed. Upper Saddle River, NJ: Prentice Hall, 2000.

56. World Health Organization, "Press Release: World Health Report 2000." Available at http://www.who.int/why/2000/en/press release.htm.

57. *The World Factbook.* "Country Comparison: Life Expectancy at Birth," U.S. Central Intelligence Agency, https://www.cia.gov/library/publications/the-world-fact-book/rankorder/2102rank.html. Retrieved September 24, 2011.

58. Cited in Richard G. Wilkinson, *Unhealthy Societies: The Afflictions of Inequality.* London: Routledge, 1996.

59. World Health Organization, "World Health Report 2000."

60. "Rank Order—Infant Mortality Rate." Available at http://www.politinfo.com/ infodesk/rankorder/2091rank.html.

61. T. J. Matthews and Marian MacDorman, "Infant Mortality Statistics from the 2007 Period," U.S. Department of Health and Human Services, Centers for Disease Control, *National Vital Statistics Report,* vol. 59, no. 6., June 29, 2011.

62. Marc Miringoff and Marque-Luisa Miringoff, *The Social Health of the Nation: How America Is Really Doing.* New York: Oxford University Press, 1999.

63. World Resources Institute, *World Resources 1996–97: A Guide to the Global Environment: The Urban Environment.* New York: Oxford University Press, 1998.

64. Dennis Cauchon and Kathy Kiely, "Prescription Imports Get Big Approval," *USA Today,* July 20, 2000, 13A.

65. Theodore R. Marmor and Jerry L. Mashaw, "Canada's Health Insurance and Ours: The Real Lessons, the Big Choices," in R. Heiner (ed.), *Social Problems and Social Solutions: A Cross-Cultural Perspective.* Needham Heights, MA: Allyn and Bacon, 1999, 185–195.

66. T. R. Reid, "5 Myths about Health Care around the World," *Washington Post,* August 23, 2009, http://www.washingtonpost.com/wp-dyn/content/article/2009/08/21/ AR2009082101778_pf.html. Retrieved September 27, 2011.

67. Chris McGreal, "Revealed: Millions Spent on Lobby Firms Fighting Obama Health Reform," *Guardian,* October 1, 2009, http://www.guardian.co.uk/world/2009/ oct/01/lobbyists-millions-obama-healthcare-reform. Retrieved September 21, 2011.

68. Ibid.

69. Justin Akers Chacón and Mike Davis, *No One Is Illegal.* Chicago: Haymarket Books, 2006, 77.

70. Quoted in ibid., 175.

71. Ibid., 187.

72. Federal Reserve Bank of San Francisco, Economic Letter 99-20, June 25, 1999, http://www.frbsf.org/econrsrch/wklyltr/wklyltr99/el99-20.html. Retrieved July 11, 2008.

Chapter 4: Problems of the Family

1. Mary Ann Mason, Arlene Skolnick, and Stephen D. Sugarman, *All Our Families: New Policies for a New Century,* 2nd ed. New York: Oxford University Press, 2003.

2. Arlene Skolnick, *Embattled Paradise: The American Family in an Age of Uncertainty.* New York: Basic Books, 1991, 8.

3. Stephanie Coontz, *Marriage, a History: From Obedience to Intimacy or How Love Conquered Marriage.* New York: Penguin/Viking, 2005, 1.

4. Quoted in Felix Berardo and Constance Shehan, "Family Problems in Global Perspective," in George Ritzer (ed.), *Handbook of Social Problems: A Comparative and International Perspective.* Thousand Oaks, CA: Sage, 2004, 258.

5. John Demos, "Myths and Realities in the History of American Family Life," in H. Grunebaum and J. Christ (eds.), *Contemporary Marriage: Structure, Dynamics and Therapy.* Boston: Little, Brown, 1976, 9.

6. Skolnick, *Embattled Paradise.*

7. Demos, "Myths and Realities," 29.

8. Ibid.

9. Stephanie Coontz, *The Way We Never Were: American Families and the Nostalgia Trap.* New York: Basic Books, 1992, 15.

10. Ibid., 43.

11. Cited in Skolnick, *Embattled Paradise,* 11.

12. Coontz, *The Way We Never Were,* 11.

13. Demos, "Myths and Realities."

14. Ibid., 24.

15. Ibid.

16. Ibid., 25.

17. Mason et al., *All Our Families,* 2.

18. Skolnick, *Embattled Paradise,* 8.

19. Coontz, *The Way We Never Were,* 25.

20. Quoted in ibid., 26.

21. Skolnick, *Embattled Paradise,* 53.

22. Ibid., 52.

23. Coontz, *The Way We Never Were,* 9.

24. Carol Warren, *Madwives: Schizophrenic Women in the 1950s.* New Brunswick, NJ: Rutgers University Press, 1987.

25. *The Fifties.* "Let's Play House," television series broadcast on The History Channel, written and directed by Alex Gibney, The Fifties, 1997.

26. Coontz, *The Way We Never Were.*

27. Murray Straus, Richard Gelles, and Suzanne Steinmetz, *Behind Closed Doors.* New York: Anchor Books, 1980.

28. Coontz, *The Way We Never Were.*

29. Steven J. Pfohl, "The 'Discovery' of Child Abuse," in D. H. Kelly (ed.), *Deviant Behavior,* 3rd ed. New York: St. Martin's Press, 1989, 40–51.

30. Coontz, *The Way We Never Were.*

31. Ibid., 30.

32. Ibid..

33. Sylvia Ann Hewlett and Cornel West, *The War against Parents: What We Can Do for America's Beleaguered Moms and Dads.* Boston: Houghton Mifflin, 1998, 97–98.

34. Julie Matthaei, *An Economic History of Women in America.* New York: Schocken Books, 1982, 213.

35. Bureau of Labor Statistics, "Employment Status by Marital Status and Sex, 2002 Annual Averages." Available at http://www.bls.gov/cps/wlf-tables4.pdf; Bureau of Labor Statistics, "Employment Status of Women by Presence and Age of Youngest Child, Marital Status, Race, and Hispanic Origin, 2002." Available at http://www.bls.gov/cps/wlf-tables6.pdf. *Statistical Abstract of the United States, 2011–2012, Table 599.*

36. W. Norton Grubb and Marvin Lazerson, *Broken Promises: How Americans Fail Their Children.* New York: Basic Books, 1982, 248.

37. Bryan Strong, Christine DeVault, and Barbara W. Sayad, *The Marriage and Family Experience: Intimate Relationships in a Changing Society,* 7th ed. Belmont, CA: Wadsworth, 1998.

38. Philip Cowan and Carolyn Pape Cowan, "New Families: Modern Couples as New Pioneers," in M. A. Mason, A. Skolnick, and S. D. Sugarman (eds.), *All Our Families: New Policies for a New Century.* New York: Oxford University Press, 1998, 179.

39. Ibid., 171.

40. Ibid.

41. Ibid.

42. David Elkind, *The Ties That Stress: The New Family Imbalance.* Cambridge, MA: Harvard University Press, 1994, 4.

43. Juliet Schor, *The Overworked American: The Unexpected Decline of Leisure.* New York: Basic Books, 1992. Schor's estimate dates to 1992. A more recent estimate from the Economic Policy Institute (July 24, 2000) indicates that "the typical married-couple family with children...worked 256 more hours per year in 1997 than in 1989." Available at http://www.epinet.org/briefingpapers/labor99.html.

44. Elizabeth Warren and Amelia Warren Tyagi, *The Two-Income Trap: Why Middle-Class Mothers and Fathers Are Going Broke.* New York: Basic Books, 2003, 6–7.

45. Warren and Tyagi, *The Two-Income Trap.*

46. Ibid.

47. Donald Barlett, James Steele, Laura Karmatz, Andrew Goldstein, and Joan Levinstein, "Soaked by Congress," *Time,* May 15, 2000.

48. Ibid.

49. Arianna Huffington, *Pigs at the Trough: How Corporate Greed and Political Corruption Are Undermining America.* New York: Crown, 2003.

50. James Suroweiecki, "Going for Broke," *New Yorker,* vol. 84, no. 8, April 7, 2008. Retrieved online June 2008.

51. Warren and Tyagi, *The Two-Income Trap.*

52. Ruth Sidel, "Family Policy in Sweden: Lessons for the United States," in R. Heiner (ed.), *Social Problems and Social Solutions: A Cross-Cultural Perspective.* Needham Heights, MA: Allyn and Bacon, 1999, 112.

53. Josh Chetwynd, "Day Care Gets a Muted Cheer," *U.S. News and World Report,* vol. 122, no. 14, April 1997, 38.

54. Lawrence Mishel, Jared Bernstein, and Heather Boushey, *The State of Working America: 2002/2003*. Economic Policy Institute. Ithaca, NY: Cornell University Press, 2003; and the Clearinghouse on International Developments on Child, Youth and Family Policies at Columbia University, http://childpolicyintl.org.

55. Sidel, "Family Policy in Sweden."

56. "Leave Policies and Research," International Network and Leave Policies and Research, http://www.leavenetwork.org/lp_and_r_reports/?S=ohne%3Ftype%3D98%3Ftype%3D98. Retrieved October 29, 2011.

57. Sheila B. Kamerman and Alfred J. Kahn, *Starting Right: How America Neglects Its Youngest Children and What to Do about It*. New York: Oxford University Press, 1995, 136.

58. David Whitman, "Waiting for Mary Poppins," *U.S. News and World Report*, vol. 123, no. 20, November 24, 1997, 10.

59. "Occupational Employment and Wages, May 2007, http://www.bls.gov/oes/current/oes399011.htm and "Child Daycare Services," Bureau of Labor Statistics (no date given), http://www.bls.gov/oco/cg/cgs032.htm; and "Career Guide to Industries: 2010–2011 Edition," BLS, http://www.bls.gov/oco/cg/cgs032.htm#earnings. Retrieved October17, 2011.

60. Cost, Quality, and Outcomes Study Team, "Cost, Quality, and Outcomes in Child Care Centers: Key Findings and Recommendations," *Young Children*, May 1995, 40–41.

61. Kamerman and Kahn, *Starting Right*, 198.

62. Paul Wellstone, "The Quiet Crisis," *Nation*, vol. 264, no. 23, 1997.

63. *Statistical Abstract of the United States, 2008.*

64. National Center for Children in Poverty, Columbia University, http://www.nccp.org/topics/childpoverty.html. Retrieved July 18, 2008; The Children's Defense Fund, *The State of America's Children, 2005*. Income, Poverty, and Health Insurance Coverage in the United States, 2010, Table 4, U.S. Census Bureau, P60-239, Issued September 2011.

65. Based on author's calculations from data from U.S. Census report (Ibid.).

66. Kamerman and Kahn, *Starting Right*, 9.

67. Quoted in ibid., 4–5.

68. Children's Defense Fund, *The State of Children in America's Union: A 2002 Action Guide to Leave No Child Behind*. Washington, DC: Children's Defense Fund, 2002.

69. Kamerman and Kahn, *Starting Right*.

70. Hewlett and West, *The War against Parents*, 66.

71. Rebecca Blank, "Poverty and Policy: The Many Faces of the Poor," in C. R. Strain (ed.), *Prophetic Visions and Economic Realities*. Grand Rapids, MI: Erdman, 1989, 160.

72. Grubb and Lazerson, *Broken Promises*.

73. Arloc Sherman, *Poverty Matters: The Cost of Child Poverty in America*. Washington, DC: Children's Defense Fund, 1997.

74. Cited in ibid.

75. Clive Cookson, "Poverty Mars Formation of Infant Brains," *Financial Times*, February 15, 2006. Retrieved June 10, 2008.

76. Ibid., 1.

77. Greg Duncan, Jeanne Brooks-Gunn, and Pamela Kato Klebanov, "Economic Deprivation and Early Childhood Development," *Child Development*, vol. 65, no. 2, 1994, 296–318.

78. Sherman, *Poverty Matters,* 15.
79. Ibid., 34.
80. James W. Russell, *Double Standard: Social Policy in Europe and the United States.* Lanham, MD: Rowman and Littlefield, 105.
81. Kamerman and Kahn, *Starting Right,* 20.
82. William H. Scarborough, "Who Are the Poor? A Demographic Perspective," in J. A. Chafel (ed.), *Child Poverty and Public Policy.* Washington, DC: Urban Institute Press, 1993, 63.
83. Children's Defense Fund, *The State of Children,* xvii.
84. Ibid.
85. Russell, *Double Standard,*109.
86. Kamerman and Kahn, *Starting Right,* 44.
87. Sidel, "Family Policy in Sweden," 116.
88. Kamerman and Kahn, *Starting Right,* 26.
89. Hewlett and West, *The War against Parents,* 92.
90. Edward Luttwak, "Turbo-Charged Capitalism Is the Enemy of Family Values," *New Perspectives Quarterly,* vol. 12, no. 2, Spring, 1995.
91. Martha Nussbaum, "A Right to Marry? Same-Sex Marriage and Constitutional Law," *Dissent,* Summer, 2009, 43.
92. Ian Robertson, *Sociology,* 3rd ed. New York: Worth, 1987.
93. Nussbaum, "A Right to Marry," 43, 44.
94. Joseph Gusfield, *Symbolic Crusade: Status Politics and the American Temperance Movement,* 2nd ed. Urbana: University of Illinois Press, 1986.
95. David Lauter, "Support for Gay Marriage Continues to Rise," *Los Angeles Times,* November 3, 2011, http://articles.latimes.com/2011/nov/03/news/la-pn-pew-same-sex-marriage-20111103. Retrieved November 5, 2011.
96. Sally MacIntyre and Sarah Cunningham-Burley, "Teenage Pregnancy as a Social Problem: A Perspective from the United Kingdom," in A. Lawson and D. L. Rhode (eds.), *The Politics of Pregnancy: Adolescent Sexuality and Public Policy.* New Haven: Yale University Press, 1993, 61.
97. Jane Mauldon, "Families Started by Teenagers," in Mason et al., *All Our Families,* 39–65.
98. Deborah L. Rhode, "Adolescent Pregnancy and Public Policy," in Lawson and Rhode, *The Politics of Pregnancy,* 301–336.
99. Lawson and Rhode, *The Politics of Pregnancy,* 3.
100. Susan E. Harari and Maris A. Vinovskis, "Adolescent Sexuality, Pregnancy, and Childbearing in the Past," in Lawson and Rhode, *The Politics of Pregnancy,* 23–45.
101. Rhode, "Adolescent Pregnancy and Public Policy."
102. Ibid.
103. Ibid., 301.
104. Diana M. Pearce " 'Children Having Children': Teenage Pregnancy and Public Policy from the Woman's Perspective," in Lawson and Rhode, *The Politics of Pregnancy,* 47.
105. Guttmacher Institute, *Sex and America's Teenagers.* New York: Alan Guttmacher Institute, 1994.
106. Ibid.
107. MacIntyre and Cunningham-Burley, "Teenage Pregnancy as a Social Problem," 59.
108. Ibid., 65–66.

109. Ann Phoenix, "The Social Construction of Teenage Motherhood: A Black and White Issue," in Lawson and Rhode, *The Politics of Pregnancy*, 74–97.
110. Ibid., 74.
111. Mauldon, "Families Started by Teenagers."
112. Phoenix, "The Social Construction of Teenage Motherhood."
113. Elliott Currie and Jerome Skolnick, *America's Problems: Social Issues and Public Policy*. New York: Longman, 1997.
114. Mauldon, "Families Started by Teenagers."
115. Rhode, "Adolescent Pregnancy and Public Policy"; Mauldon, "Families Started by Teenagers."
116. Ibid.
117. Joseph V. Hotz, Susan Williams McElroy, and Seth G. Sanders, "Mothers: Effects of Early Childbearing on the Lives of the Mothers," in R. Maynard (ed.), *Kids Having Kids: Economic Costs and Social Consequences of Teenage Pregnancy*. Washington, DC: Urban Institute Press, 1997, 55–94.
118. Mauldon, "Families Started by Teenagers," 51.
119. Quoted in Phoenix, "The Social Construction of Teenage Motherhood."
120. Frank Furstenburg, *Destinies of the Truly Disadvantaged: The Politics of Teenage Childbearing*. New York: Russell Sage Foundation, 2007, 161.

Chapter 5: Crime and Deviance

1. Emile Durkheim, *The Rules of Sociological Method*. Translated by S. A. Solovay and J. H. Mueller, edited by G. E. G. Catlin. New York: Free Press, 1966.
2. Jack P. Gibbs, "Conceptions of Deviant Behavior: The Old and the New," in D. H. Kelly (ed.), *Deviant Behavior*, 5th ed. New York: St. Martin's Press, 1996.
3. Clellan S. Ford and Frank A. Beach, *Patterns of Sexual Behavior*. New York: Harper, 1951.
4. J. M. Carrier, "Homosexual Behavior in Cross-Cultural Perspective," in J. Marmor (ed.), *Homosexual Behavior: A Modern Reappraisal*. New York: Basic Books, 1980, 100–122. See also Roger N. Lancaster, *Life Is Hard: Machismo, Danger, and the Intimacy of Power in Nicaragua*. Berkeley: University of California Press, 1992.
5. David F. Musto, *The American Disease: Origins of Narcotic Control*. New York: Oxford University Press, 1987. See also Troy Duster, "The Legislation of Morality: Creating Drug Laws," in D. H. Kelly (ed.), *Deviant Behavior*, 3rd ed. New York: St. Martin's, 1989, 29–39.
6. James A. Inciardi, *The War on Drugs II: The Continuing Epic of Heroin, Cocaine, Crack, Crime, Aids, and Public Policy*. Mountain View, CA: Mayfield, 1992.
7. Duster, "The Legislation of Morality," 32.
8. For a discussion of cross-cultural variability in drug consumption, see Ed Knipe, *Culture, Society, and Drugs: The Social Science Approach to Drug Use*. Prospect Heights, IL: Waveland Press, 1995.
9. Stuart A. Kirk and Herb Kutchins, *The Selling of DSM: The Rhetoric of Science in Psychiatry*. New York: Aldine de Gruyter, 1992, 88.
10. Patricia A. Morgan, "The Legislation of Drug Law: Economic Crisis and Social Control," in J. D. Orcutt (ed.), *Analyzing Deviance*. Homewood, IL: Dorsey Press, 1983, 358–371.
11. Musto, *The American Disease*, 244.

12. Craig Reinerman and Harry Levine, "The Crack Attack: America's Latest Drug Scare, 1986–1992," in J. Best (ed.), *Images of Issues: Typifying Contemporary Social Problems.* New York: Aldine de Gruyter, 1995, 147–186. See also Arnold S. Trebach, *The Great Drug War: And Radical Proposals That Could Make America Safe Again.* New York: Macmillan, 1987.

13. Alan Elsner, *The Gates of Injustice: The Crisis in America's Prisons.* Saddle River, NJ: Pearson, 2006, 20; *Crime in the United States,* 2007, FBI, http://www.fbi.gov/ucr/cius2007/arrests/index.html. Retrieved November 7, 2008; Jacob Sullum, "Yet Another Record for Marijuana Arrests," *Reason,* September 15, 2008, http://www.reason.com/blog/show/128793.html. Retrieved November 7, 2008.

14. Eric Schlosser, *Reefer Madness: Sex, Drugs, and Cheap Labor in the American Black Market.* Boston: Houghton Mifflin, 2003, 29.

15. Ibid. and the National Organization for the Reform of Marijuana Laws, http://norml.org/index.cfm?wtm_view=&Group_ID=4570. Retrieved July 14, 2008.

16. Schlosser, *Reefer Madness* 26.

17. Ibid., 23.

18. Gary W. Potter and Victor E. Kappeler, *Constructing Crime: Perspectives on Making News and Social Problems.* Prospect Heights, IL: Waveland Press, 1998.

19. Ibid.

20. Steven Beschloss, "TV's Life of Crime," *Channels,* September 24, 1990.

21. Piers Beirne and James Messerschmidt, *Criminology,* 3rd ed. Boulder, CO: Westview, 2000.

22. Debra Seagal, "Tales from the Cutting-Room Floor: The Reality of 'Reality-Based' Television," *Harper's Magazine,* vol. 287, no. 1722, November 1993, 52.

23. Ibid., 51.

24. Quoted in Beschloss, "TV's Life of Crime," 14.

25. Craig Haney and John Manzolati, "Television Criminology: Network Illusions of Criminal Justice Realities," in E. Aronson (ed.), *The Social Animal.* New York: W. H. Freeman, 1988, 125.

26. Joel Best, "Missing Children, Misleading Statistics," in W. Feigelman (ed.), *Readings on Social Problems: Probing the Extent, Causes, and Remedies of America's Social Problems.* Fort Worth, TX: Holt, Rinehart and Winston, 1990, 11–16, at 11.

27. Ibid., 12.

28. Ibid.

29. Ibid.

30. Ibid.

31. Phillip Jenkins, *Using Murder: The Social Construction of Serial Homicide.* New York: Aldine de Gruyter, 1994, 61.

32. Ibid., 64.

33. Ibid.

34. Ibid., 22.

35. Ibid., 17.

36. Trebach, *The Great Drug War*; Reinerman and Levine, "Crack Attack."

37. Erich Goode and Nachman Ben-Yehuda, *Moral Panics: The Social Construction of Deviance.* Cambridge, MA: Blackwell, 1994, 205.

38. Reinerman and Levine, "Crack Attack."

39. Trebach, *The Great Drug War*; Reinerman and Levine, "Crack Attack."

40. Richard Smith, "The Plague among Us," *Newsweek,* June 16, 1986, 15.

41. Reinerman and Levine, "Crack Attack," 152.

42. Ibid., 155.
43. Ibid.
44. Ibid., 164 (emphasis in original).
45. Ibid.
46. Katherine Beckett, "Setting the Public Agenda: 'Street Crime' and Drug Use in American Politics," *Social Problems,* vol. 41, no. 3, 1994, 425–447.
47. Beckett, "Setting the Public Agenda"; Reinerman and Levine, "Crack Attack."
48. Reinerman and Levine, "Crack Attack," 170.
49. Steven F. Messner and Richard Rosenfeld, *Crime and the American Dream,* 2nd ed. Belmont, CA: Wadsworth, 1997, 22.
50. Ibid.
51. David H. Bayley, "Lessons in Order," in R. Heiner (ed.), *Criminology: A Cross-Cultural Perspective.* St. Paul, MN: West, 1996, 3–14, 6.
52. Messner and Rosenfeld, *Crime and the American Dream,* 22–23 (emphasis in original).
53. Ibid.
54. Robert K. Merton, "Social Structure and Anomie," *American Sociological Review,* vol. 3, 1938, 672–682.
55. Edwin M. Schur, *Our Criminal Society: The Social and Legal Sources of Crime in America.* Englewood Cliffs, NJ: Prentice Hall, 1969, 187.
56. Philippe Bourgois, "Just Another Night on Crack Street," *New York Times Magazine,* November 12, 1989, 65.
57. Elsner, *The Gates of Injustice,* 13.
58. Steven R. Donziger, *The Real War on Crime: The Report of the National Criminal Justice Commission.* New York: HarperCollins, 1996.
59. 59 . Becky Pettit and Bruce Western, "Mass Imprisonment and the Life Course: Race and Class Inequality in U.S. Incarceration," *American Sociological Review,* vol. 69, 2004, 153.
60. Based on calculations from *Crime in the United States,* Uniform Crime Reports, 2010, Table 43a, Federal Bureau of Investigation, http://www.fbi.gov/about-us/cjis/ucr/crime-in-the-u.s/2010/crime-in-the-u.s.-2010/tables/table-43. Retrieved October 22, 2011.
61. Jay Livingston, *Crime and Criminology,* 2nd ed. Upper Saddle River, NJ: Simon and Schuster, 1996, 123.
62. Based on calculations from *Criminal Victimization in the United States,* 2008 Statistical Tables, Bureau of Justice Statistics, U.S. Department of Justice, NCJ 231173, May 2011.
63. William Julius Wilson, *The Truly Disadvantaged: The Inner City, The Underclass, and Public Policy.* Chicago: University of Chicago Press, 1987.
64. Ibid.
65. Elliott Currie, *Crime and Punishment in America.* New York: Owl Books, 1998, 32.
66. Carl Husemoller Nightingale, *On the Edge: A History of Poor Black Children and Their American Dreams.* New York: Basic Books, 1993, 137.
67. Charles Derber, *The Wilding of America: Money, Mayhem, and the New American Dream.* New York: Worth, 2004, 43.
68. Donziger, *The Real War on Crime,* 101.
69. Nightingale, *On the Edge,* 130.
70. Gresham M. Sykes, *The Society of Captives: A Study of Maximum Security Prison.* Princeton, NJ: Princeton University Press, 1958.

71. *Sourcebook of Criminal Justice Statistics.* Washington, DC: 1996, 2002. *Sourcebook of Criminal Justice Statistics Online,* Table 6.13, 2007, http://www.albany.edu/sourcebook/pdf/t6132007.pdf. Retrieved July 14, 2008; and *Statistical Abstract of the United States,* 2008, Table 338. "Prisoners in 2009," Bureau of Justice Statistics Bulletin, NCJ 231675, December 2010.

72. "Local Governments Spend More on Criminal Justice Than State Governments or the Federal Government." Bureau of Justice Statistics, Office of Justice Programs, U.S. Department of Justice, http://www.ojp.usdoj.gov/bjs/glance/tables/expgovtab.htm. Retrieved July 18, 2008.

73. Joseph Hallinan, *Going Up the River: Travels in a Prison Nation.* New York: Random House, 2003, xiii.

74. "Prisoners in 2009," Bureau of Justice Statistics Bulletin, NCJ 231675, December 2010.

75. Richard A. Oppel, "Sentencing Shift Gives New Leverage to Prosecutors," *New York Times,* September 25, 2011, http://www.nytimes.com/2011/09/26/us/tough-sentences-help-prosecutors-push-for-plea-bargains.html?_r=1&nl=todaysheadlines&emc=tha2.

76. Ibid.

77. Robert W. McChesney, *Rich Media, Poor Democracy: Communication Politics in Dubious Times.* New York: New Press, 1999, xx.

78. Jeremy Seabrook, *The No-Nonsense Guide to World Poverty.* Oxford: New Internationalist, 2003, 15.

79. Ibid.

80. For a detailed discussion, see Nils Christie, *Crime Control as Industry: Towards Gulags, Western Style.* London: Routledge, 1993.

81. Eric Lotke, "The Prison-Industrial Complex," *Multinational Monitor,* vol. 17, no. 11, November 1996.

82. Richard Swift, "Crime and Civilization," an interview with Nils Christie, *New Internationalist,* no. 282, August 1996.

83. Ibid., 11.

84. Lotke, "The Prison-Industrial Complex."

85. Donziger, *The Real War on Crime,* 95.

86. Christian Parenti, *Lockdown America: Police and Prisons in the Age of Crisis.* New York: Verso, 2000, 231.

87. Hallinan, *Going Up the River,* xiv.

88. Quoted in Lotke, "The Prison-Industrial Complex."

89. Quoted in Fox Butterfield, "Study Tracks Boom in Prisons." *New York Times,* April 30, 2004. http://www.nytimes.com/2004/04/30/us/study-tracks-boom-in-prisons-and-notes-impact-on-counties.html. Retrieved March 20, 2012.

90. Joseph Dillon Davey, *The New Social Contract: America's Journey from Welfare State to Police State.* Westport, CT: Praeger, 1995.

91. Ernest Boyer, *Myth America: Democracy vs. Capitalism.* New York: Apex Press, 2003, 13.

92. Isaac Erlich, "Participation in Illegitimate Activities: An Economic Analysis," in C. S. Becer and W. M. Landes (eds.), *Essays in the Economics of Crime and Punishment.* New York: National Bureau of Economic Research, 1974; Peter Greenwood and Allan Abrahamse, *Selective Incapacitation.* Santa Monica, CA: Rand Corporation, 1982.

93. Davey, *The New Social Contract,* 60.

94. Scott Jaschik, "Prisons vs. Colleges," Inside Higher Ed, February 29, 2008, http://www.insidehighered.com/news/2008/02/29/prisons. Retrieved November 6, 2011.

95. Heiner, *Criminology*, 197.

96. Nader Entessar, "Criminal Law and the Legal System in Iran," in Heiner, *Criminology*, 163–171.

97. Cesare Beccaria, *On Crime and Punishments*. Translated by H. Paolucci, facsimile edition. Upper Saddle River, NJ: Prentice Hall, 1998 (originally published 1764).

98. Lawyers Committee for Human Rights, "Criminal Justice with Chinese Characteristics," in Heiner, *Criminology*, 172–181, at 178.

99. David Downes, "The Case for Going Dutch: The Lessons of Post-war Penal Policy," in Heiner, *Criminology*, 243–253, at 245.

100. Downes, "The Case for Going Dutch."

101. Quoted in ibid., 248.

102. Marie C. Douglas, "The Mutter-Kind-Heim at Frankfurt am Main: Come Together—Go Together," in Heiner, *Criminology*, 254–260. Piers Hernu, "Norway's Controversial 'Cushy Prison' Experiment: Could it Catch on in the UK?" *Mail Online*, July 25, 2011. http://www.dailymail.co.uk/home/moslive/article-1384308/Norways-controversial-cushy-prison-experiment--catch-UK.html. Retrieved March 21, 2012.

103. Thomas Szasz (interview), in F. W. Miller et al. (eds.), *The Mental Health Process*. Mineola, NY: The Foundation Press, 1976.

104. Thomas Szasz, *The Myth of Mental Illness*. New York: Harper and Row, 1974, 12.

105. Richard Hughes and Robert Brewin, *The Tranquilizing of America: Pill Popping and the American Way of Life*. New York: Harcourt, Brace, Jovanovich, 1979. Richard DeGrandpre, *The Cult of Pharmacology: How America Became the World's Most Troubled Drug Culture*. Durham, NC: Duke University Press, 2006.

106. 106. Jane Prather, "The Mystique of Minor Tranquilizers," paper presented to the U.S. Senate Subcommittee on Health and Scientific Research, September 1979; Hughes and Brewin, *The Tranquilizing of America*; Richard Tessler, Randall Stokes, and Marianne Pietras, "Consumer Response to Valium," *Drug Therapy*, February 1978.

107. Richard Warner, *Recovery from Schizophrenia*, 2nd ed., London: Routledge, 1994, 148.

108. Ronald C. Kramer, "A Prolegomenon to the Study of Corporate Violence," *Humanity and Society*, May 1983, 166.

109. Mark Dowie, "Pinto Madness," in J. H. Skolnick and E. Currie (eds.), *Crisis in American Institutions*, 9th ed. New York: HarperCollins, 1994, 23–38, at 37.

110. Frederic Tulsky, "Shades of Pinto," *MOJO Wire*, 2000. Available at http://bsd.mojones.com/mother jones/JF94/tulsky.html.

111. Stuart L. Hills, *Corporate Violence: Injury and Death for Profit*. Totowa, NJ: Rowman and Littlefield, 1987, 5.

112. "What Is Terrorism," *Economist*, vol. 337, no. 7955, March 2, 1996, 23.

113. Paul Butler, "Terrorism and Utilitarianism: Lessons from, and for, Criminal Law," *Journal of Criminal Law and Criminology*, vol. 93, no. 1, Fall 2002, 3.

114. Richard J. Goldstone, "International Law and Justice and America's War on Terrorism," *Social Research*, vol. 68, no. 4, Winter 2002, 1045–1054.

115. Dan Smith, *The Penguin State of the World Atlas*, 7th ed. New York: Penguin Books, 2003, 70.

116. However, there is controversy as to whether Vesey actually hatched such a plot or whether other slaves were forced to falsely testify to Vesey's plot. See Jon Wiener, "Denmark Vesey: A New Verdict," *Nation*, March 11, 2002. Available at http://www.thenation.com/doc.mhtml?i520020311&s5wiener.
117. Butler, "Terrorism and Utilitarianism," 10.

Chapter 6: Problems of the Environment

1. Stewart Udall, Foreword, in William R. Catton, Jr., *Overshoot: The Ecological Basis of Revolutionary Change.* Urbana: University of Illinois Press, 1980, xiv.
2. Terrence R. Fehner and Jack M. Holl, *The United States Department of Energy, 1977–1994: A Summary History.* Washington, DC: DOE/HR, 1994.
3. Udall, Foreword, in Catton, *Overshoot*, xv.
4. Sheldon Ungar, "Bringing the Issue Back In: Comparing the Marketability of the Ozone Hole and Global Warming," *Social Problems*, vol. 45, no. 4, 1998, 510–527.
5. Ibid.
6. Quoted in Mark Hertsgaard, *Earth Odyssey: Around the World in Search of Our Environmental Future.* New York: Broadway Books, 1998, 13.
7. "Climate Change 2007: Synthesis Report, Summary for Policymakers," IPCC, 2, http://www.ipcc.ch/pdf/assessment-report/ar4/syr/ar4_syr_spm.pdf. Retrieved July 8, 2008.
8. See Markku Wilenius, "From Science to Politics: The Menace of Global Environmental Change," *Acta Sociologica*, vol. 39, no. 1, 1995, 5–30. See also, Hertsgaard, *Earth Odyssey*.
9. "Past Decade Warmest on Record," NOAA, July 28, 2010, http://www.noaanews.noaa.gov/stories2010/20100728_stateoftheclimate.html. Retrieved October 23, 2011.
10. Sharon Begley, Eve Conant, Sam Stein, Eleanor Clift, and Matthew Philips, "The Truth about Denial," *Newsweek*, vol. 150, no. 7, August 13, 2007, 20–29. Downloaded from Academic Search Premier.
11. Daniel Faber and James O'Connor, "Capitalism and the Crisis of Environmentalism," in R. Hofrichter (ed.), *Toxic Struggles: The Theory and Practice of Environmental Justice.* Philadelphia: New Society, 1993, 14.
12. Sharon Beder, *Global Spin: The Corporate Assault on Environmentalism.* White River Junction, VT: Chelsea Green, 1997, 17.
13. Ibid., 19.
14. Ibid., 21.
15. Frederick H. Buttell and Peter J. Taylor, "Environmental Sociology and Global Environmental Change: A Critical Assessment," *Society and Natural Resources*, vol. 5, 1992, 223.
16. Gerald Markowitz and David Rosner, *Deceit and Denial: The Deadly Politics of Industrial Pollution.* Berkeley: University of California Press, 2002, 10.
17. "Toxic Deception: An Interview with Dan Fagin," *Multinational Monitor*, vol. 20, no. 3, March 1999, 3.
18. Beder, *Global Spin*, 109.
19. Ibid., 114.
20. Ibid., 115.
21. John Stauber and Sheldon Rampton, *Toxic Sludge Is Good for You: Lies, Damn Lies and the Public Relations Industry.* Monroe, ME: Common Courage Press, 1995, 2.

22. Martin A. Lee and Norman Solomon, *Unreliable Sources: A Guide to Detecting Bias in News Media.* New York: Carol, 1992, 66.
23. Ibid.
24. Ibid., 65.
25. Beder, *Global Spin,* 116.
26. Ibid., 112.
27. Ibid., 32.
28. "Public Interest Pretenders," *Consumer Reports,* vol. 59, no. 5, 1994, 318.
29. Ibid., 316.
30. Beder, *Global Spin,* 29.
31. Sharon Beder, *Global Spin: The Corporate Assault on Environmentalism,* revised edition. White River Junction, VT: Chelsea Green, 2002.
32. Arianna Huffington, *Pigs at the Trough: How Corporate Greed and Political Corruption Are Undermining America.* New York: Crown, 2003.
33. Quoted in Stauber and Rampton, *Toxic Sludge,* 5.
34. Ibid., 8.
35. Ibid., 9.
36. Ibid. 12.
37. Ibid., 10.
38. Beder, *Global Spin,* 1997, 63.
39. Ibid.
40. George Pring and Penelope Canan, *SLAPPS: Getting Sued for Speaking Out.* Philadelphia: Temple University Press, 1996.
41. Ibid., xi.
42. Calvin Exoo, *The Politics of the Mass Media.* St. Paul, MN: West, 1994, 88.
43. Ibid.
44. Beder, *Global Spin,* 1997, 180.
45. Exoo, *The Politics of the Mass Media.*
46. Michael Parenti, *Inventing Reality: The Politics of News Media,* 2nd ed. New York: St Martin's Press, 1993.
47. Lee and Solomon, *Unreliable Sources,* 60.
48. Ibid., 78.
49. Edwards, Foreword, in Beder, *Global Spin,* 1997, 9.
50. Quoted in Mark Hertsgaard, "While Washington Slept," *Vanity Fair,* May 2006. Retrieved online July 11, 2008.
51. John Hannigan, *Environmental Sociology: A Social Constructionist Perspective.* London: Routledge, 1995, 68.
52. Paul Rauber, "The Uncertainty Principle," *Sierra,* vol. 81, September–October 1996, 20.
53. Hertsgaard, "While Washington Slept."
54. Hertsgaard, *Earth Odyssey,* 274.
55. Juliet Schor, "Can the North Stop Consumption Growth? Escaping the Cycle of Work and Spend," in V. Bhaskar and A. Glyn (eds.), *The North, the South and the Environment: Ecological Constraints and the Global Economy.* New York: St. Martin's, 1995, 70.
56. Quoted in Richard Smith, "Creative Destruction: Capitalist Development and China's Environment," in R. Heiner (ed.), *Social Problems and Social Solutions: A Cross-Cultural Perspective.* Needham Heights, MA: Allyn and Bacon, 1999, 355.
57. Mary Mellor, "Building a New Vision: Feminist, Green Socialism," in Hofrichter, *Toxic Struggles,* 41.

58. Ynestra King, "Feminism and Ecology," in Hofrichter, *Toxic Struggles*, 77.

59. Hertsgaard, *Earth Odyssey*, 196.

60. Douglas J. Goodman, "Consumption as a Social Problem," in George Ritzer (ed.), *Handbook of Social Problems: A Comparative International Perspective*. Thousand Oaks, CA: Sage, 2004, 228.

61. Quoted in Gary Ruskin and Robert Weissman, "The Cost of Commercialism," *Multinational Monitor*, vol. 20, no. 1–2, January–February, 1999.

62. Goodman, "Consumption as a Social Problem," 228.

63. Ibid.

64. Ruskin and Weissman, "The Cost of Commercialism."

65. Michael Jacobson and Laurie Ann Mazur, *Marketing Madness: A Survival Guide for a Consumer Society. Boulder, CO: Westview, 1995.*

66. Quoted in Beder, *Global Spin*, 2002, 163.

67. Ruskin and Weissman, "The Cost of Commercialism."

68. Alain Lipietz, "Enclosing the Global Commons: Global Environmental Negotiations in a North-South Conflictual Approach," in Bhaskar and Glyn, *The North, the South and the Environment*, 119.

69. Patrick Tyler, "The Dynamic New China Still Races against Time," *New York Times*, January 2, 1994, 4E.

70. Ibid.

71. Hertsgaard, *Earth Odyssey*; Smith, "Creative Destruction."

72. Elizabeth Colbert, "Running on Fumes: Does the 'Car of the Future' Have a Future?" *New Yorker*, November 5, 2007. Retrieved online June 10, 2008.

73. Bruce Einhorn, "Rolls-Royce Targets China's Really-Rich," *Business Week*, May 7, 2008. Retrieved online June 12, 2008.

74. Hertsgaard, *Earth Odyssey*, 186.

75. Jane Holtz Kay, "Cars Cloud Kyoto," *Nation*, vol. 265, no. 19, December 8, 1997.

76. Smith, "Creative Destruction."

77. Hertsgaard, *Earth Odyssey*.

78. Ibid.

79. D. Stanley Eitzen and Maxine Baca Zinn, *Social Problems*, 8th ed. Needham Heights, MA: Allyn and Bacon, 2000.

80. Hertsgaard, *Earth Odyssey*, 106.

81. Ibid., 106.

82. Wilenius, "From Science to Politics," 26.

83. Clifford Cobb, Ted Halstead, and Jonathan Rowe, "If the GDP Is Up, Why Is America Down?" in R. Heiner, *Social Problems and Social Solutions*, 372.

84. Paul Ekins and Michael Jacobs, "Environmental Sustainability and the Growth of GDP: Conditions for Compatibility," in Bhaskar and Glyn, *The North, the South and the Environment*, 23.

85. Michael M. Bell, *An Invitation to Environmental Sociology*. Thousand Oaks, CA: Pine Forge Press, 1998.

86. Jeremy Rivkin, *The European Dream: How Europe's Vision of the Future Is Eclipsing the American Dream*. New York: Jeremy P. Tarcher/Penguin, 2004.

87. Ibid.

88. Annie Leonard, *The Story of Stuff: How Our Obsession with Stuff Is Trashing Our Planet, Our Communities, and Our Health—And a Vision for Change*. New York: Free Press, 2010, xxi.

89. Bell, *An Invitation to Environmental Sociology*.

90. Marshall Sahlins, *Stone Age Economics*. Chicago: Aldine-Atherton, 1972, 1–2.

91. Schor, "Can the North Stop Consumption Growth?"
92. Ibid., 81.
93. Ibid.
94. Ibid., 70.
95. Ibid., 71.
96. Bhaskar and Glyn, *The North, the South and the Environment*, 4.
97. Carita Shanklin, "Pathfinder: Environmental Justice," *Ecology Law Quarterly*, vol. 24, no. 2, May 1997, 333–376.
98. Robert D. Bullard, "Anatomy of Environmental Racism," in Hofrichter, *Toxic Struggles*, 25–35.
99. Martin Lewis, "The Promise and Peril of Environmental Justice" (Book Review), *Issues in Science and Technology*, vol. 15, no. 3, Spring 1999.
100. Scott Kuhn, "Expanding Public Participation Is Essential to Environmental Justice and the Democratic Decision-Making Process," *Ecology Law Quarterly*, vol. 25, no. 4, 1999, 647.
101. COSSMHO Reporter, "NIH Omits Hispanics in Farmworker Study," *National Coalition of Hispanic Health and Human Services Organizations*, vol. 18, no. 2, 1993.
102. Christopher Foreman, Jr., "A Winning Hand? The Uncertain Future of Environmental Justice," *Brookings Review*, vol. 18, no. 2, 1996.
103. Foreman, "The Uncertain Future of Environmental Justice."
104. Bullard, "Anatomy of Environmental Racism," 28.
105. "Ongoing Efforts to Prevent Childhood Lead Exposure," *Journal of Environmental Health*, vol. 61, no. 10, June 1999, 44.
106. Bullard, "Anatomy of Environmental Racism," 26–27.
107. "The Five Worst Environmental Threats to Children's Health," *Journal of Environmental Health*, vol. 60, no. 9, May 1998, 46.
108. World Resources Institute, *World Resources 1996–97: A Guide to the Global Environment. The Urban Environment.* New York: Oxford University Press, 1998.
109. "The Five Worst Environmental Threats."
110. King, "Feminism and Ecology."
111. Tam Hunt and Kevin Lunde, "The Stanford Committee on Law and Human Rights and the International Environmental Legal Consortium's 1998 Global Challenges Forum: Access to Justice and Environmental Protection," *Journal of Environment and Development*, December 1998.
112. Faber and O'Connor, "Capitalism and the Crisis of Environmentalism," 18.
113. Quoted in Stephen Huebner, "Storm Clouds over the Environmental Horizon," *Society*, vol. 36, no. 3, March/April 1999, 57–67.
114. Robert D. Bullard, "Just Transportation: New Solutions for Old Problems," *Environmental Action Magazine*, vol. 28, no. 1–2, Spring–Summer 1996.
115. 115. Robert D. Bullard, "Differential Vulnerabilities: Environmental and Economic Inequality and Government Response to Unnatural Disasters," in R. Heiner (ed.), *Conflicting Interests: Readings in Social Problems and Inequality.* New York: Oxford University Press, 2010, 280.
116. 116. Ibid., 290.
117. 117. Ibid., 282.
118. Geoffrey Lean, "It's the Poor That Do the Suffering…While the Rich Do All the Protesting," *New Statesman*, vol. 127, no. 4407, 1998.
119. World Resources Institute, *World Resources 1996–97.*
120. Ibid.

121. *Ibid.*
122. "Children and Water: Global Statistics," UNICEF, http://www.unicef.org/wes/index_31600.html. Retrieved July 9, 2008.
123. Daniel Litvin, "Dirt Poor," *Economist,* vol. 346, no. 8060, March 21, 1998.
124. Noreena Hertz, *The Silent Takeover: Global Capitalism and the Death of Democracy.* New York: Free Press, 2001, 8.
125. World Resources Institute, *World Resources 1996–97.*
126. Ibid., 66.
127. World Resources Institute, *World Resources 1996–97;* Lean, "It's the Poor That Do the Suffering."
128. Alfred de Montesquiou, *Washington Post,* June 22, 2007. Retrieved online July 9, 2008.
129. Bhaskar and Glyn, *The North, the South and the Environment,* 2.
130. Frank Amalric, "Population Growth and the Environmental Crisis: Beyond the 'Obvious,' " in Bhaskar and Glyn, *The North, the South and the Environment,* 99.
131. Ibid.
132. Wilenius, "From Science to Politics."
133. Martin Khor Kok Peng, "Economics and Environmental Justice: Rethinking North-South Relations," in Hofrichter, *Toxic Struggles,* 221.
134. Buttell and Taylor, "Environmental Sociology and Global Environmental Change."
135. Hertsgaard, *Earth Odyssey,* 77.
136. Mellor, "Feminist, Green Socialism," 37.
137. "Local Control or Global Plunder" (Interview with Anil Agarwal), *Multinational Monitor,* vol. 15, no. 9, September 1994.
138. *Population Summit of the World's Scientific Academies.* Washington, DC: National Academy Press, 1994.
139. Amalric, "Population Growth and the Environmental Crisis," 88.
140. Asoka Bandarage, *Women, Population and Global Crisis: A Political-Economic Analysis.* London: Zed, 1997.
141. Ibid. (Figures rounded to the nearest percent.)
142. "India's Top Birth Control: Still Sterilization," *Wall Street Journal* citing a 2009 study by the Max Planck Institute of Demographic Research, May 5, 2010, http://blogs.wsj.com/indiarealtime/2010/05/05/indias-top-choice-for-birth-control-still-sterilization/. Retrieved October 23, 2011.
143. Bandarage, *Women, Population and Global Crisis.*
144. Ibid.
145. Ibid., 71.
146. Bureau of Statistics, Treasury Department, *Statistical Abstract of the United States.* Washington, DC: GPO, 1997.
147. Hertsgaard, *Earth Odyssey.*
148. Bill Weinberg, "Population as a Propaganda Device," in Heiner, *Social Problems and Social Solutions,* 340–348.
149. Ibid., 345.
150. Eduardo Galeano, *Open Veins of Latin America: Five Centuries of the Pillage of a Continent.* Translated by C. Belfrage. New York: Monthly Review Press, 1973, 14.
151. "UN Millennium Project," The United Nations, http://www.unmillennium-project.org/. Retrieved October 24, 2011.

152. Reed Boland, "The Environment, Population, and Women's Human Rights," *Environmental Law,* vol. 27, no. 4, Winter 1997.
153. Bandarage, *Women, Population and Global Crisis.*
154. Boland, "The Environment, Population, and Women's Human Rights."

Chapter 7: Conclusions

1. Douglas Kellner, "The Media and Social Problems," in George Ritzer (ed.), *Handbook of Social Problems: A Comparative International Perspective.* Thousand Oaks, CA: Sage, 2004, 218.
2. Quoted in Craig Aaron, "Cash and Kerry," *In These Times* (online edition), July 27, 2004. Available at http://www.inthesetimes.com/site/main/article/cash_and_kerry/.
3. Ibid.
4. Ibid.
5. Ellis Jones, Ross Haenfler and Brett Johnson, *The Better World Handbook.* Gabriola Island, BC, Canada: New Society Publishers, 2007, 34.
6. Ibid.
7. "Consumers Punishing Abusive Companies," *USA Today Magazine,* vol. 129, no. 2671, April 2001, 16.
8. Noreena Hertz, *The Silent Takeover: Global Capitalism and the Death of Democracy.* New York: Free Press, 2001, 116.
9. Ibid., 126.
10. Donald L. Barlett and James B. Steele, *America: Who Stole the Dream?* Kansas City, MO: Andrews and McNeel, 1996, 30–31.
11. International Energy Outlook, 2011, U.S. Energy Information Administration, September 19, 2011, http://csis.org/files/attachments/110919_IEO2011.pdf. Retrieved October 8, 2011.

INDEX